# THE
# BEST
# KIND OF
# LOVING

# THE BEST KIND OF LOVING

## A Black Woman's Guide to Finding Intimacy

### DR. GWENDOLYN GOLDSBY GRANT

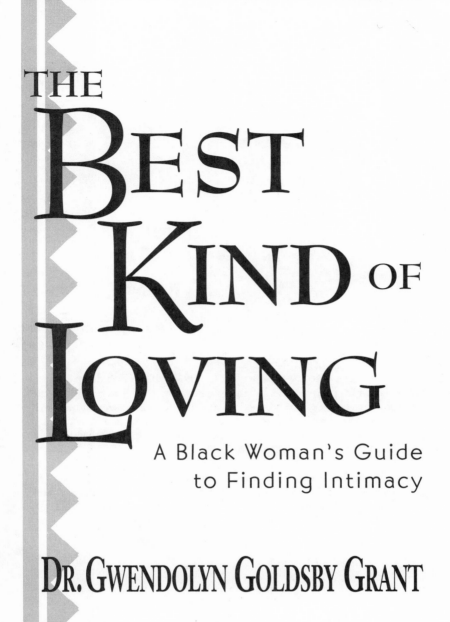

HarperCollins*Publishers*

HarperCollins books may be purchased for educational, business, or sales promotional use. For information, please write Special Markets Department, HarperCollins Publishers, Inc., 10 East 53rd Street, New York, NY 10022.

FIRST EDITION

*Designed by Alma Hochhauser Orenstein*

---

LIBRARY OF CONGRESS CATALOGING-IN-PUBLICATION DATA

Grant, Gwendolyn Goldsby.
    The best kind of loving : a black woman's guide to intimacy / by Gwendolyn Goldsby Grant
        p.   cm.
    ISBN 0-06-017088-3
    1. Man-woman relationships—United States. 2. Afro-American women—psychology. 3. Afro-American women—Sexual behavior.
HQ801.G66   1995
306.7'089'96073—dc20                                                94-40707

---

95 96 97 98 99 ❖/HC 10 9 8 7 6 5 4 3 2 1

For my late parents, Ethel Lee Mixon Goldsby and Esters Vaughn Goldsby, both born in Woodstock, Bibb County, Alabama, in an area commonly known as Big Springs, and to my mother's late cousin, Joel Threet, who introduced them.

Mama and Daddy were my first relationship role models. Black men and women such as these paved a way out of no way to give us all courage to hold on to families and the cultural fabric of our lives. The legacy these warrior brothers and sisters left for each of us to remember is: YOU CAN MAKE IT IF YOU TRY TO FIND THE BEST KIND OF LOVING.

# Contents

# Acknowledgments

To my distinguished, loving husband and dear friend, Dr. Ralph T. Grant, Jr., who always encouraged me to spread my creative wings and soar, I am extremely grateful for his steady support. I would also like to thank our three wonderful children, all United Negro College Fund college graduates, Ralph III, Sally-Ann, and Dr. Rebecca, veterinarian.

I am also truly indebted to Irene B. Eagleton of Riviera Beach, Florida, my 90-year-old "village mother," supporter, and prayerful confidante. She represents the African village wisdom that we all need more of in our lives. My continual gratitude also goes to a family friend, Florence Henderson, who, from the time I was a teenager, helped to shape my sense of womanhood and beauty by her example.

I want to express my sincere thanks to all the sisters who allowed me to interview them for this book; their contributions were very much on target. Although their real names have been omitted, I hope their experiences provide sister insights that herald truth and nothing but the truth.

My thanks and appreciation for the audiotape transcriptions go to Leslie Peters of Newark, New Jersey. The taped interviews provided real sister voices that I hope the reader will be able to relate to. Special mention goes to my typist of many years, Gwenda Davis, who is my spiritual treasure and to whom I am grateful.

Susan L. Taylor, editor-in-chief of *Essence* magazine, has been a source of great encouragement and I want to thank her for her talent and grace, and all of the *Essence* family for expressing confidence in my expertise and sharing a vision of better things to come for all sisters. To *Essence* co-founders Ed Lewis and Clarence Smith, I am grateful for the opportunity to be part of their positive promotion of Black women in the world community. I also want to express special thanks to Linda Villarosa for her encouragement.

My literary agent, Barbara Lowenstein, deserves my everlasting gratitude for her persistence and guidance for the completion of this project. Barbara made the right connections for me. Barbara and Madeleine Morel were both attentive and tireless in seeing this project through and maintaining the highest standards at the same time. I also want to thank the rest of the staff at Lowenstein Associates, particularly Norman Kurz and Bob Ward for all their help.

Janet Goldstein and her assistant, Betsy Thorpe, at HarperCollins and all the editors, copyeditors, publicity people, and others, like fashion expert Ionia Dunnlee who worked on the cover photo and art director Suzanne Noli, are women who have my continual praise and thanks for their help. My appreciation extends to Ann Gaudinier and Rick Harris and all those who assisted in the audiotaping of this book, and Lorie Young for her patience in answering queries, as well as my publicist, Wende Gozan.

Certainly I thank all the men and women from various ethnic backgrounds who have attended my relationship seminars all around the country and in West Africa because their reality-based experiences allowed me to understand that we can learn from each other despite cultural differences.

This book is written for the sisters, but it has a message for America and the rest of the world: THE BEST KIND OF LOVING IS GOOD FOR ALL, NO MATTER WHAT YOUR PORT OF CALL.

# Introduction: Kitchen Talk

Dear Sisters:

Over the years I've been with so many of you talking about what you feel, what you hope, what your disappointments are, what you want for yourselves, and what you want for your children. I've talked with so many sisters that sometimes it feels as though I know every one of you personally; that's why I want to have this conversation with you in the old "kitchen talkin' time" fashion. Like many of you, I'm worried about all of us as Black women of African descent, and I'm worried about the African American family. Women have the great burden of being the carriers of our culture. When we build strong lives, we can build strong relationships. When we build strong relationships, we can be a strong community.

Almost every sister I meet reveals to me that she is searching for ways to keep both her heart alive and her culture alive. These are not easy goals, and when you are born Black and female, you don't need anybody to tell you about the special trials you regularly face. No matter how beautiful, strong, talented, smart, or joyful we may be, as women of African descent, we have a unique set of inequalities, burdens, and challenges that are ours and ours alone. And probably nothing is more of a challenge right now than what is taking place in our romantic relationships. As many of you know, I've been a columnist for *Essence* magazine for more than ten years. Before that, I had a live radio call-in show three days a week from 2 A.M. to 5 A.M., and I was always amazed by the number of people who were describing the same kind of pain in different anonymous voices. Now, as I go around the country, leading seminars and workshops on male-female relationships and sexuality, what I'm still hearing is one tale of woe after another. Sisters are searching for intimacy and finding alienation. As a result, I hear you telling me that you feel defeated and angry. The effort of trying to find or maintain a nurturing relationship with a man is leaving you emotionally exhausted and thoroughly confused.

It's always been my belief that every time White America catches a case of the sniffles, Black America comes down with walking pneumonia. This means that our communities and families suffer from just about every malady that plagues White America, but we always seem to get it worse. Think about what this means for us as women who are trying to lead productive lives and enjoy satisfying relationships.

We all know about the intimacy problems in male-female relationships in general: inadequate communication, sexual confusion, infidelity, abandonment, commitment fears, conflicting goals, anger, betrayal, loss of trust, and unrealistic expectations. The list of ways in which men and women in America are failing each other seems to go on forever. These problems take on additional meaning when you look at research that reflects what's going on in our African American families and communities. If you're hoping for a loving family life, the chilling statistics you see on television or read about in the daily papers are but small reminders of what you experience personally in your day-to-day life. Whether you are married or single, a parent or childless, you can't help but feel alone and burdened by the double-jeopardy status of being Black and female.

Relationship issues among Black women and Black men are even more complex than those among white women and white men. Although there are certainly tremendous overlaps in many of the fundamental issues we all struggle with, such as self-esteem, loneliness, fear, control, and power, there are also profound differences. Here's a truth we all recognize: In addition to the social dynamics that affect male-female communications in general, as African Americans, we carry the added burdens of myths and stereotypes that grow out of our real history of slavery, second-class citizenship, and economic disenfranchisement.

You can't, for example, talk about the relationships between Black women and Black men without acknowledging the relationship between the African American and the white culture in this country. The two are so powerfully intertwined that they can never be regarded as totally separate, despite any racial tensions.

No matter how materially successful any of us may become, no matter how many professional accolades we may acquire, as Black women, we carry with us a shared history that has created shared fears and expectations. These common issues will ultimately affect every romantic relationship any of us enter.

In other words, when sisters talk about self-esteem, we must acknowledge how our self-esteem has been specifically shaped by living in a predominantly white culture. When we talk about expectations, we must acknowledge how the Black culture and the white culture have shaped different and sometimes conflicting expectations. When we talk about societal role models, we must acknowledge how a Black woman's earliest relationship role models were affected by the pressures of racism. And when we talk about our relationship to money, we must acknowledge the roles that money and diminished earning power have played in the Black family.

Too many men and women of African descent have unwittingly bought into destructive cultural myths, with the result that we sometimes see each other as stereotypes, rather than as people. These myths, perpetuated not only by the white European culture, but also within the African American community, have made it extraordinarily difficult for us as Black women and Black men to see each other clearly or speak to each other honestly.

Obviously, I believe much can be done to improve our interpersonal relationships. From where I sit, the male-female relationship isn't just about two people; it's about the cohesion of the community. We've got to relearn ways of constructing strong male-female relationships, strong families, and strong communities. We've got to relearn the brother-and-sister principle, so we stop fighting with each other and go back to working together.

It's important for all of us to keep in mind that before the 1960s, our families were intact. They were stable units that supported one another. We must have been doing something right back then, and we can do it again. After slavery, when our families were split up by forces we certainly couldn't control, we established benevolent organizations to help us find each other, connect us to our relatives, and put our families back together. Black people historically have always recognized the importance of these primary bonds.

Obviously, now something has gone terribly wrong in the way we connect to one another; where once the Black community fought together against seemingly insurmountable odds to hold our families together, we are now falling apart. If you are a typical Black woman, struggling with your own relationships, nobody feels this more intensely than you. The question is, What can be done about it?

In your own relationships, how can you establish dialogues that don't turn into heavy mouth battling? How can you find and keep long-term intimacy and love? How do you resolve your own internal conflicts and your own tendencies to run away from potentially good relationships? How can you learn to avoid the men who will cause you pain? What can you do to heal and protect yourself? And how can you contribute to the healing and protection of the Black community as a whole?

Our problems are real, but we've fixed real problems before. And we did it together. We have to remember that Black men and women have a history of being social equals because we come from an egalitarian cultural experience. During slavery, the shared-load philosophy was our saving grace. Now, more than ever, all of us must cling to the historical egalitarian, supportive brother-sister principle.

If sisters are going to be able to establish viable romantic relationships, we have to learn to see the ways in which we've internalized the leftovers of slavery and the myths of oppression. We have to stop mouthing the clichés that perpetuate ugly stereotypes even among ourselves and within our own communities. All of this public fighting means that we have a lot of private work that needs doing. And as Black women of African descent, we had better start doing it.

When I was growing up, I remember hearing people say that there is nothing like a Black woman with a made-up mind. Most of us are sisters with made-up minds. We are determined to find better ways of living and loving. Sisters engaged in this search know that they are facing some major challenges. Our relationships and our families are in crisis. We need to find ways to save them, and we need to find ways to save ourselves. That's what this book is about. Trying to find the best kind of loving, all the while continuing to celebrate life. Long ago, the sisters closed ranks on the plantation and saved a Black nation. Today, it is still nation-building time, and a Black woman's task is just as essential now as it was then. I want to remind my sisters that they have the thread of history in their hands and that they can sew a nation back together again. My hope is that this book will help provide a stitch in time.

# Sisters Going Through Changes

"What's missing in my life right now is a positive relationship with a loving Black man. I am definitely ready for a genuine one hundred percent African American prince, but I'm not finding him. It seems like the brothers keep passing me by, and I don't know what to do about it."

—CHERYL, 28

## Where Is the Man for Me?

Every sister I know wants an intimate love relationship. Every sister I know deserves an intimate love relationship. But it's not always happening, and we don't need to hear Bessie Smith singing the blues to understand what loneliness feels like. When you're searching for the best kind of loving and what you're finding instead is pain and frustration, it affects everything you do and everything you feel. You know what you're missing, and you carry that sadness and heartache around with you wherever you go.

When Cheryl, for example, says that Black men are passing her by, she is testifying to her strong feelings of confusion and loneliness. In the most profound sense, these men *are* her brothers, as well as potential husbands and lovers. Yet, she feels as though she has been left out in the cold, without a mate, to fend for herself. In short, she feels betrayed as well as abandoned.

Her sense of disappointment is shared by Black women who live in large cities, Black women who live in the suburbs, and Black women who live in rural areas. It is shared by sisters who are still struggling to get off welfare and make better lives for themselves, and it is shared by sisters who have pulled themselves up to places where they have shining careers, solid finances, and glamorous lifestyles. All across America, women of African descent have the same kinds of concerns and the same kinds of hopes. We want to form loving partnerships with loving Black men, but all too often we end up feeling disappointed and shortchanged.

What has happened to our relationships? What is going on in the African American psyche that is making love so hard to come by and even harder to hold on to? Why are there so many lonely and defeated women and so many unavailable and unyielding men?

By now we have heard all the gloomy statistics and read the magazine and newspaper articles telling us that there is a crisis in our families and in our communities. We've seen the books that set us against each other—"all the brothers" against "all the sisters"—and we've watched the television talk shows featuring individual African American men and women who yell at each other and blame one another for relationships that failed. What does all this mean for the typical Black woman who is working hard and trying to do right? Like you, this sister is not a statistic. She's a living, breathing human being who wants to find the love she deserves and the family life she craves.

Like you, she's frustrated and tired of emotional turmoil. She wants answers and solutions, and she wants them now. She's tired of blaming, and she is tired of being blamed. She's willing to work hard at her relationships, but she doesn't know what to do next.

# Looking for Creative Solutions

If there is one thing the typical Black woman knows how to do, it is work. You know how hard we've worked, how hard our mothers worked, and how hard our grandmothers and great-grandmothers worked. Whether it is the high-profile sister working in today's corporate or entertainment world or the anonymous sister of an earlier generation picking cotton in the summer sun, hard work is part of who we are. We've hoed, chopped, and quilted, and we've washed, polished, and scrubbed. Let's not forget that our legacy includes the memories of sisters who kept house for much of America. We've raised our own children and everybody else's children as well. We've done men's work and women's work. And we've done windows. Running from job to job, place to place, and back home to take care of her own family, the African American woman performed the first working-woman juggling act.

You also know that Black women know how to be creative and innovative. We've had to be. We've had a long history of taking what looks like nothing much and turning it into something special. We've taken discarded flour sacks, bleached them out, and stitched them into pillowcases, nightgowns, and dresses. We've taken turnip tops that were tossed away as being not worth eating and we've turned them into a pot of greens. We turned entrails into chitlins and neck bones into delicious meals. The rest of America thought that a chicken's feet were just for walking, but we turned those feet into stew and had a strut-your-stuff party to celebrate. We did it to survive, physically and spiritually.

Right now Black America has a new survival problem, and you know it. You read the newspapers; you watch the news. You see what's happening around you: Black men and women are complaining about each other; Black men are dating inter-racially because they say it's "easier"; Black women are dating interracially because they say they have "no choice." You know what kind of trouble you're experiencing in your own relationships. You know when the brothers are passing you by, you know when the brothers are giving you grief, and you know when the brothers just don't seem worth keeping. You know how hard it is to find a decent date, let alone a good husband.

Here's our problem: How do we take all of our joined experiences, our fine energy, and our good intentions and put them together, so we can find a way to forge new and better relationships that will sustain us and help restore our families and our communities. We need to work together to pull together everything we know and everything we've experienced.

## *Learning from Experience (Yours and Others')*

You know how when you watch girlfriends make choices and decisions that threaten to mess up their lives, you often can see exactly what they should be doing instead. It's easy when it's someone else's life. Now I'm going to ask you to take your skill at analyzing what others are doing and use it to figure out what is going wrong and what is going right in your own relationships.

What I want you to do is take a look at the lives of some typical sisters to see which of their characteristics you share. Let's see what they are feeling and doing. We're going to see if we can get some insight into how we, as Black women, typically handle our personal lives. Let's try to find the common denominators in this puzzle, so we can find some workable solutions to the problems we all share.

# Different Backgrounds, the Same Feelings

As you read about the women in this book, you will notice that some of the similarities among them are very obvious, whereas others are much more subtle. You may identify with one or more, or you may feel that your particular situation isn't adequately represented. Please understand that we all have different kinds of family backgrounds, different financial realities, and different hopes, and it would be impossible for any one book to cover all the ways in which we are different from one another. Each of us is special and unique, and any sister who has ever listened to the testaments remembers Jesus assuring us that "even the hairs on our head are numbered." And I believe that's true.

However, despite our individual "specialness," we recognize the common themes that keep playing out in our relationships. We hear girlfriends complain, and we hear when we're saying the same thing even when we use different words. In short, everywhere in America, sisters are feeling the same thing. There are good reasons for this. If you grew up Black and female, in all likelihood you have shared specific types of experiences and emotional crises with other women of African descent.

Typically, we are trying to forge relationships to men of African descent, all of whom also share similar trials and hardships in the contemporary world. And, let's never forget that all of us, male and female, share a common history that left us with emotional traumas and a psychological legacy that we can't deny. It's easy to see why we're all having similar feelings and disappointments.

# Sisters Talking About What They Feel

Black women have a long-honored tradition of sharing their personal experiences with each other. Men who don't see the positive value of this kind of communication often complain about it and call it "hen talk." I call it "kitchen talk" and believe that it has its roots back in the plantation kitchen. There, in the only inviting room of the house, working with other women, a sister knew it was safe to be herself and to tell the truth as she saw it. This ability to share the experiences of pain, joy, sorrow, and humor with other Black women is an extraordinarily positive part of who we are. Our great-grandparents even carried it into our churches, where testimony service became a regular part of Sunday morning. I've spent many an hour, as a child and as an adult, listening to women share their experiences, both woeful and triumphant.

In my opinion this experience of sharing played an essential role in the establishment of a strong functioning sister network. Generations of Black women have networked with other sisters whom they trusted. Historically, sisters have always trusted each other to share work, cooking, cleaning, and child care. But equally important is the way we've trusted other sisters to hear us out when we talk about what's going on and help us sort out what's happening in our lives. When you're able to tell the truth about your life as you see it and another sister identifies with it, it's a gratifying and empowering experience. Who but another sister is going to understand the experiences you've had? Who but another sister is going to be able to help you make decisions about your life? Who but another sister is going to be able to laugh with you, hurt with you, and cry with you? Who but another sister is going to understand the intense and often contradictory reactions you experience toward the men you let into your life?

What follows are stories of three sisters who are searching for love and not finding what they want. As you read about these women, see how many of the feelings they express are ones you share.

## Three Sisters Who Are Still Searching

### CHERYL, A SISTER WHO BLAMES HERSELF

Cheryl, a 28-year-old single mother, says that she is feeling completely disgusted with the way her personal life is turning out. As she looks back at the major events that made her feel this way, she concludes that she's always too late in figuring out what's happening. She blames herself even when it's not her fault. She says:

"I never 'get it' soon enough. I'm always there, like a fool, believing what I'm being told, and then one day it's like bam, I wake up. I figure it out, but it's always too late."

Cheryl, who is an administrative assistant in a large hospital, has many solid accomplishments, including a beautiful 10-year-old daughter and a job with a future. However, she wants more. She wants to build a life with a man who loves her and her child. As much as she yearns for a solid permanent relationship with an African American man, she complains that "most black men are up to no good."

She says: "I've never really witnessed a good relationship. And I can't help but think this is part of my problem. My daddy left home when I was eight, and he moved in with a lady who was my mama's best friend, or so she thought. He's always been embarrassed about how he did my mother, and I think he was too guilty about not having money for us ever to pay much attention to me or my brother. I can't say he doesn't mean well, but he's never been much of a father. I used to try to get to know him better because I wanted him to be part of my life, but he's so passive there's no reaching him."

Cheryl has been in counseling, and this has helped her to see the ways in which her behavior with men is connected to her childhood experiences. She realizes, for example, that when she was an adolescent, she was much too anxious to tie herself up with one relationship—trying to get a sense of security by finding a man to hang on to. Like most of us, she discovered that the only way to find security is within yourself. But this lesson, which she keeps relearning in different ways, didn't seem real to her when she was 15 and she met a 17-year-old brother named Lloyd.

"Lloyd got me pregnant the first time when I was only sixteen. It's probably lucky for me that I lost that baby, but Lloyd got me pregnant again in less than a year. I'm happy about it though. My daughter is the most important person in my life, and she forced me to get my life together. If I didn't have her, I don't know where I'd be. And I've been lucky with her because I've had my mother and aunt to help me."

As much as Cheryl loves her mother, she is concerned about repeating her patterns in relationships. She says: "As far as men are concerned, my mother always rolled over and played dead. She doesn't think she's that way; she thinks she's tough. But I'm telling you she never took care of herself. Don't get me wrong. My mother is a wonderful woman who always managed to find a way to put food on the table. She cleaned houses, she cleaned offices. She did whatever she had to do to keep it together. She always taught me to believe in myself, and she's made me keep going no matter what."

Anyone who has ever found herself alone with a young child can understand how difficult it was for Cheryl to maintain a positive attitude after her baby was born. She was just a teenager who had to find a way to support herself and her child. Lloyd, the father of her child, was coming around to see her less and less often, and she was feeling a sense of loss and abandonment. She was very hurt, but she tried not to let it show. Cheryl told me that although she didn't want to face it at first, she knew in her heart that she and Lloyd didn't have a real future by the way he acted toward her and their baby.

"Lloyd would tell people that I was his fiancée, but even so he started disappearing on me right away. When I was young and didn't have a child, he was grabbing at me all the time, but once the baby came, it was different. It was like he didn't care anymore. At first, I was all bothered about it, but in the end I didn't mind that much. If he didn't want to be there, I sure didn't need him! Besides, right after you give birth, you're into your mother role, and sex isn't big on your mind. But no matter how he was with me, I still wanted Lloyd to be more involved with our daughter. But that's not his thing.

"My aunt says it's a blessing Lloyd isn't with me. . . . This way, at least he's not hanging around expecting me to do for him. She says I don't need two babies, one of them a full-grown man. She's right, and I guess I can understand what happened with Lloyd. I trusted him, but we were both kids. I still miss him, but I can't get that angry. It's the men I've met after Lloyd who really kept me confused and mad."

Once Lloyd stopped being important in her life, Cheryl got involved with two other brothers who, she says, didn't give her enough to make it worth her while. One of them, Roger, was a tall, handsome man she met when he came to install cable television.

After a lot of hard work, Cheryl had taken the necessary courses and tests to get a job in the hospital system, and she had been promoted to a level where she could finally afford an apartment of her own. And then came Roger to, as she put it, "mess me all up." It took her a year to figure out that on many of his jobs Roger was installing more than cable. She says: "The way I figure it, with half the women in the town, whenever they watch MTV or BET, they're thinking about Roger. Two of my girlfriends tried to warn me about him, right off, but I thought they were only jealous because he was so good-looking."

Cheryl had hoped it would get more serious with Roger, but when she finally saw the writing on the wall, she read it right, and she ended the relationship. It wasn't long, however, before she ran into another brother. His name was Donald, and his biggest drawback was that he was already living with a woman upstate.

"Donald would come down to New York every week or two and spend a few days. At first, he was all sweet talk, indicating he was going to be real generous with me. It was all, 'Baby, baby, there's no one like you.' Then I found out through a friend that he had another woman he was 'engaged' to. He said she didn't matter, and at first I believed his tall tale about leaving her and moving to live with me. But after six months, it didn't take a genius to figure out he was playing us both.

"Whenever he was in New York, he was sitting around

my apartment, eating my food and telling me what to do. He never followed through on *any* of his promises. I might have still gone for it, but he wasn't good to my daughter. And that's where I draw the line. He didn't hurt her or anything; he just ignored her. I figured, who needs this! I wasn't asking him to be my baby's daddy; she knows who her daddy is. But she's not an object like a coffee table that you can just walk around."

As disappointed as Cheryl was by her experiences with Lloyd, Donald, and Roger, nothing upset her quite as much as something that happened last week with Lester, an administrator who works at the same hospital. She says that when she first met Lester, even though he was married, he represented exactly the kind of man she wanted in her life: "Lester is very good-looking and very successful. But I knew he was married, and I never expected anything from him. We were just friends, and I thought we were good friends. Sometimes we worked late together, and we would have something to eat, and we talked. He would tell me about how he went skiing on weekends, and it sounded like something I would like to do. I even told him about Donald, and he would listen. He always told me Donald wasn't good enough for me. The way he said it made me believe him."

Cheryl says that the way this man connected with her made her feel attractive and important and it fulfilled some real emotional need. Then last week, Lester's wife—a blue-eyed white woman—came into the office, and Cheryl was overwhelmed by what she felt.

"I thought this guy was decent, and it gave me hope that maybe someday there would be somebody for me. I knew he was married, and I didn't expect—or want—anything more from him. But when I saw him with his wife, I knew he would never find a Black woman attractive. I felt as if I had been lied to . . . as if he'd been playing a game with me. I know he was embarrassed when his wife was there because he couldn't look me in the eye. Another brother who talks Black and sleeps white. There's no hope—I feel like I'm the last woman in the line."

Cheryl says that she is so "disgusted" by her experiences that she feels like giving up on men altogether. Like many other Black women, she also seriously questions whether there are any available men. As she puts it:

"There are no men for me to meet. There are a couple of other single men I've met through work, but they're never going to make a commitment. Why should they? They have women fighting over them just because they have jobs and cars.

"I really like being with a man. I like the touching and the hugging. I like to hear a man tell me I look good and that I'm important to him. But you have to pay too much to get that. It seems like every man I've known has cheated on me. I'm disgusted with myself for putting up with so much."

Right now, Cheryl is concerned not only for her own emotional future, but for the future of her daughter, a bright child who does well in school and still plays with dolls. Last year, some young girls Cheryl knows, only a little older than her own child, went to a community pool where they were surrounded by a group of teenage boys who humiliated them by pulling their bathing suits down and calling them names. And a teenage girl, down the block, was recently raped. These events made Cheryl very angry, and she asks: "What's my daughter got to expect if this is what's happening now? I'm getting tired of watching Black men disrespect Black women. I don't want it any more in my life, and I sure don't want it for my baby."

Cheryl is probably more concerned about her daughter's well-being than she is about her own. She is extremely worried about what her daughter will grow up believing and doing. Cheryl doesn't want her daughter to be as ill prepared for life as she was. As Cheryl recalls: "My mother didn't tell me anything about sex or men. At least nothing useful. She told me not to get pregnant, but she didn't tell me how you got pregnant or how to avoid it. All her information was vague like 'wash yourself down there,' and 'no self-respecting woman lets a man do certain things.' It wasn't really good information. Sometimes I think it's already too late for me, but I want my daughter to be prepared for what can go on with men."

As we read Cheryl's story, we can see how determined and positive she has been to improve her life. This sister is no slouch. She has a good job, a decent apartment, supportive relatives, and a child she deeply loves. But her feelings of loneliness overshadow all her hard work and achievements. It feels as though she's in control of everything except her romantic life, and that's what she wants the most.

### DENISE, A SISTER WHO STARTED OUT WITH HIGH EXPECTATIONS

Denise, a 35-year-old computer analyst, is struggling with the fact that she hasn't been able to establish the family she expected. Denise, who has a well-paying job with a large firm, considers herself blessed in many ways. Growing up, her parents told her that she was beautiful, smart, and deserving of a good life, and they backed up their words by making certain she and her siblings all went to college and were prepared to be independent and self-sufficient.

Because Denise's parents had secure employment, they were able to give their children a middle-class life that Denise describes as protected and sheltered. Denise was particularly close to her father, whom she describes as the ultimate family man. According to Denise, her father treated her like a princess. She recalls:

"My father had been married before and had other children who his ex-wife wouldn't let him see, so when I came along, he treated me like a princess. He even called me princess. I grew up believing in Santa Claus and happy endings, and I honestly expected to marry a prince and live happily ever. I thought once I had a good job and was able to afford some nice things, it would all come together. But it hasn't—at least not for me.

"Of course I'm surprised. I don't believe in playing games. I'm very straight, and I believe in focusing on one person at a time and doing the best you can. Nothing in my life pre-

pared me for the kind of crap that goes down in relationships. Nothing."

Denise dates her problems and insecurities with the opposite sex back to her high school years, which she says were a
lot of fun except that she never had any dates. Her explanation is an all-too-familiar one: "The school I went to was
integrated, but there were fewer Black boys than Black girls.
I have dark skin, and it didn't take long to figure out that the
boys asked out the light-skinned girls. I went to an all-Black
college, but I had the same experience there. It wasn't until
graduate school that I started to meet men who appreciated
the way I look. But I never seem to have a relationship that
lasts more than a few years. I meet somebody, we fall in love,
then he dumps me—usually for somebody else."

Right now Denise is trying to get over a relationship with
Robert, a business consultant who kept promising to settle
down, but who didn't do it. She spent more than three years
waiting for Robert to make good on his promises. Talking to
her, it's easy to see she is still very involved with this brother.
No matter what, her conversation keeps coming back to
Robert as though he is the only thing on her mind. She has
obviously spent a lot of time analyzing Robert's emotional
makeup. She feels that the relationship broke up because he
had problems with intimacy: "He couldn't handle it. Whenever we got close, he'd turn into a real crude dude—breaking
dates, not showing up, and generally disappointing me. I
knew there were reasons for his being this way, and for a
long time, I made excuses for him. He had a bad childhood,
and his father was in and out of jail for most of it. I don't
know the whole story, but I think his father was abusive to
him. He never learned how to trust."

Despite Robert's emotional limitations, Denise felt that
the two of them shared a real bond, a connection so intense
that it made her feel that they were destined to be together.
Even when he was at his worst—disappearing when she
needed him or "coming on" to her friends—she believed that
he loved her and everything would work out. He encouraged
her in this belief.

During most of their relationship, Denise devoted a large part of her energy trying to prove herself to Robert. She was always worried about figuring out what made Robert tick— what made Robert happy, what made Robert mad, what made Robert sad. She worried about what she should say, what she should wear, and what she should cook. Denise is a busy, successful woman. Even so, she waited for his phone calls, and she waited for him to show up. Robert was her real life, and everything that she did on her own was just a way to pass time until he was there. That's why she was so troubled when the relationship broke up. She says: "It wasn't just that it ended, it was how it ended. I knew he was looking for another job, and I encouraged him to do that. He was dissatisfied with his work, and he wanted to do something else. How was I supposed to know that he'd go and get a job in another city, two hundred miles away?"

Robert told Denise that his moving wasn't going to make any difference in their relationship and that they would still be together on weekends. But that's not what happened. He showed up less and less, and he never invited Denise to see his new place. And when he did come to visit her, he wasn't as passionate as he had once been. It didn't take much insight to figure out that he didn't act like a man who was missing sex. Before long, as much as Denise wanted to believe what Robert was telling her about the future they would someday share, she began to suspect that there was another woman: "My girlfriend told me I should just show up at his door, and if there was another woman, I should fight for him. I don't think any man is worth fighting over, but I needed to know what was going on. So I got on a midnight bus and knocked on his door on Sunday morning at 7 A.M. Sure enough there was another woman. She wasn't anything special to look at, but she was there, and I wasn't. I couldn't say anything when I saw her. I just turned around, got on the first bus, and came back home."

Denise says she couldn't control her crying all the way home. When she walked through her door, the phone was ringing. It was Robert saying he was sorry and telling her she had the wrong idea about who the woman was. He even promised that things would change. However, within weeks, it was apparent that the woman had moved in with him. Now Denise says she would like to meet another man and get on with her life, but she isn't feeling optimistic:

"I'm scared I'll never meet anybody and I'll end up alone. Around here there are a fair number of men who make a decent salary, drive nice cars, and own condos. But the ones I meet think they're God's gift. They know there's a shortage of Black men, and they expect you to fall over if they so much as speak your name. Sure one of these guys will take you out for a night of wining and dining, but despite all this fanfare, they're no different. They all want to end up the evening in the standard supine position. If you don't go along with it, they move on. Often they move on, even if you do go along with it.

"Some of my friends have started talking about trying to find white men, but I don't know about that. I think it would kill my parents. Besides I'm very proud of my heritage, and I've developed a more Afrocentric attitude over the years. I want a relationship with a man who is like me, and who can understand me. One firm I worked for was almost all white, and I didn't like it. It felt too foreign. I was accepted and even made some friends there, but it's not the same. Now that I'm working in a Black firm, I'm much happier. Much more relaxed. I definitely want a husband who is Black; I just don't know where to find him."

### JARNELLE, A SISTER WHO HAS TAKEN
### TOO MANY EMOTIONAL RISKS

If you met Jarnelle at church or in the small beauty parlor she owns and operates, you would never believe that she feels disappointed about anything. Jarnelle, 51, who is outspoken and direct, seems independent and sure of herself. She says she believes firmly that a woman has to take hold of herself and not depend on anyone. When it comes to making a living, she has proved to be resourceful and creative, and although she says that it is a constant struggle to maintain her business, she is careful to make certain that no one around her knows how hard it is for her to do so.

Jarnelle acknowledges that when she is upset, she tends to spend money—often charging her purchases on a credit card. She believes that buying things for herself helps reinforce her ego when it's faltering. Since the circumstances of her life frequently upset her, she is in a fair amount of debt. Being in debt makes her anxious and worried, which makes her want to spend even more money. It's a vicious cycle that many women recognize.

Jarnelle says that what is sustaining her right now is her faith, and that without her belief in God, she doesn't think she could continue. Her major concern is her teenage son, who is at an age when he is exposed to many negative influences. She says:

"My worst nightmare is trying to raise this child without a family structure. I feel lost and abandoned. And I feel angry, so I have to deal with my resentment, as well as everything else.

"You understand, I don't let anybody push me around, and I don't let anybody push my son around. But I can't be with him all the time, and he sees things, and he goes places where I can't protect him. He needs a father to take an interest in him, and he doesn't have that."

In many ways, Jarnelle blames the absence of a father figure on herself. She acknowledges that when it comes to men and business, she is like two different people. As far as her business is concerned, she thinks with her head and makes good decisions. With men, it's quite different, as she explains: "My father was verbally abusive and emotionally cold. And then my mother left him and moved in with another man who was just plain crazy. I think that made me the way I am with men. I don't believe in myself enough, and I don't think I deserve anything good. That's the only explanation I can come up with for what's happened to me."

Within the past three years, Jarnelle has had two separate experiences with men that have left her questioning her judgment and her choices. The first was with a white man, a fireman she met when there was a problem with a defective steam pipe in the basement underneath her shop. His name was Jim, and he seemed very kind and very interested in her. She says:

"I'm not even attracted to white men, but he really worked on making me like him. He never acted like he was just interested in sex or anything like that. He seemed like he wanted a real relationship. He would come 'round to the shop when I was closing up, and we would go out for a drink. He was very sweet, and I thought he was genuinely in love with me.

"There were a couple of strange things that should have made me suspect that some funny business was going on, but they made sense considering everything else. One thing, he wouldn't go to my apartment. I live in a nice building, but because it's not in a racially mixed neighborhood, he said it made him nervous, and he didn't want to look for trouble. Also he said he didn't want to meet my son until we were engaged, which I thought was very sensitive. Then I never went where he lived because he said he lived with his brother, and it wouldn't look right to bring a woman there. So when we had sex, it would always be on the sofa in the shop, or sometimes we'd go to a motel across the river.

"He kept talking about how when we were married, we would have to find a place to live where we both felt comfortable. I was seeing a lot of him, almost every day. Sometimes it was just for a few minutes. He'd drop by, say hello to me at work, and have a cup of coffee with me. He was real nice to everyone, and everyone was real nice to him.

"Then suddenly he stopped showing up, and he stopped calling. At first I thought he was dead or something. You know, I worried something happened to him on the job, but there was nothing in the papers. The only two numbers I had for him were at the station house and at his brother's, but when I called, he was never there. Finally, I went around to the station house and asked where he was. They told me he had been transferred—to another area—and they couldn't give me his number.

"Then I saw this other fireman I had met, so I asked him

if he knew where I could reach Jim. He said no, but when I was leaving, he ran down the street after me. 'Look,' he said, 'you're a nice person and you shouldn't get hurt or upset. But you should know what's going on. His wife just had a baby, and they moved to the suburbs. Jim requested a transfer to be closer to home.'

"Can you imagine that! He was giving me this big line about marriage, and he was already married!"

About a year ago, Jarnelle had another unfortunate relationship that, she says, completely soured her on men. It was with a salesman named Gregory whom she met at a Kwanzaa celebration. She says:

"I thought Gregory was a gay happy person, and then I found out that he was only gay. I was going out with him a few months when I heard that rumor about him. A girlfriend who has her hair done with me told me that her uncle told her. So I asked to meet the uncle. He told me that Gregory was always over in a restaurant near where he lives messing around with some gay guys. He said they liked Gregory, and Gregory liked them. That's all he would say about it.

"The next time I saw Gregory, I started watching his body and trying to process this information, but it didn't seem possible. I thought it was just gossip, so I put it out of my mind. You've got to understand there was nothing feminine about Gregory. He looked all man. He was so much man that women would come up to him on the street even when I was with him.

"Then a couple of months later, when I was closing the shop, there was a man waiting for me who said that he was Gregory's lover. He told me that Gregory was messing around with him, and that he wanted me to get out of the picture."

Jarnelle said she wanted to find out what was going on, so she went to Gregory's apartment, and he admitted that he had "messed around" with some gay guys, but he said he definitely wasn't a homosexual or even a bisexual. Jarnelle said he had a strange explanation for his behavior: "He told me that *he* never did anything with the gay guys but he *let* them perform oral sex on him because *they* liked it so much. He explained it like it was to pacify them, you know. He said he didn't even like homosexuals."

Jarnelle says that at this point she had enough sense to get out of the relationship. Among other things, she was scared, not only for herself but for her son, who she didn't want to know about any of this. She says: "Fortunately, after Jim, I got less trusting and very careful about birth control. So I always made Gregory use a condom. Even so I was nervous and had a blood test. I'm sure I'm OK, but I don't need this kind of trouble in my life. The problem is, there doesn't seem to be anything else. Sometimes I think I must be doing everything wrong. Why else would this kind of thing keep happening to me? I'm just about ready to give up on men altogether."

# "Ready to Give Up"

Is this how you feel? So many sisters complain about feeling totally burned out that psychologists who work with Black women have a special term for it: "sexual anorexia." This is a term coined by two prominent African American scholars from San Francisco, Nathan Hare, Ph.D., and his wife, Julia Hare, Ed.D. Sexual anorexia is a malady suffered by sisters who are reacting to being dumped on, reacting to being blamed for whatever goes wrong, reacting to a lack of respect, reacting to abuse, and reacting to a shortage of love and available men.

A sister who is suffering from sexual anorexia typically feels so much pain that she wants to withdraw from the sexual arena altogether. I'm sure that this is a place where many of you have been. Too much pain can make you want to curl up and be alone; it can even make you want to be celibate. I want you to know that there's nothing wrong with taking some time out to gather yourself and strengthen yourself.

But I want you to do this with a plan. Otherwise what often happens is that as soon as you feel strong enough to deal with the world again, you meet some man who turns you right around. Oops, there it is! Before you know it, you're right back where you started—building your life around a man. Even if it's a different man, you're the same woman. That's because you haven't done enough inner work to change the way you react.

You see, I firmly believe that if you change the way you act, there's going to be a big change in the way the world treats you. If there's one thing I've learned as a psychologist, it's that it is never the problem that defeats you—it's your attitude toward the problem and what you have to do to resolve it.

# Moving Away from Pain and Frustration

It goes without saying that there is no magic solution that will immediately remove all your pain and grief. Healing is a process. However, no matter what kind of grief, disappointments, or losses you've experienced, the only way to get better and change your life is to start this process. Every woman who has ever had to put her life together knows you have to do it one step at a time.

I hope reading about some of the difficulties that other Black women have faced reminded you that you're not alone, and I hope you are able to find strength in that knowledge. Now let's take a serious look at all the changes that have taken place in your own life, both good and bad. It's time to reevaluate the relationships you've had and start healing your emotional pain. When architects and engineers design a new structure, they need a blueprint to guide them. Sisters need their own "Blackprint" so they can restructure their lives and move on to a new and better place. Here's a ten-step plan to help you begin.

# Getting Started— A "Blackprint" for Healing

### STEP ONE: STOP AND THINK ABOUT EVERYTHING THAT HAS HAPPENED TO YOU

When I say *think*, I mean think. I want you to make a list of all your relationships and what was good or bad about them. Then reevaluate how you behaved in these relationships, how your romantic partners treated you, and how each of these relationships made you feel. Don't focus only on the man's behavior. Try to gain insight into what went wrong in your past relationships by looking at your own patterns as well as your partners'. Ask yourself why you chose the men you did and why you stayed with the relationships? Give yourself honest answers. Honesty encourages change and personal growth. Your honesty with yourself about your past is what will help protect you in the future.

Honesty promotes self-determination and the ability to think for ourselves. *Kujichagulia* is the African word that describes this principle. It means self-determination—defining, building, and thinking for ourselves. It is one of Kwanzaa's seven principles of Blackness, which are called the *Nguzo Saba*. As many of you know, Kwanzaa was created by Dr. Maulana Karenga. He is the chairman of the Department of Black Studies at California State University, Long Beach.

### STEP TWO: ACKNOWLEDGE AND FEEL YOUR CURRENT PAIN, BUT DON'T WALLOW IN IT

Not that long ago I was on a panel and I started to talk about how Black women shouldn't allow themselves to wallow in their pain. Afterward a white woman came forward and told me that she was surprised because she thought it was only white women who behaved this way. She commented that she had always believed that Black women were too strong to fall into the wallowing trap. The fact is that Black women often have too much pride and attitude to let anyone *see* them wallow, but that doesn't mean they don't do it. Hanging on to pain isn't just about being Black or being white. Very often it's about being female. This is what I call a "woman thread," and it's universal. I believe it's important for sisters to learn to feel pain without feeding it. My mama used to say, "Troubles like babies grow larger when you nurse them." This is something all women need to remember. Otherwise there is always a temptation to sit around wallowing in our own mess for too long. The fact is that if a sister spends all her time worrying about some man who hurt her, she's going to waste years of her life. So let go of your pain and start moving toward a positive future.

Here's your warning label: *Feeling the pain is OK; increasing the daily dosage is not.*

### STEP THREE: LEARN YOUR LESSONS

I really believe that when something happens to you, good or bad, it means that the experience contains a lesson that was designed specifically to give you a new way of looking at your life. The trick is to find the lesson, rather than to dwell on the loss or the pain. Life has a way of showing us that as we keep changing and evolving, our lessons change as well. Wise women recognize that no matter what level any of us reach, there's always going to be another lesson. That's what it means to be alive. So take a good look at your life and at everything that's happened to you, good and bad, and instead of dwelling on your loss, see if you can find your very own special God-given lessons.

### STEP FOUR: DON'T BLAME YOURSELF FOR WHAT WENT WRONG

I think one of the best things about the majority of Black women is their ability to see their mistakes and face up to them without whining. More than any other women, I think, sisters try to do this. However, out of this very positive quality comes another quality that can be self-defeating, and that is the tendency to blame oneself for one's difficulties. Sisters say things like "I always figure it out too late." "I must be doing something wrong." As women, we worry about whether we've given our men too much or too little.

I realize that sometimes it feels better to accept all the blame for a bad situation. When you blame yourself, it makes you feel that you can do something about the problem. You think that because you have the power to change your own behavior, you have the power to change your life. And that's true. But not always in the way you expect or want. Besides, taking all the blame tends to make sisters fall into the "good-girl syndrome." Not only do sisters tend to blame themselves, too often they also start trying to prove themselves by doing better.

Typically a sister who takes all the blame will start thinking things like, "If only I could be a little smarter, sexier, kinder, or tougher, then maybe I could get this man to change." She'll go out and go on a diet, buy some new clothes, change her hair, or start trying to be more understanding of some man who doesn't deserve her because she thinks she's responsible for everything that's going wrong. That's not how relationships work.

The fact is that in any partnership, romantic or otherwise, there are two people. The only one you can change is yourself. One of my favorite books is *Having Our Say* by Sarah and A. Elizabeth Delaney with Amy Hill Hearth. Even if you haven't read the book, many of you may remember seeing the Delaney sisters on *Oprah* or other television shows. Sadie and Bessie, as they are known, are both over one hundred years old. In the book, Bessie says, "It took me a hundred years to figure out I can't change the world. I can only change Bessie. And, honey, that ain't easy, either."

One of the first things you can start thinking about changing is your attitude toward yourself. You're a wonderful woman, so stop trying to prove yourself to anyone.

STEP FIVE: GIVE YOURSELF CREDIT FOR ALL OF YOUR STRENGTHS AND ALL OF YOUR ACCOMPLISHMENTS
There is so much every woman accomplishes every day. Think about everything you've achieved in your life. Think about the work you've done for pay, as well as all the work you never got paid for. Think about the love you've given.

Think about all the ways in which you've stood on your own two feet and give yourself the credit you are due. Make a list of all your accomplishments, and when you look at it, don't feel sorry for yourself because you've worked so hard. Just praise yourself.

### STEP SIX: ADDRESS YOUR SELF-DOUBT

In many Black women, there is always a large kernel of self-doubt that keeps them feeling powerless and unable to bring about real change. That's because self-doubt is one of the true grandchildren of slavery. No matter how good you're doing, self-doubt tends to hang around, making you worried and anxious about everything you do. It's self-doubt that keeps you always anticipating the worst possible outcome of any situation. It's self-doubt that magnifies your failures and your mistakes. It's self-doubt that keeps you from taking risks and robs you of your self-confidence.

If you're a religious person, you know that self-doubt is connected to doubt in general. If you're carrying too much doubt around, then you can't believe either in God or in yourself. If self-doubt creeps into your mind at regular intervals, address it every day. A good way to do this is to talk back to your doubt and start every day with an affirmation.

Here are three simple affirmations that I like. Repeat to yourself:

> "I see success. I am success. I hold success in my hands."
> "With God all things are possible." (Matthew 19:26)
> "Once and for all, doubt is a low-down dirty dog, and I
>    won't have anything to do with it."

### STEP SEVEN: WHEN YOU'RE HEALING, DON'T LOOK FOR SOME MAN TO JUMP-START YOU

What you need to help you get over that relationship is to find yourself another man. Right? *WRONG!!!*

When you're feeling low and alone, it's easy to think that what you need is another man. In fact, that's the last thing you need. Instead of finding another man, you've got to find yourself. This habit of looking for a man to define her and save her is what keeps a woman feeling powerless and disappointed. You've got to learn to jump-start yourself.

### STEP EIGHT: LEARN TO LISTEN TO YOUR OWN VOICE

You can begin to jump-start yourself by listening to your own voice and figuring out exactly what you need to do for you. Instead of writing letters to the men in your life, start writing letters to yourself telling you what you need to hear. Many women wait for the sound of a man's voice calling them on the telephone, or from the next room. They say that's what makes them feel alive. This kind of thinking leaves you at the mercy of some brother who probably doesn't even want this kind of power in your life. What you've got to do instead is to build your own strong voice and to value that voice. Hear what your inner voice is telling you about your feelings and your needs. Try to fulfill these needs by getting involved in your own projects and your own process.

Another way to jump-start yourself is to give yourself more praise by using what I call "personal love talk." Verbally reinforce your jump-start thoughts each time you view yourself in the mirror by saying aloud, "At last, I love the sister in the glass." This is called self-talk. What you tell yourself reflects how you feel about yourself. It's a good mental health practice to affirm yourself regularly.

### STEP NINE: LEARN TO BE WITH YOURSELF, NOT BY YOURSELF

Start going places because that's where you want to be, not because you're looking for a man. When women tell me that they don't want to go places by themselves, I remind them that they aren't by themselves, they are *with* themselves. That's a big difference. When you're with yourself, you're with a lovable, spectacularly terrific person. So enjoy being with this person. If you want to go to a restaurant for dinner, for example, don't be afraid to do it alone. Look around at your surroundings and appreciate them. Enjoy your meal. You can go to movies, museums, and dozens of other places alone. Don't be nervous because you think people are staring at you because you're by yourself. Remember, you're not by yourself, you're *with* yourself.

STEP TEN: DO YOUR SPIRITUAL WORK

There's a difference between being religious and finding your spiritual center. Religion has to do with praising God and doing work for Him; spirituality has to do with acknowledging and working on your inner self. Black women usually are more comfortable doing outside work than inside work. When a sister starts having trouble with a man, for example, she often works at finding practical solutions. It doesn't occur to her to spend an equal amount of time working at finding her own inner spirit or center.

History has traditionally told the African American woman to "stay in your place, girl." Time and time again, you've been told that you reside in a place where you don't count, where you and your needs aren't taken seriously. We've been programmed to put everyone else's needs before our own. I'm telling you to turn that around. Instead of *"staying* in your place," I'm telling you to start *finding* that precious inner place where your own spirit resides.

Your spirit is your life force, and it needs protecting. If you don't take care of it, value it, and give it the importance it deserves, your center will always feel fragmented. You're always going to feel as though you need a man to give your life meaning. You don't. What you need is your own spiritual center, where you know your value as a thinking, loving human being who takes herself and her needs seriously. Directions: Spiritual work is an inside job.

# 2

# Looking Back: There's a Lesson in Here for Me If I Can Just Find It

"I'm wondering whether some guy I met last night is going to ask me out next week? What does something that happened to my great-great-great-grandmother back in 1864 have to do with that?"

—DEIDRE, 23

## Looking at the Past So You Can Move Forward into the Future

I know some of you agree with Deidre and believe the past is the past and it doesn't have anything to do with your current life. You don't want to waste any more of your precious energy blaming your relationship difficulties on racism or historical events. In fact, just hearing someone mention how Black men and women were exploited in this country triggers a mechanism inside you that makes you want to turn off and stop listening. All you want to do is try to get along with everybody and move on with your life in a productive, constructive fashion. Your problems are here-and-now problems, and you want here-and-now solutions.

I can certainly empathize with that point of view. We all want to move on to better relationships and a better life, and nobody wants to stop the blaming more than I do. Yes, of course, many of the things that go right or wrong in relationships between Black men and women go right or wrong in *all* relationships, whether the participants are Black, white, Asian, or Latino. People have trouble getting along, and I think it's important that we acknowledge the times when our male-female conflicts are a direct result of being human, no matter what our ethnic or racial group.

However, many of the ways in which we as Black women—and men—*handle* what goes right or wrong in our relationships are directly connected to our common experience as people of African descent. Knowing this is not about blaming; it's about understanding.

Your great-great-grandmothers and great-great grandfathers, your great-uncles and great-aunts, and your distant cousins had experiences that made them relate to each other in very specific ways. How the world treated them, as well as how they treated each other, left indelible impressions on their children, who, in turn, passed this way of behaving on to their children until eventually it got passed on to you. When you think about it this way, it's easy to understand how many of our problems, as well as many of our strengths, come from the history we carry with us from generation to generation.

# How the Burdens of History Become the Burdens of Self

We often hear people referring to someone with a bad relationship history as someone with a lot of baggage. As far as

I'm concerned, most of us had our bags packed before we even entered this world, let alone started having relationships.

When sisters talk about moving forward without spending more time on "ancient history," I remind them that they are carrying around baggage that is directly connected to our common history as Black Americans. This baggage is so heavy that it is keeping them stuck in one place: They *can't* move. The fact is that you can't walk with all that weight, and you sure can't fly because no airline will be able to accommodate so much excess poundage.

Carrying around all this heavy emotional "stuff" while trying to have good relationships is like trying to get through the world lugging invisible five-hundred-pound steamer trunks. Because you can't see them, you don't know what's making you immobile. All you feel is exhausted, angry, and completely frustrated. There's only one way out of this dilemma. *Instead of Black men and women taking out their frustrations on each other and beating each other with this heavy baggage, we've got to start unpacking all this old stuff and start looking at what's inside.* You're going to be surprised at what you find. Yes, there are negative painful memories and feelings that everyone would rather forget. But you're also going to find hidden treasures and family heirlooms. Trust me, buried down underneath all the pain and misuse of the Black experience is some pure gold. We have a history of love, generosity, mental health, emotional stability, humor, and intelligence in dealing with our personal relationships. Otherwise we wouldn't have survived.

Before 1960, the Black family was, if anything, known for its strength, endurance, and stability. Relationships between Black men and women were tightly bonded on the basis of experience and mutual respect. Our relationships were genuine partnerships. Black men and women modeled manhood and womanhood as an equal working unit, not on who was the major breadwinner. Our ancestors knew that when everyone works, everyone wins.

In our communities, the terms *brother* and *sister* were

about creating family life and secure bonds even when no blood ties existed. We were safe with each other, in our homes and in our communities. We were able to find love with each other. There are lessons in that love that all of us need to remember, unpack, and hold on to. But we can't fool ourselves about the negative behavioral patterns that developed as a direct result of our experiences. We need to unpack those first, so we can examine them, understand them, and discard them before they cause more problems in our relationships. Know what you're carrying, and don't become an emotional bag lady.

# Before You Can Go Anywhere, You Have to Know Where You've Been

*"Glory, glory Hallelujah, since I laid my burden down*
*I feel better, so much better since I laid my burden down."*

—OLD BLACK SPIRITUAL

No matter how materially successful any of you may become, no matter how many professional accolades you may acquire, as Black women, you carry with you shared experiences and memories that, in turn, have created shared fears and shared expectations. This situation has created common issues that will ultimately effect every romantic relationship you enter.

If you're going to end up in a place where you have better and more fulfilling relationships, the history of Black men and Black women in America will provide you with a priceless road map. Without looking at that map, you can't help but go around in circles and repeat patterns that were started long before you were born.

What follows are some of the markers on that map. These are major issues that are typically important to Black women like you, sisters who are searching and still not finding the love they deserve. In all likelihood, they are important to you, too.

# Trust Has a Special Meaning for You

Yes, all women want to be able to trust, but it's even more important for a sister. Typically, it's difficult for you to trust, and when your trust is betrayed—even a little bit—you become hurt and defensive. To understand why trust is such a highly charged issue, you have to think about how you feel when you trust someone. You feel safe, right? Trusting implies confidence that you're not going to be hurt physically or emotionally.

There are so many times in life when each of us has felt scared and worried, even in situations that outwardly may appear harmless and nonthreatening. On the most obvious level, that of physical safety, just about every sister grew up hearing messages that the world wasn't safe for Black people. Depending on your age and what part of the country you lived in, you heard regularly about Black men who were either beaten or lynched or shot. These tragedies, which are a frightening part of the landscape we inhabit, can't help but haunt us. Hearing these kinds of stories told and retold provided graphic warnings that we carry with us, no matter where we are.

No matter what your age or where you lived, you also heard stories about what could happen to Black women who weren't careful or lucky, stories about women who were raped or abused. You personally may have even experienced some form of abuse. Recently, Black-on-Black violence has visited our communities. In all likelihood, this kind of information or experience has left you anxious and concerned about what can happen in your environment or to you personally.

But we all realize that trust brings up more complicated

issues than physical safety. An environment that is safe is one that is accepting of who you are and what you are. And it's a rare sister who hasn't had to face hostile situations caused by racism, either open or disguised. You know full well that it's impossible to feel trust in this kind of hurtful atmosphere. The defense systems we've built to protect ourselves against the possibility of racism are so well ingrained that most of the time we don't even know they are there. All we know is that we are wary and that there are few places in which we feel totally relaxed, comfortable, and trusting. Whether you are conscious of it or not, you carry this wariness with you—even into your romantic involvements.

Lately, as we all know, a further complication has arisen: Some Black women have had to face disrespect and hostility in their own communities, where they have been subject to name-calling and unkind stereotyping. Defending yourself against the boy next door is a lot harder on your psyche than defending yourself against strangers. But sometimes we've had to do it, further eroding our sense of trust.

That brings us to what is perhaps the most important example of trust—trusting the man you love. When you love someone, you want desperately to be yourself and not to worry about being hurt. There are so few places in which sisters have been able to feel safe, doesn't it make sense to want to feel safe with the man you love? You want to be able to trust him with your heart and everything in it. You want to know that he won't play games with you, use you, take advantage of you, or reject you. You want to know that he won't betray you. This is of primary importance to the typical sister. Perhaps because you want so much to be able to trust someone totally, you have a tendency to give your trust too quickly or inappropriately, and you've been taken advantage of. You may have to learn how to hold back and wait until a man earns your trust. In the chapters that follow we are going to explore ways of knowing when and how to trust.

*Your History Lesson:* Don't let what has happened before determine what will happen in the future. If you've been hurt in your relationships, you now have to relearn how and when to trust. Even more essential, you first have to learn to trust yourself. You need to be sure that your judgment is so sound that it can be trusted; you need to trust your ability to think and make good decisions. Treat yourself and your life with respect, so you will be able to make decisions that can be trusted.

# Attitude Is Your Way of Concealing Vulnerability

When your trust has been shattered, you are typically left with a defensive wall that is often defined as "attitude." Attitude is perceived as a message to the world that says, "I can take care of myself." There are no two ways about it, attitude is definitely a learned response with historical significance. Even during slavery, sisters were using attitude as a weapon to protect themselves, as may be seen in the memoirs of Cornelia, a former slave, who said: "The one doctrine of my mother's teaching which was branded upon my senses was that I should never let anyone abuse me. 'I'll kill you, gal, if you don't stand up for yourself,' she would say. 'Fight, and if you can't fight, kick; if you can't kick, then bite.'"

When Cornelia's mother, a slave named Fanny, gave her daughter this advice, she believed it was essential for her daughter's safety and well-being that she learn to protect herself any way she could. She knew that Cornelia was going to face many situations in life in which someone would try to put her down or hurt her. Her gift to her daughter was a lesson in maintaining attitude.

Sisters are always listening to people (usually men) tell them they have an "attitude problem." Individually and as a group, we've been called bitchy, bossy, and evil. I think Susan L. Taylor, editor-in-chief of *Essence* magazine, stated it best when she said, "Black women aren't Black and evil. They're Black and tired." She's right.

We're tired of man troubles and money troubles and work

troubles. We're tired of having people play games with our heads, our bodies, and our feelings. We're tired of feeling anxious, and we're tired of being worried. We're tired of working so hard and being blamed for so much of what goes wrong. We're tired of feeling powerless, and we're tired of being disappointed, and we're tired of being called too strong. Typically, when we're so tired inside that we don't know what else to do, we open our mouths to speak our piece, and let me tell you, sometimes what comes out is amazing! Perhaps you grew up surrounded by women who frequently seemed angry and always knew how to say what was on their minds. With these role models, you came by your attitude almost by osmosis, and when it comes to defending and protecting yourself, attitude is definitely a primary skill.

There is another kind of attitude that was also taught to young women by different kinds of protective mothers. Many mothers who wanted to protect their daughters advised them always to keep their own counsel. If someone tried to hurt them, they were told to "hold on and hold out." These mothers believed that there were ways of fighting back without being confrontational. The motto in these households was "In silence, there is strength." And this motto sometimes produces another kind of attitude—a silent anger that can be maintained almost as a weapon.

Whether your attitude comes out as confrontational anger or silent anger, both of these attitudes were learned as a means of self-protection against a hostile, exploitative world. With this thought in mind, as Black women, we need to remember that having an attitude isn't always negative, no matter what we're told. Positive attitude, which I like to call "truth telling," comes out of real strength and is an example of how Black women have managed to use their righteous and justifiable anger to empower themselves through all these hard years. Positive attitude helps you get what you need and deserve. We all want more of this kind of attitude.

Attitude becomes negative and self-defeating when it ends up hurting you and those you love. It's negative when it creates a defensive posture that you put around yourself, like a wall, to keep from feeling any more pain or loss. When we get confused about who and what it is that we are resisting, our weapons get turned against our own relationships and, consequently, against ourselves.

This kind of attitude drives people away, sometimes even people who love and care about you. A sister with this kind of negative attitude can use her words and thoughts to make sure that nobody else can hurt her or leave her because she'll get them first. She can use nagging to push lovers and children away. She can use her short temper to keep her family and friends nervous, fearful, and distant.

From where I sit, when a sister shows a lot of attitude, there is always an underlying reason. Usually, she is overwhelmingly hurt and disappointed by everything that has happened to her and everything that she has seen. Often her self-esteem and her personhood have taken such a beating that she feels she's got nothing much left to lose, so she might as well show her rage. Sometimes she does this with words; frequently she's funny and clever—a real piece of work. Other times she shows her anger with a resounding silence.

Whichever method she chooses, she passes this attitude on to her daughters, who grow up, experience their own pain, and fall back on attitude to help them deal with everything bad that happens to them. In short, when a sister shuts out the people around her, it means that deep down she's angry, she's in pain, and she doesn't know any other way of expressing herself. As much as she may speak out, she's still hiding a hurting heart.

*Your History Lesson:* Recognize that attitude separates you from your true feelings. When you worship at the altar of the attitude goddess, what you're doing is using conflict to deny your pain. What you often end up with is more conflict and more pain. You have to start thinking about finding new ways to work on your self-esteem and deal with your fears of being disappointed or abandoned. And you have to find new and more effective ways of communicating your feelings to those you love.

# Whether You're Conscious of It or Not, Plantation Psychology Still Resides in Your Psyche

We all know that stereotypes about Black people's skills, talents, abilities, and interests were set up on the plantation. Slave owners, who needed to feel comfortable with themselves about the way they were exploiting us, established the pecking order that determined that there were two separate sets of slaves: house slaves and field slaves.

By definition, this separation created conflict and division between these two groups. To complicate this unusual situation, Black women were often impregnated by their masters, and the issues of color, light and dark, were introduced. Now there was yet another way to set up patterns of envy and competitiveness. When we responded by bickering among ourselves, the owners reaped the rewards of this extraordinary divide-and-conquer system.

It's easy to see that the plantation structure was an enormous setup that left our ancestors powerless to change their fates. The only way to better oneself was to identify with the oppressor. Only by getting closer and being more like white people could you hope to lessen your afflictions. There was no other alternative. Psychology teaches us that when one feels powerless against the larger system, one tends to vent anger and rage against those who are close. And that's what happened; we lashed out and took out our frustrations on each other.

A pattern of behavior was established in our communities. Competitiveness, faultfinding, and finger-pointing took over: "What makes her think she's so special; she's no better than me." "She thinks she's white." "He's acting like a damn Uncle Tom." This pattern of competitive attack against one's own people, those who are nearest and dearest, continues today.

We compete against our mates, we compete against our

friends, we compete against our family members, we compete against strangers on community street corners. All too often these face-offs are some form of leftover plantation madness that strikes angry people who don't know what to do about their justifiable frustrations. When we fight about who's got the best system for cleaning a house, or who's got the most information about what to do with money, or who's smarter about life, or who's showing the most disrespect, we fight as though our entire future depends on it. Whether it's in our marriages or in our friendships, too often instead of joining forces to get to a better life, we compete with each other and limit progress.

*Your History Lesson:* Unless you are careful, you will continue to play out the plantation psychology in all your personal relationships. Color bondage; divide-and-conquer bondage; blame bondage; envy and jealousy bondage; breadwinner bondage; and, most of all, hate bondage. This kind of thinking was masterminded back on the plantation, and it's got to go.

We must reach out and help one another. We need to understand that one brother's or sister's progress does not defeat another brother's or sister's purpose. Two sisters who understood this were Mary Church Terrell and Josephine St. Pierre Ruffin, who founded the National Association of Colored Women's Clubs earlier in the century. The organization's motto, "Lifting as We Climb," is still applicable today. As I used to say on my radio show, "We are family."

# You've Been Conditioned to Expect the Worst from Black Men

In all likelihood you've been listening to complaints about Black men for your entire life. Probably without realizing it, you've internalized so many of these complaints that you are overly suspicious and judgmental about men. Think about the following statements:

- Black men are always late.
- Black men never call when they say they will.
- Black men are full of jive.
- Black men are always on the prowl.
- Black men tell stories.
- Black men lack follow-through.
- Black men spend too much time with the boys.
- And let's not forget the ever popular, all the good Black men are taken; the rest are gay, on drugs, or in jail.

You may have started out hearing these things when you were still a child. You heard the women complaining in church, in the beauty parlors, in their kitchens. Mothers, aunts, older sisters. You didn't realize it, but all the messages you've heard have prepared you for romantic disappointment. These messages may have even set up an expectation of poor treatment from men.

When you were young, you probably didn't like it when you heard the women around you attack men, and you may have even vowed that when you grew up, you would be different. You would have good relationships, and you weren't going to find fault with men. Because you were different, the man in your life was going to be different.

Then you met the real world, and a real man, and he was less than the perfect prince you dreamed of, and here you are sitting in the kitchen with the girlfriends bitching up a storm. Or doing something that's a lot less fun—nagging at your man in the living room or, worse, in the bedroom. How did this happen?

The way I see it, the typical sister is rightfully angry at Black men about many things—so many things, in fact, that her head is filled with what I see as little simmering pots filled with unspoken rage and disappointment. Some of what is cooking in these pots are the destructive things that have happened to her personally, but also included are all those things that she heard happened to other women with other men, past and present. Then along comes a brother who fails her in some way, and she says, "Uh-huh, that's right." The flame goes up, the pot starts boiling over, and it all comes out.

If you have experienced a lot of romantic disappointment or if you've seen too many other women get hurt, your anger and resentment can be so close to the surface that all a man has to do is be five minutes late once, and you'll jump on him for every time every Black man has ever been late with any Black woman. He'll want to go out with the boys once a month, and you'll react as though he is out every night until bar closing. He'll lose a job, and you'll be thinking you're always going to be supporting the family while he spends the rest of his life sitting on the couch watching television.

Anyone who has run or attended as many relationship seminars or has been on as many television panels as I have knows that Black men don't hold a special claim on lateness, laziness, or womanizing. Calling all Black men lazy is just reinforcing a stereotype that was imposed on the Black workforce during slavery, and don't you forget it.

I was on *Oprah* a few years back, when a woman in the audience kept referring to lazy out-of-work Black men. I let her go on for a while and then decided that a historical correction was called for. I reminded her that this false stereotype of laziness was invented to reinforce the mind-set of white slave owners. Did she honestly believe that anybody would travel all the way to another continent to bring back a group of *lazy* people to pick cotton? As Black people, we all know that what she now sees on the street corners of America is a used-up labor force, suffering from chronic unemployment and without hope. Charlie, one smart young brother from the "hood" calls this modern condition "sophisticated slavery."

When you're talking about Black men, you should also keep in mind that there are just as many white women complaining about white men as there are Black women complaining about Black men. White women also say that men try to tell them what to do and don't help around the house. They complain about men who don't do anything but watch TV, hang out with the guys, drink beer, and chase other women. Doesn't that all sound familiar? However, the truth is that nobody judges a man as harshly as a Black woman does when she has been taught to expect the worst and doesn't know how to work for the best.

*Your History Lesson:* Don't be so quick to label a brother and reject the whole man when you reject the behavior. Take a lesson from Lorraine Hansberry's award-winning play *Raisin in the Sun.* In the play, Beneatha is talking about her unemployed brother Walter Lee, who has used up the family's funds. She says there is nothing about Walter Lee left to love, when Mama makes her healing statement: "Child, when do you think is the time to love somebody the most; when they done good and made things easy for everybody? Well then, you ain't through learning—because that ain't the time at all. It's when he's at his lowest and can't believe in hisself 'cause the world done whipped him so. When you start measuring somebody, measure him right, child, measure him right. Make sure you done taken into account what hills and valleys he come through before he got to wherever he is."

# Historically You've Received Little Protection from Anyone

It's hardly news that the institutions in this country have never fully protected Black people. Sisters, who have the double-jeopardy status of being Black and female, often feel that they can't depend on anybody for protection—not the white community; not the Black community; and, too often, not even the men they love. The typical sister can't help but believe that she is less protected than other women; this makes her feel alone, vulnerable, and resentful. As Black women, we keep hearing how strong we are, and we are strong. But when the typical sister stops to consider all that strength, what she's usually thinking is that nobody needs to have gone through what she's gone through to be that strong! In fact, when she looks around, she feels as though everybody else is surrounded by safety nets while she's all alone on a high wire.

Sometimes when we look at the fantasy world depicted by magazines, television programs, and films, it seems as though all we see are women, usually white, who are being put on pedestals and handed diamonds and other tokens of affection by men who are doing everything they can to take care of them.

The fact is that the white community isn't all that protective of the majority of white women either, but the mass media and advertising show us a lot of pseudoprotection. And it makes you feel bad. It makes you feel that you're the only one in the whole world who is standing alone, without a protective man helping you fight life's battles. You start feeling like you've got problems from which you need saving— whether your problems stem from loneliness, financial stress, sexual longings, or just a sense that the world holds too many terrors for a woman alone.

*Your History Lesson:* Recognize that wishing and hoping for protection can make you particularly vulnerable to bad choices because this leaves you open to fantasy thinking. You start looking for a man who's going to surround you with protection and care and "say it with diamonds" like the advertisements tell us to expect. You start looking for fantasy figures like the Black prince or the Black knight in shining armor. The problem is that there are a great many men, both Black and white, who will sweet-talk a sister into believing they are going to be able to save her. It's a nice fantasy, but it's not one any woman can count on.

# History Has Made You Self-Conscious About Your Appearance

No matter what her physical type or shade of skin color, the typical sister is tuned in to internal voices telling her she is too tall, too short, too light-skinned, too dark-skinned, too fat, or too skinny. Far too many sisters remember having clothespins put on their noses to narrow them and bleaching cream as a skin lightener. In short, it's a rare Black woman who is 100 percent comfortable with the way she looks.

Listen to some of the messages you heard in childhood:

"Look at that child, she's got the nappiest hair I've ever
    seen."
"That girl's skin is so dark, she turns blue in the sun."
"Her nose is so wide . . . "
"Her lips are so thick . . . "
"Her butt is so big . . . "
"Her legs are so skinny . . . "

These voices follow us all our lives. As we all know by now, the African American community's obsession with physical appearance started when our ancestors internalized white attitudes toward beauty. Our ancestors first compared beautiful Black women against the white women who lived in the big (plantation) houses and later against those who appeared in advertisements and in the movies. As one would expect, the Black woman responded by becoming insecure. She started trying to straighten her hair, lighten her skin, and disavow her body type. Most distressing, within our communities there was altogether too much talk about skin color. Sometimes men and women were even told that they were supposed to find partners who were "lighter," so they could lighten the race. "Light, bright, and damned near white" was the color standard. I call this color codifying, and it is designed to destroy self-esteem.

Then, thank the Lord, there was a backlash. Suddenly, the Black Is Beautiful movement emerged, and for a very brief period it looked as though we were going to stop putting emphasis where it didn't belong. Finally, it looked as though there was going to be an end to this kind of illogical thinking. But that didn't happen because some people still hung on to what I call the "white standard" while others began to focus on how Black was Black, which further complicated the appearance issues. That's when men and women with light skin started hearing that they weren't Black enough!

To rid ourselves of color games, we need to understand that Black refers to race, not color. Those of African descent belong to the Black race, which contains all hues of the color spectrum. There is no such thing as Blackupmanship!

Recently I read a book by a sister named Yelena Khanga (written with Susan Jacoby) entitled *Soul to Soul*. I had the fortunate experience of meeting this sister at a convention for the Association of Black Journalists. I think what broke the ice between us was my speaking my few words of Russian to her. Yelena had the unique experience of growing up Black in Russia. Coming to this country, she had to deal with what it means to be Black in America. One of the things that struck her was our emphasis on color. In her book she says:

> Soon after arriving in Boston in 1987, I lost my way on a tram and asked a handsome young black man for directions to the *Monitor*. He noticed my accent and asked where I was from. He wanted to hear more about Russia, so he offered to walk me to my office. I was a little bit excited by the encounter. I'd met a good-looking black guy just by asking for directions! Who knew, maybe Prince Charming would turn out to be a black American.
>
> As he began explaining his version of black America, I realized he was only interested in the Russian part of me. He talked about his own circle of successful black friends and told me all of them had light skin. "You, for instance," he remarked almost casually, "would be too dark for me. My friends would be surprised if I turned up with a girl who looked like you." I was amazed. . . . Was it possible that I, coppery me, right in the middle of the black-American color spectrum, would be considered too dark by a black man? What sort of looking glass had I fallen through?

Yelena Khanga's book shows us how a Black woman from another country responds to our color madness. Too often

Black Americans have internalized this kind of foolish thinking. The end result of all this focus on physical appearances that do or do not measure up to some impossible ideal is that the typical sister is always selling herself short. There has been so much overpowering information about what a sister should look like that it's small wonder that she often believes she's not measuring up. She feels as though she can't compete with other women because there is always something wrong that she can't fix.

*Your History Lesson*: Stop believing that you have to *fix* or change the way you look. This sense of wanting to *fix* yourself means that you're always picking yourself apart. These toxic feelings of insecurity can't help but spill over into your relationships, to your disadvantage. Focus on your African beauty and walk your graceful African gazelle walk through the city jungles or in the shade-tree suburbs. A lot of music has been written celebrating Black womanhood. Just think to yourself that wherever you walk, the earth is filled with the music of "Sweet Georgia Brown." Listen to the music about you. Poet Mona Lake Jones begins your concerto when she advocates: "A room full of sisters, like jewels in a crown, Vanilla, cinnamon, and dark chocolate brown . . ."

# History Has Made You Accustomed to High Drama

The good news about this situation: The changes that the typical sister has lived through have made her a genius at crisis-oriented decision making; the bad news: When nothing is going wrong, sometimes she is the one who stirs the pot. Claudia, a sister I know, describes it this way: "You've heard the expression 'sh—— happens'; well, in my family it *really* happens."

Claudia is not alone. Let's face it, our ancestors didn't lead calm lives, and even today, the average Black family has significantly more ups and downs than any roller coaster anybody I know is going to pay to ride on. Since generations of Black Americans have grown up not knowing what was going to happen next, it's a rare sister who has been blessed with security, stability, or a sense of continuity.

Of course, there are elements in everyone's life that are somewhat out of control, but from slavery on, so many things have been out of our control: where we lived, how we lived, where we worked, if we worked, where we went to school, where we raised our children. The list of ways in which our choices and consequently our economics have been limited is endless.

This sense of not being able to control your destiny can't help but effect the way you view the world. It can't help but make you feel that since there is little you can count on, it doesn't make sense to try to plan ahead. Besides, because so much is always going on that needs managing, how can a sister stand still long enough to think ahead?

All of this has been compounded for the typical sister simply because she is a woman, and traditionally so much that happens in the home is determined by her children and the man she loves. The typical sister is thinking about everybody's problems. You know what that's like: If your man or your kids are having difficulties, you're expected to help provide solutions. Even when the problems are monumental and seem completely beyond your control, you're supposed to be able to jump right in and fix everything. One woman told me that she felt as though she were leading her life *trapped* in a three-ring circus.

The ability to deal with crisis efficiently and effectively is a wonderful quality. But there are several downsides. For example, when a sister leads her life from crisis to crisis, she can become accustomed to an emotional Ferris wheel. There's always a drama or a side show, there's always something causing a sinking feeling in her stomach or a jubilant sense of being on top, if only for a moment. If it all stops, sometimes it feels as though something is missing.

Sometimes a Black woman will create even more troubles for herself because she's so used to chaos that she doesn't notice it unless it's totally out of control. She may let emotional chaos pile up in her personal life because she figures she is so strong and so skilled at crisis management that she will always be able to deal with it. She may choose the wrong guys, run up too many bills, or generally lead her life much too close to the edge. The end result: She's always trying to dig herself out of one mess or another.

If you feel as though you have no power to control your life, you will always feel like a victim. You may not be able to stop other people from bringing crisis into your life, but you can start controlling the kind of people you allow to enter your life.

*Your History Lesson:* Hard experience has given you admirable skills for coping with drama and crisis management. What our history has eroded is the ability to think in terms of long-term goals. You need to work at developing better skills at life management and planning ahead. Think about *crisis prevention* and protect yourself by conserving your resources, both financial and emotional. Get positive, don't be victimized by chaos, and start thinking about your life with an in-charge attitude. Make sure the people you team up with, male and female, are people who will work with you to make good plans for the future.

# You Find It Difficult to Separate from Those You've Loved

Even when a relationship is destructive or finished, the typical sister has so much separation anxiety that she finds it heartbreakingly difficult to move on and let go of her feelings. Because of our history with slavery, I believe we start out our lives programmed to feel overwhelmingly anxious at the idea of losing someone who is close to us. Engraved into our memories are loud, clear messages about our ancestors having been separated and sold away from each other. Women losing husbands, mothers losing children, children losing fathers and mothers, sisters and brothers losing each other: Such a deep sense of loss is built into our emotional structure that it feels as though it's part of our DNA. When we think about it, it's terrifying.

Sometimes a sister has this global sense of loss, reinforced by her own childhood experiences. Statistics tell us that a sister has often been separated temporarily or even permanently from a parent. Perhaps she was raised in a household where no father was present, or perhaps her father was physically present but was so distant that his spirit seemed to have walked out the door.

In other words, as a Black woman living in America, you come from a heritage of loss, and this fact is going to reverberate throughout your life in very specific ways. As men move in and out of your life, they are going to push buttons and trigger responses that may be much more intense than they deserve. I've heard sisters say, "I didn't even want him around, but the minute he walked out the door, I thought I was going to die from the pain." Sisters often wonder why they put up with so much, rather than end a relationship. They question why they grieve for a man for what can seem to be a lifetime. Here's an answer:

The idea of separation creates an inner drama that brings up all the loss you're carrying around with you. It triggers a mechanism that makes you feel as though you're losing not just a man, but you're also losing bits and pieces of yourself. Every time somebody leaves, it brings up all those unconscious memories of what our ancestors experienced. There's only so much loss that anybody can bear, and you feel loss so strongly that it makes you feel separated from yourself and sold away from yourself. All this pain chips away at your inner core, at your inner sense of self. It makes you feel as though when you are searching for a man, you're not just searching for a mate; you're also searching for yourself. It feels like a game of blind man's buff.

*Your History Lesson:* There are lingering anxieties running around in the hearts and minds of Black people that few of us will ever fully examine or make conscious. Preeminent psychologist and president emeritus of the Association of Black Psychologists, Na'im Akbar, Ph.D., refers to this condition as the psychological chains of slavery. Some of our anxieties are directly related to what I call the auction-block syndrome. The auction block was the place where our ancestors were judged and sold with no thought to their human dignity or feelings. It's extremely painful to think about the indignities these dignified people suffered. Yet these experiences are part of what some experts describe as genetic memory and consequently affect the psyche of each African American. Your reluctance to examine these terrifying memories can give them more power in your life than they deserve. Spend some time thinking about your genetic memory, and you may discover that these collective fears are at the very core of your need for security and power in your relationships with others.

Once you have faced these fears and acknowledged your anxieties concerning them, I believe you will be able to see how they have influenced your personal decision making. No sister should ever be so afraid of losing a man that she tolerates inappropriate or destructive behavior. Carry this fact around with you: You can't be sold away from yourself. Find your own center and your own powerful voice, and no man will be able to use your fear of separation as a means of controlling you. Break the psychological chains of slavery that separate you from your reliable Afrocentric self.

# History Has Given You Many Confused Messages About Sex

When we watch television or read books, we see Black sexuality portrayed as hot and steamy. We hear jokes about the myth of the Black man with the big genitals. We see stereotypes of Black women as big, sexy Mamas and hot-to-trot Miss Looseys. As far as the media are concerned, the "Mandingo Syndrome" is alive and well. Then we read surveys about the differences between white America and Black

America as far as sexuality is concerned, and we discover that Black America is significantly more conservative. Why is there so much distance between the myth of sexuality that is wild, steamy, and abandoned and the reality of sexuality that is frequently unsatisfying and often repressed?

There's a simple answer. African Americans had their sexuality controlled, manipulated, and supervised by others for over three hundred years. Coming through an experience like that, we can't help but be confused about our sexual identities. Even in our own communities, we've bought into the stereotypes and the mythology to such a degree that some of us have completely internalized them.

Yes, once again we have to travel back to the plantation to get to the root causes of our confusion. The truth is that our African ancestors derived their sexual values from their religious values, and sex was seen in the context of rite and procreation. But the white slave owners thought our great-great-great-grandparents were so primitive, wild, and passionate that they needed controlling in all ways, particularly sexual. And control they did!

To produce even stronger slaves, the strongest and healthiest Black male was often chosen to serve as a stud for the women. Frequently, sex with him was the only sex that was approved. That's how young women with surging sexual hormones found themselves competing for the favors of the plantation "Buck." Women who followed orders and had more children not only were given trinkets or small favors in return, they also received higher status. As we all know, the white owners frequently used the mythology of the sexually primitive out-of-control Black woman as a rationalization for their own institutionalized sexual abuse and rape. To continue the color game, they used their mythology to support their biology.

Mothers who experienced this kind of abuse worried for their daughters. Wanting to shield them, they typically issued a series of extremely repressive conservative messages aimed at nullifying this stereotype and protecting their daughters from sexual exploitation.

In the meantime, after several generations of being rewarded as baby makers, Black men absorbed and internalized the messages about their sexuality, placing inappropriate value on the roles of stud and baby maker.

More than 150 years after slavery, we're still dealing with the same kinds of sexual issues, the same kinds of stereotypes, and the same kind of thinking. All too often, Black men and Black women do not communicate their sexual feelings. For example, we hear many brothers complain that they are being used as studs, while we hear scores of sisters complain that they need tenderness more than they need sex.

*Your History Lesson:* Learn how to break out of the roles that internalized white values have forced on you. Sex isn't just something we do between our legs. Sex is about the whole person. How we take that message and translate it to somebody else is our sexuality. Sex is many things. Sex is a sincere conversation with somebody who understands what you say and is able to embrace your feelings. Sex is being alone and dancing in your nightclothes. Sex is your essential self, and it's no stereotype!

# When You Know Better, You Do Better

Didn't someone once say, "Those who forget the past are destined to repeat it"? I think it's important for each of us as African American women to remember the lessons that history has taught us, so that we can shape and mold our futures in a better direction.

An African American's life always has three components operating simultaneously: the historical experience that shaped the person's present-day socio-economic status; his or her current economic, educational, social, and political conditions; and the attitudes—positive or negative—that come from these factors and consequently shape one's life.

Understanding these vital connections will ultimately

empower our individual and/or collective responses. In our intimate relationships, the strong *collective response* is our SECRET WEAPON. Without this knowledge, we tend to feed on each other's fears and maintain oppression by victimizing each other. *Umoja* is the first principle of Blackness. *Umoja* means unity or togetherness.

Black people have always loved truth. Time and time again, our ability to see and tell the truth has been our salvation. Self-knowledge implies the ability to see the truth about who we are as Black women of African descent. Our history is part of our truth; understanding it is part of understanding who we are and how we got this way. From a psychological point of view, history can help explain behavior that is out of our conscious reach, and it can help us heal our relationships.

My Uncle Charlie and Aunt Bea used to sing an old spiritual that exhorts, "My soul looks back and wonders how I got over." That makes me believe that all these many painful experiences in the Black American's past are not predictors of the future. Rather, these trials and tribulations that were survived give us hope for the future, coping skills for the present, and a made-up mind for the journey. Don't be a sister who feels the pain and never learns the lesson. Learning your lessons is an excellent way to avoid what I call pain addiction, which creates the climate for the blues or chronic depression. When you learn your lessons, you feel a sense of pride and accomplishment as well as hope for the future.

# 3

# Looking Inward: Figuring Out What You Want from a Man

"I think I've figured something out. Almost every time I've got a man in my life, the people around me have something to say about him. Everyone told me that one man who liked me was way too ugly, even though he had a good body; another wasn't making enough money and wasn't driving a 'name' car. Now I don't have anybody, and I'm wondering why I ever paid any attention to what anyone had to say about what I do. I really should learn to take care of my own business."

—DANIELLE, 32

## When You Let Someone Else Do Your Thinking

When Danielle says that she let other people's opinions about her boyfriends influence her thinking, she's telling us something about herself. She's telling us that she is always looking to others to confirm or negate what she is doing. In other words, she's telling us that she doesn't have a secure enough sense of self to make her own judgments and her own evaluations.

Danielle is not unusual in paying too much attention to what others think. Let's get straight about something: Anyone who has ever been oppressed is not going to have a strong sense of self. As someone who is both Black and female, Danielle is a member of two large groups that have suffered oppression. Before she can think about finding a man, she has to think about finding herself.

# Second-Guessing Your Own Judgment

When you don't have a strong sense of self, you keep questioning yourself and others, "Am I doing the right thing?" "Do you think that man's right for me?" Even when you know what you should do, you ask, "What do you think I should do about this situation?" When a man pursues you, you don't evaluate him for yourself. Instead you think to yourself, "He seems to like me, so I guess I should like him."

A sister often believes she will have more value as a woman if she has a man to confirm her as a woman. Then she measures the man against what her friends think. If he doesn't measure up, she's caught in a dilemma: Is she worth more because a man likes her, or is she worth less because he's not rich enough or good-looking enough to impress the people she knows. This kind of thinking comes with not having a strong sense of self.

If you are Black and female, you may always have to fight this tendency to question yourself and your judgment. That's because women have been conditioned to believe that what they hear from others is more valid than what they think for themselves. For example, all women—Black, white, and every shade in between—have historically denied their intellect in order to fit into a male interpretation of what femininity should be. All women have been told to define themselves in terms of men and in ways that satisfy male-dominated societies. Women are taught that they need to have men to feel like women and that they need successful men if they want to feel successful.

For an African American woman, these issues are doubly toxic because we live in a society where Black people, both male and female, always have to deal with other people's interpretations of our reality. Here's a fact: As long as other people interpret your world, you're letting someone else tell you what to do. As long as you're worried about what someone else thinks, you will never be free. As long as you let someone else tell you how to run your life, you will never make good decisions.

# How My Mother Taught Me to Think for Myself

When I was in the tenth grade, I had an experience that I believe changed my life and helped me develop my capacity to shape my own behavior and make my own decisions, and I'd like to share it with you. As a teenager in a mostly white high school, I really felt as though I needed approval from my peers. The approval that I wanted most of all came from two teenage Black girls and their little clique. I wanted to belong to this group, and I was willing to do just about anything to be accepted by them.

Because I am light-skinned, I had what was perceived as a problem, and these two girls made fun of me because of it. They determined in their minds that if I didn't show enough of an attitude in class with my gym teacher, they would give me a hard time. These were the kinds of color games that "colored girls" (as we were then called) played when I was growing up.

Having my Black identity questioned was very distressing to me because I was raised to have a strong African-based identity. I was brought up in the north by two southern parents, in what I call an Alabama-African environment. I was even fortunate enough to know my great-grandfather, Deamos Caffee, who was born into slavery before the Civil War and who lived until he was 110. Everything in my life confirmed my Black identity and where I came from.

Because I wanted so desperately to fit in, I tried to prove myself to these classmates by giving the teacher a lot of attitude. I put my hand on my hip, I let my backbone slip, and I kimboed my way through class, mouthing off the whole time. Well, after a few days of this behavior, I got what I wanted; I started to get a reputation as a troublemaker, so I gained the approval of this clique of girls. However, I sure wasn't getting what I needed for my own well-being.

The teacher called my mother, who came to school; together they quickly concluded that I was trying to prove myself to the group. When I got home, I got my punishment. My mother told me that it was going to be difficult enough for me in life to be Black and female; I didn't need to be Black and a fool. My mother was a beautiful woman with dark brown skin and an Afrocentric attitude long before Stokely Carmichael ever raised his fist as a Black power symbol. She told me that only a fool would buy in to and continue to play the color games of slavery. She said that as punishment for my inability to think for myself, I was going to have to be alone for a full month. That meant no visits with friends, no phone calls, and no social activities of any kind for thirty days. My mother said that I had to be with myself until I came to myself and learned to think for myself.

I regard that month I spent alone as an extraordinarily valuable lesson. After four weeks of this solitude, I really did have a different attitude. The experience made me see that I had other choices. I could find other friends, and I could behave differently with them. There were other Black teenagers who were prepared to accept me for who I was. As a result, I began to expand my horizons and started availing myself of other opportunities that high school could offer. The world wasn't limited by a clique of girls who wanted me to prove myself. It was an empowering experience, and it really did provide a turning point in my life because it forced me to look at the information that I was getting from these girls I wanted as my friends, and it made me realize that following their advice wasn't going to get me anyplace.

# Bad Information Is All Over the Place

As Black women, we sometimes think that the only ones we have to worry about telling us what to do are society as a whole or men in particular. We know how to monitor bad information when it's coming from an obvious racist point of view, and we've all developed indicators that tell us when some guy is being a total sexist jerk. What we don't have are good ways of sifting information when it's coming from the mass media or from friends, family members, and people in our community who look like us. So we listen to friends who sometimes also have been listening to the wrong advice, and we listen to family and members of the community who may also be making their judgments based on the wrong kind of information.

Because we don't know how to sift through everything we're told, we don't always distinguish between good information that is supportive and helpful and bad information that is negative and potentially destructive. There is a lot of information out there telling you what you need from a man. Let's see if we can take a look at it and figure out the difference between the good advice and the bad advice.

# How You Figure Out What You Want from a Man

You didn't enter this world full grown and talking about how you want a guy who is tall, dark, handsome, smart, and rich and who is going to satisfy all your needs for a wonderful, exciting, stimulating life. These thoughts were created by many different outside influences. To understand how complicated these influences are, think about how you form your attitudes toward something simple. For example, whether you send all your laundry out or do it yourself, you probably have some strong notions about how it should be done.

These ideas of yours about how to handle wash were formed by a complicated selection of conflicting advice, mixed messages, and personal experience. You probably received some advice from the women around you, you may have read up on washing machines and dryers in periodicals like *Consumer Reports*, and you may have paid close attention to the messages in television commercials by companies that were trying to sell detergent and appliances. Finally, putting all this information together, you discovered through hard experience what works for you when it comes to getting your clothes clean.

If it's this complicated figuring out whether you should put Tide, Cheer, or Wisk into your GE, Kenmore, or May-tag washing machine, imagine how complicated it is to process really important information about love, commitment, and relationships among Black people. Our goals and our expectations have been formed by such a variety of different forces that it's worth looking at some of them in more detail.

## The Voices We Hear Around Us

It would be much easier for all of us if we had some solid source of advice that we could rely on, and as children that's what we look for—a reliable information source. Elizabeth, a

Jamaican sister, talks about her search for dependable answers: "Growing up in the West Indies, it seemed as though the grown-ups around me had an answer for everything that anyone might ever want to do, whether it was the right way to make a meal or the right way to treat a man. Some of what they said was good and practical, but sometimes what they said was totally off the mark. Nevertheless, because I was looking for answers, for a long time I took every word as gospel."

You notice that Elizabeth started out believing everything she was told by her elders. This is true for most of us, even when we don't remember ever having been young enough to feel that way. The fact is that as Black people, we have a tradition of listening to our elders. Probably the most enduring model or archetype in our culture is that of the wise older person, be it a man or a woman, who holds secrets and information. We believe this kind of person can tell us things we need to know.

For our ancestors in Africa, the wise old men and women of the village taught the secrets of the world and individual destiny. They relayed the facts about reproduction, birth, the meaning of life, death as it relates to life, sickness, health, love, and passion. They carried a large body of knowledge, as well as "rules" about how to live right.

These elders passed on their wisdom to the next generation, who passed it on to the next, who passed it on to the next, until it became a chant of common wisdom that everyone heard. Within the villages, men and women used the common wisdom conveyed in these chants as a way of measuring themselves and their achievements. If you followed the behavioral and societal guidelines set down in these chants, you were "doing right." When you didn't, you were doing wrong. In life, there were only two ways to go—African right or African wrong. That's just the way things were.

I call this chanting "the Village Chorus," and it still goes on even though the kinds of things that are repeated in these chants have changed significantly. I want to make it clear that I don't think of the Village Chorus as a group of people. No, it's just a collection of disembodied voices that have become totally embedded in our thought processes. These voices are no longer giving advice as much as they are disseminating messages.

## Searching for Answers and Listening to the Village Chorus

Black men complain that sisters are always taking advice from others. In a way, their complaint is true, but Black men do exactly the same thing. The capacity to look for answers, to seek knowledge and information, and to search for meaning is one of the most beautiful characteristics that we share in our Black culture.

Most of us want to know what's right and wrong, what should be and what shouldn't be. We want to make intelligent choices based on intelligent information. This desire for wisdom is very precious. However, it can also leave us vulnerable to the wrong kind of advice and the wrong kind of judgment.

It seems obvious to say that when you're searching for answers, it's important to find good advisers. Here's where the problem comes in: Although there is a great deal of wisdom in our communities, there is also a great deal of confused thinking, and much of that confusion is heard in the voices that make up the modern village chorus. What we have now is a village chorus that has seen too many movies, watched too much television, and bought into too much advertising. I've always believed that conflicted thinking is the burden of the oppressed. Listen to some of the conflicted messages we hear.

"If he's got a fine car, the brother is living large, and you will, too."
"Take up with him, and you're going to have to provide for him and pay the bills, too! Girlfriend, that car's going to cost you plenty!"

"Find a man who is a good breadwinner."
"Don't judge a brother by how much money he makes."

"Black men know how to treat a sister."
"Find a white man. They really know how to treat a woman."

"He's something else, the way he knows how to romance a woman."
"Romance without finance becomes a nuisance."

"Uh-huh, he's slammin' fine-looking."
"He's just another pretty boy looking for a dumb girl."

"Build a brother's ego by telling people what he does right."
"Don't tell what your man can do because another woman might want to try him, too."

"Be honest with your man."
"Don't ever tell him what you're really thinking. He'll end up throwing it in your face."

"Let him know from jump street that you have your own money, honey."
"Don't tell him about your money or else he'll be trying to get into your pockets as well as your drawers."

These messages aren't coming from a place that contains a tradition of sound advice about doing right. Instead, they are coming from a place that has been influenced by a mishmash of media hype, Eurocentric thinking, and unrealistic fantasies.

## Two Messages That We Need to Take with a Grain of Salt

If you look at most of the advice that has been directed to us as Black women, you'll notice that it tends to reflect two separate and distinct points of view:

- Have "attitude" (protect yourself because you can't trust anybody).

- Have "faith" (trust everybody and put your faith in fairy-tale endings).

Message that reflect these two points of view are typically delivered by people who sound as though they are repeating gospel. Everywhere we go we hear messages like, "A real man is supposed to take care of his woman" and "Take care of *yourself*, sugar; every tub stands on its own bottom." These messages have been repeated to us so often that we have internalized them without realizing it, and we repeat them even to ourselves.

When you hear both of these messages (have attitude and have faith) and you're not comfortable living your life according to either one, the conflict between them can make you go back and forth in your own head. "Am I being too strong and independent?" you ask yourself. "Or am I putting my faith in pipe dreams?" This kind of conflicted thinking is further complicated by our awareness of two major stereo-types—the strong Black woman who can take care of herself, as well as everybody else, and the silly hysterical Black woman who can't even handle chump change.

Typically what a sister does in her own life is to start looking for a romantic good-looking man who is both willing and able to take care of her. Then when she doesn't find someone who fits this bill, she becomes disgusted and goes about the business of taking care of herself and builds her romantic fantasies in her own head.

There is a third alternative that I want to encourage sisters to think about. When it comes to men, I think sisters need to spend less time developing attitude or maintaining faith in storybook endings. I think they should develop a new system of dealing with men based on *common sense*.

## DEVELOPING COMMON SENSE
My grandmother used to call common sense "mother wit" or "good sense." Common sense means that you take every situation you encounter with a man individually and you

assess it for yourself. Common sense (not so common) is what gives you the ability to see the differences between one person and another. It's what keeps you from making generalizations about all Black men or all Black women.

When you're using common sense to evaluate a potentially romantic relationship in your life, you have to let it develop gradually because common sense tells you that you need plenty of information to assess what is happening. Common sense tells you to hold back your feelings, your expectations, and your final judgments until you know what a man is all about. Doing this is practicing good "border control" in your own life.

If Danielle, whom we met at the beginning of this chapter, had been using common sense, she wouldn't have rushed to any judgments about a man being "way too ugly." She would have gotten to know him, she would have allowed a friendship to develop, and she would have been able to see for herself what this man's positive and negative characteristics were as a potential partner. Besides, anybody who has been married for any length of time could tell her that in a long-term relationship, it doesn't take long for looks to recede.

Right now, more than ever, you and other sisters like you need to be able to decode what's going on with male-female relationships. If you're going to recognize a good man when you see one or protect yourself from a destructive relationship before it becomes overwhelming, you have to use common sense. If you go into your closet in the morning and pull out a dress only to discover that there is a big stain on it, common sense tells you that the only way you're going to get that stain out is by cleaning it. You're not going to wish it away, and it's not going to disappear by itself. Because you don't want to wear a stained dress, you put on something else. That's common sense. If you can't figure out for yourself whether your dress is clean or dirty, you can't see for looking. A romantic situation is no different. You have to use your own common sense, or mother wit, to figure out what's going on in your own life.

# The First Commonsense Question to Ask Yourself Is: Does the Man You Want Actually Exist?

"I'd like to find a relationship with the right man, but nobody I meet reminds me of Bryant Gumbel or anybody else I'd want to be with. Growing up, even with this pretty face, I knew I was too skinny and dark ever to be Miss America, but I thought for sure I'd end up being Mrs. Somebody Wonderful. Even though I had a hard life, I picked myself up and got a good profession and a good lifestyle. Now I want a family, but I need to meet a brother who will match me. The problem is I can't find him. Maybe he's not even there."

—CARRIE, 41

Carrie raises an interesting point. Recently I was leading a workshop and I asked each woman to make a list of what she wanted from a man. One stylishly dressed woman stood up and started talking about what she expected. She said that she believed in setting her sights high, so she wanted a tall, dark, handsome man who would wine her, dine her, and give her presents. She wanted walks in the park and Sundays at the museum. And she wanted to go places. She wanted to go to the Grammy Awards, the Essence Awards, Black Expo, Soul Train Awards, and the NBA playoffs—to name just a few.

When she finished talking, the woman next to her blurted out, "Honey, you think you want a husband, but what you really want is a TV set."

Setting our sights on fantasy men who don't exist can't help but make us conflicted about what we want from the real men in our lives. Do we want a traditional family life, sitting home with the husband and the kids, or do we want an out-every-night running-and-doing kind of life? Do we want day-to-day settled, stable love, or do we want roller-coaster passion and excitement? Do we want too much, or do we expect too little? Are we carrying shopping wish lists for men who don't exist except on daytime TV?

# What Television Programs Tell Us We Want

I'm not alone in believing that the media, particularly television, has special meaning for you as a Black woman. In fact, surveys have found that Black Americans spend more time in front of the tube than does any other group. What does this finding mean? Well, everyone agrees: If you watch enough television, you can't help but be influenced by what you see. By definition, whether you're aware of it or not, this means that you are personally forming expectations based on a media version of the world.

The necessary task of the media, particularly television, is to sanitize and homogenize everything and to present all America as one big happy Brady Bunch, whose members have the same wants and needs. For the media, this is a powerful selling tool. But when sisters absorb and accept this kind of thinking, it separates them from the real world, as well as from the values that are part of our heritage.

For example, we know how much we hate it when a brother passes up a fine Black woman and chases after a Cindy Crawford look-alike. Well, as women of African descent, all too often we're guilty of the same kind of thinking, even though it sometimes looks different. Too many sisters are caught up in what I call the soap-opera syndrome. They don't notice the Black men they interact with every day. They say they don't want an everyday kind of guy. What they want for themselves are men who look and act like Thyme Lewis and other actors on daytime television.

Society feeds all women, white and Black, with a lot of fantasy about strong powerful men who will give them that swept-away feeling and fulfill their storybook fantasies. We see these images everywhere, and we're encouraged to believe in storybook endings. After all, doesn't Cinderella end up with the prince? Aren't you just as deserving as she was?

For Black women, these fantasies take on an additional twist. When we turn on our television sets, go to the movies, or pick up books, we watch or read about men and women who are living in ways that seem totally different from the ways that the people around us and in our communities live. The truth is that we have all been inundated with material and images that don't fit our lives.

The enviable people featured on television are fabulously groomed men and women who lead glamorous, exciting lives. Why shouldn't a sister want to live like them? They have incredible clothes and fancy cars. They live in big, clean houses with enough drawers and closets to fit the biggest wardrobes. And, yes, of course, most of them are definitely white. Be careful of what I call "media whitewash"!

When the *Cosby Show* came on television in the 1980s, it was a first. Suddenly, there was a Black family on television who didn't seem to be filled with caricatures or stereotypes. But it introduced the same old dilemma. Once again, Black women were presented with images that didn't jibe with what was happening in their own lives. After all, how many male Black doctors married to female lawyers living in half-a-million-dollar brownstones do you meet in your neighborhood? It's still a fantasy life even though the actors had names like Felicia Rashad and Malcolm Jamal Warner.

Terry McMillan's 1992 bestseller, *Waiting to Exhale*, was another first. It was wonderful to read about sisters struggling with life and love in a way that we could relate to. And it wasn't just Black women who related to McMillan's characters. White women read the book, too, and said, "Yes, I also go through these kinds of trials and tribulations with the men in my life." Books like McMillan's are rare, but even so, the cross-cultural implications are very clear.

For the most part, if you are a sister who wants to relax and indulge in some escapism in the form of reading or viewing, you won't find much that reflects your cultural experiences. Because of what Black women watch and read, the message they receive from the mostly white media is very convoluted: It tells them that a desirable man is a rich Black man or any average nine-to-five white man with leisure time. It certainly doesn't tell them anything that makes them appreciate the many regular guys who are working hard and trying to live right in our communities.

# Soap-Opera Thinking and the Female Fantasy Trap

The Black Knight. Mr. Wonderful. He's driving a BMW, dribbling a basketball, showing off his law degree or his medical degree or his MBA. He's tall, he's good-looking, he's well dressed, and he only has eyes for you. When he finally shows up, he's going to empathize with all your problems, pay off all your debts, help you achieve all your goals, and absolutely adore your body.

The soap-opera syndrome tends to affect many Black women, single or married. Talk to most *single* sisters, and you will notice a lot of old Black magical thinking revolving around meeting and marrying an African American superstar. Talk to most *married* sisters, and you will find they also measure their marriages and their men against fantasy expectations.

Michele, a 29-year-old bookkeeper, is a good example of a single sister who is singing, "Someday my Black prince will come." Although Michele has a good job and plenty of friends, much of the time she lives in her own head, dreaming about what she wants. She won't go out on dates because the men who ask her out don't seem desirable enough. She says she doesn't want to settle for second best. The only place she enjoys going to are basketball games because she finds many of the players attractive. Otherwise she says she'd rather stay home, watch her television shows, and read her books. Right now, even Michele admits that sometimes her own life doesn't seem as real to her as the characters she watches on television or reads about in her magazines.

Michele's attitude has been reinforced because it seems as though every time she gets involved with a real man, she is badly hurt. The last man who caused her pain was Carl, a bad-news dude who treated her rotten. When Michele met Carl, he already had one wife and one steady girlfriend. Even so, because Carl was "very good-looking" and "very sweet-talking," Michele thought he was the perfect picture of what a Black man should be, and for two years she accepted his coming around once every few weeks.

Carl had a lot of "big" plans about what he was going to do with his life, and he spun a real line. Because Michele was hooked on fantasy to begin with, she fell for it. When he talked to her about his dreams, she was mesmerized by what he said. Michele wanted to believe in Carl so much that she attached all of her belief systems on to him and treated him like he was some kind of god.

When he was with her, Carl was attentive and sexy. When he wasn't, Michele thought about him constantly and kept setting up scenarios in her head in which she was able to get him away from the other women in his life. But instead of responding to her wishes and ultimatums, what Carl finally did was to get himself still another girlfriend. That's when Michele was forced to face the fact that he was never going to change.

As a result of this disappointing experience, Michele became even more depressed and withdrawn from the world of dates and sex. Although she likes to hear her friends talk about the men in their lives, nothing available to her in the man department seems worth much. The men she meets aren't handsome young doctors or rich tycoons, which is what she currently wants for herself.

Before she met Carl, Michele would develop crushes primarily on basketball players. For a long time, she focused on Magic Johnson, but that particular crush ended when he got married. Later, when he announced that he was HIV positive, she told herself that she was "lucky" that she didn't marry him as she had dreamed she would—although for a brief period she wondered how it would feel to be "standing by his side, helping him overcome his hardships." You can see from all this that Michele is a *real* "dream girl."

Within the past year or two, Michele seems to have grown out of her sports crushes. Now she says she wants to meet someone with a more stable lifestyle. If she doesn't meet someone like that real soon, Michele says that she's considering getting pregnant and having a baby because she thinks that motherhood is definitely on her agenda.

When we meet single sisters like Michele, it's clear that they are allowing fantasy to rule their lives. We look at the life-size posters of Black stars—actors, sports figures, musicians—on their walls, we hear their conversations about what's going to happen when they finally meet the men of their dreams, and we can see how they are wasting time and emotional energy with daydreams that are keeping them from finding real-life men and going about the real business of living. They have allowed what I call soap-opera thinking to take over their lives.

Soap-opera thinking is something that most women fall into at one time or another. From my point of view, women are socialized to fall into this trap. Soap-opera thinking means that someone has lost the ability to make judgments and good decisions based on concrete reality.

# Married and Still Dreaming

Single sisters tend to believe that once a woman is married, everything is resolved and fantasies will take a backseat to real life. Not so. Karen, a 37-year-old working mother, is a case in point. When Karen and her husband, Jordan, were first married ten years ago, she thought they were very much in love. However, as time has gone on, Karen has started to question her commitment. Even though she and her husband have two daughters, she wonders whether she should get a divorce. Her problem: She feels lonely and empty in her marriage. She no longer feels the kind of excitement and passion that she expected.

She says that both she and her husband use all the right words. They both say, "I love you" and "I miss you." They are affectionate and caring with each other. Her husband is a good father and a committed husband, but she feels lonely and bored. As far as she's concerned, her life lacks excitement. Even the sex life that she and her husband share seems boring and dull.

Karen isn't sure whether the problem is her husband or the lifestyle they share. Although they have a comfortable life, neither she nor her husband make enough money to take vacations or do any of the things she thought she would be doing in her marriage. She dreams about living in a big house with beige carpeting and mirrored walls. She wants to go dancing, and she wants something more from her life— something she is not getting, but she's sure it's something that only a man can give her. She loves her husband, but she wants a different kind of life.

What Karen needs to do is get over her fantasies and start doing her own work to find ways to make her own life more interesting. In soap-opera thinking, a man comes along, turns a woman on, and everything changes. Karen needs to realize that this is a fantasy, and she's got to find ways to turn herself on to life. I always recommend that sisters repeat the words "You turn me on" to themselves as a self-motivator that will condition them to look inward for their stimulation and motivation.

# How Poor Male Parenting Makes You Vulnerable to Soap-Opera Thinking

Any woman—Black or white—who grows up with inadequate parenting, particularly from her father, is going to have a tendency to weave fantasies around the men she meets as an adult. When a Black child is born, there is a higher-than-average chance that he or she will be raised in a household with a male parental figure who has withdrawn in some way. That kind of upbringing makes sisters particularly vulnerable to soap-opera thinking.

Perhaps your particular male parental figure was in so much personal pain that he was emotionally unavailable; perhaps he compensated for his lack of power in the world by becoming overly controlling at home; perhaps he had too many rules and was impossible to please; perhaps he withdrew from the world by becoming addicted to alcohol or drugs; perhaps the whole family suffered because of his inability to earn a living wage; perhaps he was physically abusive; perhaps he was emotionally abusive and insensitive to your psychological well-being; or perhaps he simply wasn't there.

When you grow up with poor parental role models, you typically respond in one of two ways:

- You may duplicate the patterns you were exposed to and continue the cycle of inadequate or destructive relationships.
- Because you want something different for yourself, as a child you fell into fantasy creating idealized situations in your own head; you continue this pattern as an adult.

If you grew up with no flesh-and-blood male parental figure who related to you in a positive loving way, you have no way of evaluating what a solid reality-based intimate relationship feels like. You have no sense of how real men behave; you don't know how men treat women in general and how a man is going to treat you specifically. So you make it up, often using television images or other kinds of images that look attractive.

If you grew up with a male parental figure who was actually destructive or unavailable to you, the tendency is to do much the same thing: You create a more acceptable model of male-female behavior in your head, and you often base this model on your own fantasies—again influenced by what you have seen or read.

When you don't have a real man to relate to in a positive way, the men you create in your head are apt to be larger than life. They are so perfect, so strong, so supportive, so giving, so exciting, so stimulating that it's almost impossible for any real man to measure up to the superman you've imagined. Believing these men exist keeps you forever stuck in a dream-girl status. If you want real intimacy with real male partners, here are some suggestions to help you start figuring out, *for yourself*, what you really need in your life.

# Doing Your Own Thinking— A "Blackprint" for Realistic Choices

## Step One: Make a Determination to Start Thinking for Yourself

Thinking for yourself is empowered thinking, and that's something that sisters aren't used to doing. They simply do not have enough opportunities to develop the necessary skills, and often when they do think for themselves, they are accused of being selfish. Even if you started out as a young girl with a mind of your own, circumstances tend to make it hard to continue being this way, and you get out of practice. Here's a mental exercise to help you empower your thinking:

The first thing you need to do is to get a view of your situation from a different perspective. To do this, you have to get into a different position. When sisters have a situation they're considering or a problem they need to think about, they tend to consider them as worries that are weighing them down. Everyone with a lot of thinking to do knows that when you've got worries sitting on top of you, you feel so burdened that you can't think.

Start by mentally getting yourself out from underneath

your worries. Close your eyes and envision yourself sitting on top of the problem or the situation that you want to think out. You want to be on top where you can see clearly what's going on, not underneath where you can't think straight. On top is the posture you need to achieve if you're going to think something through. So create a mental picture of your-self getting on top of this pile of confusion and looking down and starting to sort things out.

Not all women can immediately create this kind of mental picture. Of course, some of them have enough bounce in them that they can see themselves jumping right on top of their situation. But many others feel so burdened that they can't make it so fast. If that's what happens to you, remember Jacob's Ladder, and construct a mental picture of a ladder reaching up to the top of your worries and start climbing it one rung at a time.

Think of each rung as somebody who hasn't let you think for yourself and climb on past each and every rung until you get to the top. You may have to get past your mama, past your daddy, past your boyfriends, past your girlfriends—in short, past everybody who has ever tried to tell you what to do or how to think about what you do. Just get a clear mental image of yourself climbing up and keep on going.

When you've finally pulled your mind up to where you're on top of what it is that you're trying to think through, start looking at it clearly from above. See what your good sense makes of what you see.

## Step Two: Stop and Ask Yourself What You Really Need from a Man

What do you really need in your life? Forget what you've heard that you should want. Forget about all the things you've read in romance novels. Be real and be practical. If you want to start a family, for example, you should look for someone who shares this desire. If you want a career, you need a man who supports this goal. If you already have a child, more than anything else, you may need someone who loves children and is prepared to help you raise yours. If you can't find someone like that, you may be better off staying by yourself, just dating and enjoying your friends until your children are grown. So when you think about what you need from a man, take *your* own specific situation into account.

On a piece of paper, write down the characteristics that describe who you are and where you are in life. After that, think about your life goals. Write down where you would like to be in five years, ten years, twenty years, and so on, until you finally reach the end of your life. What's important to you, and what kind of life do you want to have lived?

Then make a list of everything you want from a man to help support you emotionally in what you want for yourself. Finally, condense that list into eight major qualities that you must have in a man. Carry that list with you in your wallet to help you stay on target with what you want for yourself. Write your requirements—what you want and why you want it—down in their order of importance. Here's a list of what my friend Jackie, a practical nurse who wants to return to school, wants from a man:

- kindness (particularly to her children)
- intelligence (she wants someone who shares her interest in learning more and becoming better educated)
- humor (she's an outgoing, funny woman, and she wants someone who will laugh along with her)
- generosity (her ex-boyfriend was tight with money, and she doesn't want to have to deal with that again)
- religious conviction (she wants someone who will go to church with her)
- shared values (there are so many different kinds of values that Jackie has another list of them—she wants to maintain her African-based value system, for example, as well as her liberal politics; she also wants to make sure that any man she ends up with shares her family values, her honesty, and her capacity for fidelity)
- great sex (hey, why not!)

- financial security (it would be nice to have a man who could take care of himself, as well as help her)

This list will help remind Jackie that when she meets an unfaithful man who has lots of money, but no religious convictions, no sense of humor, and no brains, that she needs to stop and think before she gets involved. Her list reminds her that ultimately fidelity and humor are going to matter more in her life—no matter how great looking the guy is and no matter how great the sex!

## Step Three: Stop Judging Men by How They Look and the Labels They Carry

When you automatically assume that good-looking men or men with good labels are better men, you're not practicing commonsense thinking. You may believe that you're thinking for yourself, but you're not. All you're doing is thinking the way you've been programmed to think. Black women are thoroughly conditioned and sensitized to believe that keeping up appearances is one of the most important things in life. Sometimes this conditioning causes you to think more of men who look good than of men who would be good to you.

Growing up, I remember walking with my mother and hearing her tell me, "Pick up your feet, girl, and look like you're going somewhere!" She wanted me always to look as though I had the appearance of having a direction. She wanted me to look confident and sure of myself.

In all likelihood, you were also constantly reminded how important it was to be proud and hold your head up, no matter what was going on in your life. This is part of our heritage. Generations of Black women have routinely struggled against a sense of depression that made them want to just plain give up. But they knew they couldn't give up, and part of their survival was their ability to keep up appearances and stand tall.

Our communities have always encouraged and applauded

men and women who "looked good" and walked with style. This is a wonderful characteristic. Certainly, it's one that we can all admire and respect. In fact, traditionally it's often been associated with people whose spiritual life is so strong that they can't be destroyed, no matter what happens. Where we get into trouble is when we translate this spiritual quality into the material side of life. Whereas "looking good" once meant showing spirit and pride, now it frequently means showing labels and advertising material values. And that's what too many of us are doing, particularly with the men we find attractive.

Often, we look at the labels a man is sporting and don't notice whether he's going to last through the wash-and-wear of ordinary life. We examine a man's credentials and don't notice his capacity for love and commitment. Black men complain about sisters who report back to their friends, saying: "I'm dating a doctor," "I'm dating a lawyer," "I'm dating a computer analyst." They say they rarely hear a sister proudly announce, "I'm dating a nice guy named Jim." Is it true that we hear a lot about good dressers, good dancers, good talkers, but we don't hear enough words like sensitive, kind, thoughtful, considerate, sharing, and loving?

When a sister looks at the advertising a man carries with him and doesn't look at his character, chances are she's going to end up feeling hurt and defeated—no matter how good it all looks to the rest of the world. Don't ever forget that what looks good doesn't always act good.

## Step Four: Stop Automatically Thinking More of Men Who Seem to Have More Money

Here's a truth I wish weren't so: In our communities, a direct connection is often drawn between money and self-worth. Ultimately, how you value money and how you value yourself get all mixed up. Financial hardship has been the lot of so many Black men and women that it's easy to see how money and what it can buy has assumed too much importance in how we think about relationships.

It's not so much that having money is associated with everything that's good. But we get confused and start thinking that not having money is something to be ashamed of. Money gets directly connected to how you esteem yourself and how you esteem others. Although you don't really equate money with your basic values, you somehow think you're going to need more money before you can get in touch with your true self and your real values.

This kind of attitude can mess up your thinking when it comes to men. Trust me, when your measuring stick for a man's value is his material worth, you're going to make some major mistakes in the men you go out with. First, with young men, you can't even tell where they're going to end up financially. Second, lots of men flash money around, but they may not end up with any security either. Third, and perhaps most important, having this kind of attitude will cause money to become a major issue in your relationships. You may end up evaluating your relationship with a man not on the love between you, but on the possessions you share or exchange. Too many sisters think that marriage symbolizes "shopping for the house," and what ultimately happens are a lot of arguments and resentments centered on money issues. Finally, if you are getting your sense of self from what you buy, there's a good chance you will buy more than you can afford and end up in debt, singly or as part of a couple.

There is a clear message in the advertising that has been directed at our communities: Put on the trappings of success, and you won't look poor, you won't look dejected, and you won't look bent out of shape. We're told that "designer" women will get more men and have more fun. We're made to believe that a designer suit or a good car or a gracious apartment is a substitute for genuine self-esteem, and that is just not going to work! We all need to bring our money issues out into the open and talk about why not having enough money makes us feel bad. We need to be certain that money doesn't become such a major concern in our lives that it sabotages our chance at happiness.

## Step Five: Try to Overcome Your Tendencies to Indulge in Romantic Fantasies

You can start by examining your childhood. Did you turn to fantasy to cover the absence of positive male parenting? What kinds of a relationship did you have or not have with your male parent? If any of the following are true, then you are a prime candidate for fantasies about men: Was your father withdrawn or unavailable emotionally? Was he abusive, mean-spirited, or demanding? Do you feel that he abandoned you in some way? Did he abandon you by leaving and showing no interest in your well-being? Do you feel abandoned because your father died when you were young? Do you feel abandoned because he paid no attention to you or your upbringing, except to find fault?

This kind of experience with your primary male parent has an unconscious carryover that you need to think about. We don't consciously say that because my daddy treated me this way or that, that's why I'm with this kind of man. But unless you consciously work on changing your pattern, your relationship with your father will frequently affect how you are with other men. For example, sometimes a female child will idolize a male parent who is not there and construct whole scenarios in which she is reunited with her missing father. These feelings of loss and found love can be so intense that they can carry over into the way she is as a grown-up. She may reach maturity confusing intense longing with fulfilled loving.

If you grew up without good male parenting, there is a good chance that you are going to be especially vulnerable to men who trigger the feelings that come up in your fantasies. This kind of man typically isn't just a regular guy. He's someone who is high profile in his behavior toward you. For example, "Jeffrey Jive," a good-looking, fast-talking brother, is toxic for women who have these kinds of issues because he has such a well-practiced line of seduction. When he meets a woman he finds attractive, he says what every woman with rich fantasies dreams of hearing. He knows exactly which buttons to push, and to make matters worse, Jeffrey seems sincere because he is *also* addicted to fantasy—he *believes* these things *when* he's saying them. The problem: He wakes up the next morning and knows he was just jiving. You don't.

The fact is that you can't think clearly when you're always sitting on a pink cloud of imagination. Save your creative thinking for some creative endeavor that is more fulfilling. What you need in your life is a real man, not a made-up one.

You can get practice in improving your relationships with real-life men by trying to get more pleasure from the real-life things that happen to you every day. Learn to enjoy the simple things you do and get as much from them as you can. Develop all your positive relationships, no matter how unimportant they may seem. Become friendlier with co-workers and other people you see routinely. In other words, stop saving all your emotional skills and all your best experiences for relationships that exist mostly in your dreams.

## Step Six: Start Developing Your Own African-Based Wisdom and Common Sense

There is an Ashanti proverb that says: "He who cannot dance will say, the drum is bad." In this case, it's not a bad drum, it's incorrect thinking. Your own personal drumbeat should be coming from a cultural place within you, not from conflicting messages, alien values, media images, and circumstances that don't relate to your ethnicity or life experience.

In African thinking, one does not think exclusively of the man. One thinks in three parts: the man, his family, and his village. You can't separate the man from the village. Here in America in the 1990s, we tend to think only that we are looking for a man, and we don't consider all those things he brings with him. We want to see the man in advertising context, almost as we would on a television set, with no historical past, no future, nothing except what exists at that moment or what you fantasize about the future. This is pure Eurocentric advertising.

We've been conditioned to assume that because a man has a good suit, he has good values; because he has a good line, he has good manners; and because he has a sweet swagger, he won't have a bitter aftertaste. You don't realize it, but you're thinking about a man for the moment, and African common-sense wisdom will tell you that you need to think about a man for a lifetime. Lifetime men carry a different kind of advertising with them. You can recognize a lifetime man because he has already made a commitment to something real—to his family, to his community, to his extended family—in short, to the entire village.

There's something I remember my father saying: "For some people, using common sense is like trying to find a lost ball in high weeds." As far as I'm concerned, the high weeds represent the alien or non-African-based guidelines. What you've grown up with are a vast number of media images that have nothing to do with who you are, what you look like, where you came from, or what your experience is. These images have created millions of photographs in your mind that have taken the place of common sense.

On the one hand, the typical sister hopes to meet a rich man who will treat her like a queen; on the other hand, she expects so little and is so afraid of being used or abused that she doesn't know how to deal with the overlooked brother who isn't doing a number or who doesn't have a major line. When you start out unsure of your true worth as a human being—and that's how most sisters have been made to feel—it's easy to let external values and expectations cloud over the sound family and village values that are part of our heritage.

We all say we want to preserve our own values, but frequently we forget all about them and focus instead on finding someone who looks and acts like a character in a soap opera. To do this is risking a Hollywood fade-out to black with no real man remaining on the screen. You need a man for the journey, not for the moment.

# 4

# Looking at Brothers: What Makes Them the Way They Are

Many African American males believe they have only six options: NBA, rap, drugs, crime, the military or McDonald's.

—JAWANZA KUNJUFU, *THE POWER, PASSION AND PAIN OF BLACK LOVE*

"I gave her a chance to make an application to go out with me, but she flunked."

—A BROTHER ON A DAYTIME TALK SHOW EXPLAINING WHY HE CHOSE ONE WOMAN OVER ANOTHER

## Trying to Understand the Men You Love

Why do we love Black men so much? Here are some good reasons: We love their sweet talk and their wonderful ability to make us feel alive, feminine, and cared for. We love the way they can hustle and make money even when they have little else going for them besides wit and wisdom. We love their capacity to have fun and celebrate life. We love their banter and their way of walking. We love the way they look and the way they smell. We love it when they are able to cope with bad times with humor and grace. We love Black men who have presence, men who stand there commanding space like kings or warriors. We love it when a brother can be sensitive to our moods and has a polished awareness of the male-female courtship drama. We love all this about them. Here's the big question: *We may love them, but do we understand them?*

Sometimes it seems as though it's impossible to figure out Black men. On the one hand, we know that Black men face tremendous odds and obstacles in the world. On the other hand, when it comes to women, they can appear *so* conceited and self-centered. We've all seen how sisters sit around talking about men, trying to understand what one specific man or men in general are all about. All these conversations tend to end up with the same question marks.

When you don't know why somebody is the way he is, it's easy to get caught up in bad-mouthing and name-calling, and that's not going to help you find the intimacy you want. We all need a more constructive approach, and that calls for more understanding. Figuring out all Black men is not something that can be accomplished in the pages of one book, but there are certain common attitudes and feelings that we can try to understand and empathize with a little more.

## *Time-Out for You*

But before we start talking about men, let's talk about you again. I believe in self-empowerment for women, and part of that means knowing that before you can love and understand anybody else, you have to love and understand yourself. For that reason, when a sister asks me about difficulties she may be having with a man, I tend to discourage her from focusing on his problems. I worry that a woman can get so caught up trying to understand why a man is being the way he is that she can become obsessive about *him* and forget about herself and her own development. In other words, I worry about sisters who get stuck in bad relationships, thinking about everybody else and not taking care of themselves. The rule is that no matter how much you want to understand any one man, you should never let go of your own sense of self. However, if you're going to protect yourself and the relationship, you need information and understanding about where your partner is coming from. With that idea in mind, let's think about some of the major issues confronting Black men as a group.

# Looking at the Big Picture

In a relationship with a brother, you need a sense of the big picture and the issues that concern him on a gut level, day by day. You need to be aware of the deep emotions he has experienced, both as a man and as a person of African descent, emotions no less complicated than those you deal with as a Black woman.

Never automatically assume that a brother is the way he is because of something you're doing or something that is happening in your relationship. It's probably not so. Before the man even saw you smile, he had two very important specific sets of attitudes and feelings that you need to know more about. Although these were formed by people, situations, and forces that had nothing to do with you, they have everything to do with how much he will be able to give you or the relationship. They are as follows:

1. What he thinks about himself as a Black man in the world
2. What he thinks about Black women in general

There is no way to avoid these two themes. They are going to affect your partner and, in turn, they are going to affect you. So for your own good, you had better get to know what his attitudes are, where they are coming from, and how you can deal with them better.

# Question 1: What Does He Think About Himself as a Black Man?

Whether the man you love is pulling down a six-figure income in a fancy firm or trying to eke out a living washing car windows on a busy cross street, the fact is that Black men as a group have suffered economic disenfranchisement and they are in a crisis because of it. I know many brothers don't look like they're in a crisis, with their smooth talking and even smoother walking. When the typical Black man is interested in a woman, he sure seems to know what to do and say to get his way. The question sisters ask themselves is an old one: If he's so good at getting me to do what he wants, why is he having so much trouble with the rest of the world?

In the late 1960s, two Black psychiatrists, William H. Grier and Price M. Cobbs, wrote what was considered a landmark book about the struggles that faced Black people. It was called *Black Rage*, and it spoke to the anger and frustration that brothers and sisters were feeling then. It still speaks to the same issues today. Talking about Black men, Grier and Cobbs said:

> For the black man in this country, it is not so much a matter of acquiring manhood as it is a struggle to feel it his own. Whereas the white man regards his manhood as an ordained right, the black man is engaged in a never-ending battle for its possession. For the black man, attaining any portion of manhood is an active process. He must penetrate barriers and overcome opposition in order to assume a masculine posture. For the inner psychological obstacles to manhood are never so formidable as the impediments woven into American society.

Let's think about this statement a bit. All African Americans, male and female, had their *personhood* stolen and diminished by slavery and the postslavery conditions in this country.

We all know what it feels like to be treated as someone who is less than equal and sometimes less than human. We all lost our rights as people. However, as women, we never lost the right to do those things that were traditionally considered feminine or female. We never lost our roles as women, and we never had our female identity stripped from us.

Whether you enjoy the so-called traditional feminine tasks or not, no one tried to keep Black women from doing them. An African American woman who was a good cook, for example, could still take pride in creating meals that people enjoyed. A woman who was a phenomenal housekeeper could still invite others to her home, knowing that they would envy the clean, orderly environment she created. A woman who sewed could create beautiful clothing over which her friends would ooh and aah. Part of femininity was always seen as the capacity to nurture and emotionally support men and children in the home—in other words, to cope with all kinds of stress with soothing words and smiles on our faces. Certainly, no one ever erected obstacles to keep African American women from doing that.

But what about the traditional male roles? Men are supposed to be able to earn a living and provide for their families. We all know about the obstacles placed in front of African American men who want to work. Historically, African American men were lynched, and not that long ago, for trying to open their own stores and improve their earning capacity. Even today, we know how difficult it is for Black men to get into unions or find good-paying construction work. No one is going to question the fact that the kinds of jobs that would allow a man to get food, clothing, and shelter for his family are simply not always available to Black men. So, that traditional piece of male identity has been denied many brothers and made more difficult for just about all of them.

How about that old macho job as protector of women and children, hearth and home? That's a role long associated with manhood. Let's consider what has gone on historically in most of this country. If you think Black men could protect their women and their children, let alone themselves, from the likes of Bull Connor and his bull horn, you've got your head in the sand. It hasn't been that long since crosses burned regularly on lawns across this land, and it's still happening.

Growing up, I had ample opportunity to watch my father, a Black man who looked like a cross between the British actor David Niven and the flamboyant Black Congressman Adam Clayton Powell, get stuck in places where his ethnicity made it difficult for him to take care of his family. It was always a struggle to support his family, and he was always running after the job market. He worked in the coal mines of Pennsylvania until they closed; then he went to the steel mills of Ohio. When the need for steel diminished, he went back to the South, where he worked as a master mechanic. In the South, the job of master mechanic was typically held only by white men because it provided benefits, such as insurance and paid holidays. When racist elements discovered that my father was holding a job they thought a white man should have, the lynch tree was held up to him. There was no arguing with the threatening phone calls made by members of the local Ku Klux Klan. I remember Daddy's rage and frustration as he went posturing about the house with his shotgun, threatening to take on every cracker on God's earth. I was so scared as a child because of everything that was happening that I hid under the bed.

Emotionally, my father was ready to take on the world for his family, but it was a futile attitude, and we all knew it. He couldn't protect us; he couldn't even protect himself. I remember my mother telling him that she wanted a live husband, not a dead hero. He had to leave, and quickly, on a Greyhound bus heading north at midnight. The rest of us followed later.

We tend to forget about incidents such as this, but the kinds of attitudes that forced my father to run for his life are still prevalent. My daddy was threatened with death because he wanted to work to support his family. It's a terrible mistake to say that was then, this is now. We have the lesson of Rodney King to teach us that violence against Black men, simply because they are Black, has not disappeared.

Although no one may be as up front about threatening to lynch brothers as they once were, African American men who want to get ahead and make a decent living still face enormous roadblocks. They know it, and it affects everything they do, including their relationships. We heard Supreme Court Justice Clarence Thomas express his sensitivity to this issue, when, during his hearings, he stated, "This is just a high-tech lynching." What he was referring to was what he perceived as extraordinary obstacles to his confirmation to a position of equally extraordinary power. His statement tells us that he was sure that these obstacles would not have confronted a white man. This does not excuse any issue of alleged sexual harassment—it only points out the power problems encountered by Black males at every level of society.

## Power, Money, and Manhood

Some people say that the quest for power is what's wrong with all men—Black, white, and every shade in between. But until we all develop more saintly dispositions, the need for power seems to come along with hormones, particularly testosterone.

If a man has power, he has control over himself and his destiny. Power means deciding for yourself where you will live and what kind of career path you will choose. When a man feels powerful, he feels strong and sure of himself. He experiences his manhood at an emotional level that makes him feel satisfied with who he is and what he does. Baseball players feel that kind of power when they hit a home run with the bases loaded; lawyers feel it when they win difficult cases; salesmen feel it when they close big sales, and gamblers feel it when they pick winners.

Obviously, for all men, power is an elusive goal. But white men are raised to believe in its possibility; Black men are raised to understand that the odds against their achieving any real power are slim at best. Even in sports, Black players were not allowed to enter the national limelight until 1947, when Jackie Robinson became the first Black baseball player in the major leagues; after that, the door started opening *slowly* for other Black players.

The traditional route to achieving power is financial. If you have enough money, people believe that you have the power to do anything you want with your life. Because there is almost no inherited wealth in Black communities, there are only a limited number of ways a brother can acquire enough money to feel a sense of power and control over his destiny. Born without equal access, he believes—and probably rightly—that money talks and money will improve his chances in the world.

The thing to remember is this: *When a brother is looking for money, a larger issue is involved. He's really looking for his chance to have some kind of equal footing with every other man in the power race.*

There is not a Black man alive in this country who hasn't confronted the issues created by racism and felt diminished as a man by the limitations placed on his ability to perform the traditional male role of protector and breadwinner. There is not a Black man alive who hasn't thought about his earning capacity and measured himself by how much or how little he can make. All these realities have an impact on your relationships because they all affect they way your partner feels about himself.

It's a simple fact: When a man feels good about himself, he's more likely to be good to the people around him. Not being able to find meaningful, financially rewarding work will, by definition, affect a man's self-esteem and, consequently, his relationships. Psychologists recognize that there's a direct correlation between unemployment and domestic violence, for example.

## Big Money/Bigger Ego

Unemployment or underemployment aren't the only economic issues that have an impact on romantic relationships.

Too much money can also be destructive of love. I hear complaints all the time from sisters who are trying to have relationships with successful men; they say that many of these brothers have gone on what appear to be ego trips. A brother with a fine job knows he is one of the lucky ones—that he is succeeding despite incredible odds. He knows the statistics, and he sees that people treat him as though he is special, a real prince. Sometimes these feelings go to his head. He may lose touch with his roots and his community, or he may see himself as a rare commodity in the dating market and take advantage of it.

How a brother sees himself and his status in the world is a determining factor in how he is going to behave in his relationships. A successful brother has to be careful or else he will end up with a major ego problem. He can start thinking about himself as such a prize that he won't be fit company for any woman. He needs a sense of balance and a sense of cultural responsibility to keep himself from too much arrogance and conceit. If you're involved with someone like this, you also have to keep a sense of priorities, always making certain that you place more emphasis on genuine cultural ties and less on materialistic goals.

## A Sense of Specialness and Power Attached to What You Own

The Reagan-Bush years had a profound effect on the economics of this nation. Statistically, for all groups of people in this country, the rich got richer and the poor got poorer. Our communities started out with little room for anyone to get poorer, yet that's what happened. Yes, some people were fortunate enough to get an education and find well-paying jobs. Typically, these brothers and sisters moved to areas where they wouldn't have to deal with violence and cockroaches on a day-to-day basis. But many more were stuck in neighborhoods where drugs, violence, and despair were getting the upper hand.

No matter where you were living, however, the 1980s

presented all people in this country with such a glamorous picture of wealth and overindulgence that everyone had rich-and-famous dreams. When they looked at those pictures of rich people on magazine covers at grocery checkout counters, brothers and sisters typically put their own frame on it. They thought, *That's what I should have.* But not everybody could have it. While one group of people was using the phrase "shop-till-you-drop," another group couldn't keep up with day-to-day living expenses.

The sight of all this money being thrown around made even people with good jobs feel as though they didn't have enough. The credit card became another symbol of power and status. The more credit cards you got, the more power you felt. Everyone wanted to feel like a high roller. Some highly paid brothers and sisters are still drowning in credit-card debt and financial anxiety because they couldn't resist the sense of power attached to those little plastic rectangles.

More and more the people in our communities seem to believe there is a connection between having expensive objects and having a sense of self-worth. This kind of thinking affects everybody, but it is particularly dangerous for young brothers. For some of them, we have seen how getting a pair of expensive sneakers could compensate for achieving bona fide self-esteem. I remember how shocked I was when I first heard stories about young brothers who killed each other over leather jackets. These jackets and sneakers were nothing but symbols. From advertising and all the other messages they received, these young people had been taught that if they owned the right stuff, they would feel as though they had the right stuff; that is, they would feel more worthy and powerful.

Adults and professional people are on the same kind of bandwagon with their power symbols—expensive cars, designer labels, fancy condominiums, and rich neighborhoods. Anyone who has problems with self-worth and power is inclined to try to get more power from what he or she owns. When such a person puts on a good "power" suit, he or she feels bigger and more serious than someone in coveralls.

To one degree or another, all of us have gone along with this destructive attitude, and it's threatening our capacity to have good relationships. Brothers think they are bigger and better when they have a power walk, and too often sisters are agreeing with them. Therefore, good, kind, loving brothers are being overlooked, and they are complaining about it. They want to know how come women are passing by the nice guys and chasing after the brother whose major attraction is that he looks like he's living large.

It's a mistake to think that Black men are not concerned about relationship issues. The typical brother wants love as much as you do. In his book, *Black Men: Obsolete, Single, Dangerous*, Haki R. Madhubuti expressed the hopes of many brothers when he wrote:

> If Black women do not *love*, there is no love. As the women go, so go the people. Stopping the women stops the future. If Black women do not love, strength disconnects, families sicken, growth is questionable and there are few reasons to conquer ideas or foe. If Black women love, so come flowers from sun, rainbows at dusk. As Black women connect, the earth expands, minds open and our yeses become natural as we seek
>
> *quality in the searching*
> *quality in the responses*
> *quality in the giving and loving*
> *quality in the receiving*
> *beginning anew*
> *fresh.*

## Love, Money, Respect, and Disrespect

No matter how much they make, Black men can't help but believe that money plays an important role in relationships. There's an old saying, "For money, you get honey." No money, no honey. Many believe, and often correctly, that sisters judge them by how much cash they are carrying. Many good men think, for example, that they can't ask a woman out if they don't have enough money to spend on a first date. Black women reinforce these feelings by expecting dinners, movies, and nights on the town and by respecting men who give them these things. When a brother can't afford to live large, sisters sometimes treat him with less respect.

If you are in love with one of the many brothers whose ethnicity has been the major contributing factor in his underachievement, it's easy to see how this situation has affected his sense of who he is in the world. A brother like this needs a superior sense of balance, priorities, and intelligence to keep from feeling self-destructive levels of rage and bitterness. The world is not giving him the kind of feedback that helps him maintain a healthy ego and good self-esteem. He may feel that he's not getting the respect he wants, and he has to be careful not to take these feelings out on the woman in his life.

There is a lot of talk in our neighborhoods about respect and disrespect. Like power, respect is as sought after as it is elusive. But it seems that people don't know what's worthy of respect. When we hear stories about young brothers buying guns so they can get more respect, we know we've got a problem. When a brother tells us that the only way he can get respect is to get money, and the only way he can get money is to start dealing drugs, we know we've got a problem.

A lot of this didn't come home to me until I was the victim of a drive-by mugging one day when I was on my way to church. Because my cultural attachments are so strong, I wanted to believe that a Black woman would always be safe in her own neighborhood. For me, community has always represented protection and safety. Traditionally, Black people worried about white neighborhoods, not about their own home ground.

But on a less personal level, the idea that so many young brothers are risking so much to take a few dollars off somebody shows how confused our values have become. Some of them seem to think that the only way they can get respect is to show disrespect to another brother or sister.

It's a tragedy when a young brother ends up in jail, or worse, because he's trying to get respect from his peers. This is a frightening omen for the future of Black people in this country. As women we have to think about what we can do to change things. Instead of complaining about all the Black men in prison or on drugs, we've got to take some action of our own.

I think there are a couple of things that sisters can start doing right now. One, you've got to get rid of your own focus on material things. You've got to think about what you respect and how you act with the men you meet. Because many Black men believe that the only time sisters respect them is when they get presents and get taken out, you've got to make the men in your life believe that you'll respect them for doing right and living right.

If your son, brother, lover, or friend is showing up with clothes, sneakers, and jewelry, you can't pretend it's coming from his imagination. You can't be so happy for the "merchandise" that you make him think he's doing what you want. You can't feel a little surge of pride when a brother starts throwing money around that came from who knows where. You have to live as though your values are different. Respect a man for who he is, not for what he owns. Change your focus. Instead of "For money, you get honey," make it "For honey, you get honey."

The other thing you can do is to encourage the brothers you know to get their respect in other ways. It wasn't that long ago that Black men, realizing they would get no respect from the white society, found their status in their own communities as solid, stable citizens. They went to their own churches, lodges, mosques, and clubs where they were deacons, ministers, elders, imams, and officers. They had the respect of their neighbors and their peers for doing right. There are still clubs, churches, and mosques. There are many ways for a man to become involved in organizations that help people. Let brothers know you will respect them more if they are better people. Encourage them to find ways within the neighborhood to get the dignity and Black intellectual stimulation that may be missing in their work lives.

The real missing link in a brother's life may be his cultural attachments. Without cultural attachments, brothers (and sisters) may develop what I call *detached behavior*, or the separated-self syndrome. If a brother loses his connections to his African identity base, he can easily fall into anticultural behavior. If he is detached from his African identity base, he can easily forget how important it is to develop and maintain appropriate relationship skills.

Detached behavior is connected to irresponsible conduct, violent and abusive behavior, self-destructive behavior, and substance abuse, as well as a disrespect for one's roots and sense of community.

## Black Men Know Their Sense of Well-Being Can Be Shattered in an Instant

There's a joke about a well-dressed brother who gets into an elevator with his dog and moves to the back. Two white women enter the car. Trying to make more room, the brother orders his dog to "Sit," and both women get down on the floor. There is another variation on this joke: Two well-dressed brothers, one a well-known performer, are in an elevator in a Las Vegas hotel. Two white men enter behind them. As they approach the floor their rooms are on, the two brothers realize they haven't pushed the button. One says to the other, "Hit the floor," and both white men do just that. Yes, these are jokes, but they make a strong statement.

Every brother, no matter how well dressed or well employed, knows that he is an object of fear and distrust. He knows that the world is filled with situations in which he will be threatened because *he is seen as threatening*. Almost every day we hear stories about Black men getting arrested, getting beaten, or getting killed simply because as Black men they were perceived as dangerous. You know the expression "armed and dangerous." Well, all across this country, the minute some people see a man with dark skin, they assume he's concealing a weapon. Brothers know how easy it is to get into a lot of trouble simply because of their skin color, and they believe that the institutions of this country are still likely to work against them.

Another issue that men, particularly young men in our communities, face is Black-on-Black violence. The number one cause of death for a young brother is homicide.

Walking down a street these days can be scary for everybody, but it's even more so for a Black man. The fear and sense of powerlessness this all engenders may be subconscious, but it's there nonetheless.

## The Cool Pose as Protection

Think about something small that you find scary—perhaps a mouse or a ride on a roller coaster. Then think about how you react: Do you scream, do you yell, do you run and hide? As a woman, you've been taught that these are appropriate reactions to fear. Think about how you would feel if every time you were nervous or anxious, you forced yourself to look brave and confront the thing that scared you.

That's what men are trained to do. They are supposed to face fear by gritting their teeth and looking more macho. The more scared they are, the less fearful they try to look. Enter the "cool pose," so no one can see their pain or their insecurity. When sisters are hiding their feelings, they show attitude; when brothers are doing so, they develop the "cool pose." It is their shield against looking vulnerable.

In 1994, when I watched the televised celebration of Nelson Mandela's election, I saw the men from the Zulu tribe holding up and waving their traditional Shaka shields. Many of you may have noticed these shields, which are named after the great Zulu chief who led his nation against the Dutch colonialists. As I watched these South African men, I thought about the way men in our neighborhoods use a cool pose as an invisible weapon against the outside world. It's so important to them that it becomes their Shaka shield, and they wouldn't think of going out without it.

The way I see it, trying to be cool is almost always a protection posture; it's a defense against feeling helpless and powerless. Some men are so good at looking "cool" that this is the way they behave all the time. It's hard for these men to access or get in touch with any of their emotions. They may try to minimize or play down anything that's important, including their true feelings toward women they care about. It's almost as if they are using the cool pose to protect themselves against everything that's real. For example, psychiatrists Grier and Cobbs reported that many Black men show a curious symptom—weeping without feeling.

When we see male family members acting as though nothing matters and there is nothing they can't handle, we usually recognize it for the protective mechanism it is. But when you see a man you're sexually attracted to acting "cool," it's easy to be fooled by the facade, to appreciate that he looks so big and strong, and not see the feelings that his pose is shielding.

## The False Hope That Is Found in Alcohol and Drugs

We can't discuss power and manhood without talking about the many brothers who retreat from desperation and hopelessness by taking up heavy drinking or drug use. In our communities, we're hard pressed to find a man who hasn't been touched by substance abuse. Drugs, for example, have become a peculiar symbolic rite of passage for many Black youths. Often boys are expected to prove themselves as men by becoming involved, in some way, with the drug culture, and these early habits continue into adulthood.

Black psychologists regularly talk about how these substances are used to relieve psychic pain and emotional distress. For a short time, liquor can provide a heady sense of strength and power, and cocaine can make someone feel invincible. A man can forget his troubles and build dreams.

He can feel as though he is a "real man" for as long as he has a buzz. The use of drugs or alcohol is his way of shaking off the shackles, if only for a few hours. Of course, ultimately, as most of us know, liquor is a depressant, and the "crashing" effect of some drugs produces a worse emotional state than the original sobriety.

It's a mistake to think that substance abuse is limited to men with economic problems. There are different kinds of addiction at all economic levels, and we've seen too many cases of accomplished men with "everything" going for them who fell into the drug trap. The only difference between these men and those with economic problems is that sometimes the drug of choice is different. Since drugs are illegal, using them brings additional risks that can impact on your life.

If you know a man who is drinking or doing drugs, don't encourage him by your behavior. To find some good ways of dealing with this problem, talk to your local drug rehabilitation center. These centers have plenty of information to help you, for example, get in touch with the kind of lying you may encounter, as well as the kind of trickery that drug use may bring on. Many communities also have alcohol rehabilitation centers. Consult with a clergyman or Islamic minister to get more information or call Alcoholics Anonymous or Al-Anon (an organization designed to meet the needs of people who are family members and friends of alcoholics). AA and Al-Anon have a great deal of literature you can get on this subject, and it doesn't cost anything to go to meetings. ACOA (Adult Children of Alcoholics) also can be very helpful in dealing with issues that touch your life if your parent was a substance abuser.

## Becoming More Sensitive to Issues That Concern the Man You Love

If our relationships are going to improve, we each have to learn to be more sensitive to our partner's needs and feelings. It is important that you try to see the world through your partner's eyes. Sometimes Black men are completely locked in to their history, and they don't even know it. That's what makes the problem so insidious.

This explanation is not a way of making excuses when a brother treats you in a discourteous, rotten, or outrageous manner. I just want you to have more information because knowledge empowers you with better decision-making skills. Obviously, I can't give each of you a specific plan that will work in your particular situation. But here are some things to think about when you think about the man in your life.

1. Has he ever worried about supporting himself, a wife, or a child? Think about how these concerns have made him feel.
2. Does he have a cool pose that he uses as protection against what he's really feeling? Think about his vulnerabilities.
3. Does he think more of himself when he's making money than when he is not? Think about what money means to him.
4. Does he have mercurial emotions (a bad temper, moodiness) that are connected to how he sees himself as a man? Think about how he feels about his own self-worth.
5. Does he believe he has more power in the world if he behaves as though he has more resources than he really does? Think about his insecurities in the world.
6. Does he ward off his financial anxieties by throwing around every penny he gets as soon as he gets it? Think about the ways you may be encouraging this behavior with your spending habits.
7. Is he so anxious about money that he overcompensates by stinginess and penny-pinching? Think about how he became so financially insecure.
8. Does he act as though there is power attached to what he owns? Think about how he gets his sense of self.
9. If he's a good provider, does he believe that earning a good living is a substitute for emotional providing?

Think about learning to talk to him about his life without becoming demanding.

10. Does he feel anger and bitterness about his place in the world? Think about ways of showing him that his life can be satisfying.

Obviously, these are all big issues, and they need more investigation than we can do here, but sometimes just bringing issues out in the open can help you deal with what's happening.

# Question 2: What Does He Think About Black Women in General?

What he thinks of you is going to be the end result of all his experiences with every Black woman he has ever known. His mother, his sisters, his relatives, his schoolteachers—all have given him expectations and patterns of behaving that will continue in your relationship. Further confusing the ingredients in this mixed bag are the stereotypes about Black women that he may have picked up along the way. If he has any negative attitudes written in concrete, they are going to increase your relationship difficulties. Ask yourself whether the man you care about has any of the following negative attitudes.

## Does He Believe That Black Women Are to Blame for Any of His Troubles?

This destructive myth has emerged in many of our neighborhoods. "Emasculating," "domineering," "bossy," and "controlling" are some of the names Black women have been called by people who say that we have created our own problems by being too strong to handle. These people point out the serious control issues that exist in our relationships, arguing that if sisters were to subjugate ourselves further to our men, our circumstances would improve. We are told that we like to mother men because we want to control them, that we put them down because we want to control them, and that we are keeping brothers from experiencing their power because we want to control them.

On an emotional level, I've even heard people say that the "macho" attitude many brothers assume is an overreaction to the way they have been treated by their women. There have even been published books that advised Black men to become *more* domineering and less sensitive to women. In my opinion, men and women accomplish more by being allies, rather than adversaries.

If you're involved with a Black man who sometimes thinks of you as an adversary or holds any negative opinions of Black women, you have to realize that you didn't put these ideas in his head. Like you, he's been influenced by the media, he's been influenced by the "village chorus" repeating incorrect information, and he's been influenced by the stereotypes set up by a racist system.

## Does He Hold Any Negative Stereotypes of Black Women?

Stereotyping can keep your partner from seeing you as a real person with real needs, feelings, and desires. Let's look at some of the common stereotypes that a brother may have.

Probably the most familiar stereotype is *Mama*. If the man you love believes all women act like Mama, he's going to expect you to cater to all his needs, both physical and emotional.

He's not going to be able to see your vulnerabilities or understand that sometimes you need him to be supportive and nurturing. Sometimes Mama appears as *Hot Mama*, an all-embracing, all-accepting sexual figure whose only intent is to satisfy her man, no matter how he acts toward her. In this man's head, a Hot Mama's sole satisfaction is in pleasuring her man, whenever he shows up, before and/or after cooking him his favorite meal. Some men are so taken with the idea of "woman as Mama" that the minute they get involved with a sister, they see her as supermama, or *Amazon*. When a man views a sister as an Amazon, she ceases to exist as a flesh-and-blood human being. Instead, he treats her as though she is so strong that no man could match her power or her ability to take care of the people around her. This kind of thinking fits in with the underlying myth in the Black community that sisters need no protection and can take care of themselves in all situations.

*Black and evil* is another favorite stereotype. Brothers often think a sister who is trying to make it in the world is Black and evil. Brothers have a problem with such a sister because she's not making them her first priority. This woman is threatening because her struggles with trying to get ahead sometimes leave her stressed out and emotionally unavailable. Brothers who believe Black women are for "handling" may deal with their concerns by making light of them. The sister may be having a problem at work, be anxious about her kids, or have a million chores to do. Instead of helping her or relating to what's important to her at that moment, a brother may try to turn her into a sexual figure by saying, for example, "You're so Black and evil today, girl, but I know what you really need."

Another frequently used stereotype is *Miss Loosey*, the loose vamp who is always hot to trot. The primitive image is of a throbbing, trembling woman. The myth is that men look at her and want to relieve her sexual distress. Sometimes it seems as though all a sister has to do is put on some makeup and a nice dress. It doesn't matter where she's going; she could be heading for church, but men assume that she is heading straight for them, and they can't see the real person underneath the cute clothes.

## Is He Stuck in a Slavery Mind Lock?

When you stop to consider how stereotypes of any kind come to be, you have to think about a giant game of Gossip, started by one or a few people who pass on a word, a phrase, or a belief. Eventually, everybody gets to hear it, and everybody comes to believe it because everybody's saying it. Here's something you've got to think about: I believe that one of the primary reasons why African American men maintain stereotypical thinking toward sisters goes back to what happened sexually on the plantations. I think African American men got their minds locked in to some wrongheaded thinking back then, and they started these sexual "rumors" about their women. That kind of thinking continues even today.

On the plantation, a man wasn't able to protect a woman sexually, no matter whether she was his mate, his mother, his sister, or his daughter. I believe the feelings he experienced were so intense that he set up a psychological mechanism whereby he could protect himself. He needed to be able to deny the truth and tell himself something that he could live with; therefore, he rearranged all the ugly facts in his head and framed them so somehow the woman became responsible. He told himself that she must have liked what happened, or else she would have stopped it. This kind of mind lock allowed him to brush off the pain of the moment and think about *her* as a "bitch in heat." I think he tried to shrug off what was going down by telling himself, his peers, and his relatives that it was OK because *she* was just a "tramp," a "bitch," or some other epithet. It is another example of a psychological cool pose. I think this kind of ugly "rumor" about African American women got passed on from generation to generation, and I honestly believe that this kind of thinking set up the justification for the name-calling and disrespect that goes on even today. Whenever a Black man is angry at a Black woman, in his head she becomes "just a bitch," a throwback to her unprotected status.

As sisters, we can discourage this kind of stereotypical thinking and disrespect by recognizing it for what it is. I also believe that it is *extremely* important that we don't become part of it and that we don't encourage the practice by using these stereotypes and names against other women.

## *Does He Believe That Sisters Are Out for Money?*

When you hear a Black man calling a sister names, there's a good chance it has something to do with jobs and money. Because the Black woman is simply not as threatening to white America as is the Black man, she has always been able to find work. If nothing else, she could either nurse or do domestic work, and most of us had grandmothers, aunts, and mothers who did just that. The Black woman has a long history of putting food on the table. Often she has been the one with money in her pocket, and she has come to be viewed and sometimes resented as the one who is connected to the power-money supply. There have been long periods in our history when men couldn't find work and couldn't get their hands on any legal money. This situation made them feel as though the only choices they had were to go to a woman, usually a mother, a lover, or a sister, or do something for which they might end up in jail.

When it comes to money, Black men tend to be angry at women for at least three reasons:

1. *They think sisters get more jobs than brothers do.* This realistic situation creates havoc in our relationships. Certainly, you can't blame a woman for it because if she hadn't been willing to go out and clean houses, often there would not have been any food on the table. Nonetheless, in many families, sisters were raised with two clear and conflicting directives: "Be strong" and "Don't be so strong that you take away from the men." As Black women have branched out and starting succeeding in fields other than domestic labor, it is frequently pointed out that working Black women are taking jobs away from unemployed brothers.

2. *There has been too much financial dependence, and brothers are afraid of more.* No matter how much money a brother makes or how successful he becomes, he has a memory and a

stereotype of Black men who have been financially dependent on women. The fact is that dependency breeds resentment and anger. The typical brother hates being dependent; he hates the idea of a Black man standing around with his hat in his hand looking for some money from a woman. There is hardly a man alive who doesn't want to be able to stand on his own two feet. A man who is dependent often stops thinking about the woman as a hardworking, struggling sister. Instead, he begins to see her as some privileged person who has a stash of money that she's treating like her own. She's resentful that she's worked so hard and has nothing left for herself, and he's resentful that money is unavailable to him and he has to go to her. Sometimes a brother's dilemma narrows down to asking a sister for a few dollars "for the cause" or going out on the street and making bad choices.

3. *They believe sisters have focused on the money and haven't understood how difficult it has been for Black men.* Brothers say things like, "All she cares about is money"; "She doesn't love me, she loves what I bring her"; "If I can't get things for her, she's going to show me that she can get them for herself"; and "She doesn't need anybody." What they mean is that sisters haven't truly related to the difficulties Black men have experienced trying to make a living.

When a sister complains about a man who isn't making enough money, acts like she wants a man to give her things, or seems to appreciate a rich man more than she does a poor one, the typical brother looks at her and sees someone who doesn't give a damn about the real hardships he has faced. He thinks: *She can't know how I feel, and if she's so stupid that she can't understand, I'm not about to tell her.* We have to remind brothers that this is a finger-pointing trap none of us deserves.

In many of our relationships, the absence of hard cash has translated into hard feelings. Because of our common experience, Black men and women tend to feel valued when they have money and the things money can buy and devalued when they don't. All of us need to do more to improve our values, so we don't allow love to become less important than cash. We have to stay sensitive to each other's feelings and not harden our hearts to each other because of money issues.

# Learning to Talk to the Man You Love About What He Feels

Women are always wondering how to get a man to open up and be honest about his emotions, good and bad. Men don't want to do it. The typical man prefers to talk about concrete things like football games or what he read in the newspaper or heard on the radio. Men like to talk about skills, action, and physicality. When he's sitting around with his friends, a brother rarely says things like, "I was so worried about the baby last night. I wasn't sure whether I should call the doctor." No matter how worried he may be, he's not going to talk about it easily, and he doesn't have much practice in discussing feelings.

If you sincerely want to get a man to talk to you, you've got to work at it. Here are some suggestions on how to get started. You aren't going to be able to get a man to talk about his feelings overnight; therefore, be patient and be prepared to spend a fair amount of time—weeks, months, and possibly years—before he starts unburdening himself. This little program is done in steps, so don't jump ahead before the man you love is ready.

1. *Engage him first in conversations about things that interest him.* This is just an exercise to get him accustomed to talking to you, so don't expect to hear anything special. Be prepared to hear about a lot of stuff that doesn't interest you in the slightest. As you are listening to him, you will probably begin to understand why you prefer to talk to your girlfriends, who talk about the things you like to talk about.

2. *Pay attention to what he is saying and don't jump on him when he says things you don't want to hear.* What you're trying to do is make him comfortable being with you. You want him to feel that he can trust you and that you are not going to "get" him if he says the wrong thing.

3. *Ask him questions about the incidents and events in his life that gave him pleasure and pride.* Get him to talk about the good emotions he experienced and the times when he felt happy and content.

4. *Support his feelings.* When he says he liked something or somebody, don't criticize him or tell him that he's wrong to feel the way he does.

5. *Engage him in shared conversations about feelings that aren't particularly threatening.* For example, you could say, "I really got scared at that movie. Did you?" You could follow that statement by asking if anything scares him and if so, what?

6. *Ask him outright about what he felt in the past.* For example, "Did you feel bad when your marriage ended or when you lost that job? Were you very happy when you graduated? What did you do? Who did you tell about your feelings?"

7. *Ask him about what he feels in the present.* Give him a chance to talk about other things besides your relationship. Talking about feelings is like anything else, the more you do it, the better you get.

To help you get a man to talk, here's a wonderful tip I got from my mother, Ethel Lee. My mother, who was very smart about life, graduated from a one-room segregated schoolhouse in Alabama and went to Tuskegee University in 1928. You can imagine how determined and intelligent she had to be to do that. She always knew how important it was to get a man to share his feelings, and she started giving me little lessons when I was a young girl. One of her favorites came from an old blues song called "In the Dark." I still remember her singing the song and telling me that the best way to talk to a man was "in the dark." She didn't mean anything sexual by that phrase; rather, she meant that it was easier for a man to speak about himself when the lights were low and a woman couldn't scrutinize his body language or the expression on his face. She said, "There are times when a man needs the comfort of darkness to relax and say what's on his mind." And I'm telling you the same thing.

# Learn the Art of Verbal Stroking

It's a fact, men love women who make them feel good about themselves. As African American women, we are sometimes deficient in this skill. We have a long history of loyalty and devotion to the men we love, but no one has ever accused us of softening our words. Many of us were born with verbal skills and abilities that are as colorful and funny as they are biting. In fact, we have a learned tendency to support the men we love with our actions while we put them down with our words. This is not conducive to good loving. We need to start being ultrasensitive to the various ways in which a brother may need verbal support and assurance. Learn how to tell the men in your life when they please you. When they're being smart, funny, or sensitive, let them hear about it. They need to hear words of love and caring as much as we do. And every once in a while, tell a brother how fine he is, so when another woman tells him, it will be secondhand information.

# 5

# Getting a Handle on Hot-and-Heavy Issues

Men wear you down to a sharp piece of gristle if you let them.

—A FEMALE CHARACTER IN TONI MORRISON'S *JAZZ*

## *You Need an Attitude to Keep from Getting an Attitude*

There are a thousand and one things that can go wrong between two people. In this chapter, we're going to take a look at lying, infidelity, and jealousy, three major issues that can affect your relationships. I want to be sure that when these hot-and-heavy issues crop up in your life, you're prepared to handle them constructively.

If you've ever argued with a man about his lying or his cheating, you know the pain and anger these issues can cause. Typically, these kinds of problems make sisters focus on what's wrong with the relationship. I have another suggestion: START FOCUSING ON WHAT'S RIGHT WITH YOU.

When I say that you need an attitude to keep from getting an attitude, what I mean is that you need a clear sense
of who you are and what you stand for. Instead of reacting
to any of the ways that a man may be causing you pain, focus
on moving forward with your own life in the direction you
want to be headed. My father used to say, "If you don't stand
for something, you'll fall for anything." This is the case in
many areas of life, but it is particularly true in romantic relationships. Where love is concerned, you've got to start out
by standing for yourself and those values you consider
important. It's your way of protecting yourself if something
goes wrong—and something always goes at least a little bit
wrong.

## Protect Yourself by Being in Touch with Your Special Self

Do you sometimes feel as though other people, particularly men, are telling you who you are? The truth is that as
you go through life, you've constantly got to be redefining
yourself in the world; either you're going to do the defining
for yourself or somebody else—often a man—is going to do
it for you. That concept is so simplistic that it's often overlooked. The person you are is your biggest protection against
romantic pain.

To help you always stay in touch with who you are, I want
you to find a special identity of your very own that you can
always hang on to. To do this, think about all the things that
are good and valuable about you. See if you can find a quality
you admire in yourself and want to cherish and then give it a
name. It can be any name, as long as it establishes that you're
talking about something special.

As an example of someone with a special identity, I think
of Sarah Vaughan, who called herself "The Divine Sarah."
See if you can find a phrase like that, something that con-
nects you to your glorious, gracious, gorgeous, very individu-
alistic self. Sarah Vaughan once wrote, "I'm not a special person. I'm a regular person who does special things." When

you choose your special name, try to find one that reminds you of the special things you can do.

I've had a special name ever since I was two years old. That's when we got a new little puppy in the house. The puppy and I started playing, and the puppy, who was teething, bit me. I became upset and cried. My mama washed the bite and told me to be careful when playing with the dog. She went back to talking to Mrs. Johnson, a neighbor who was visiting at the time. The next thing they heard was the puppy yelping. Still crying, but determined nonetheless, I had gone and bitten the puppy back. Mrs. Johnson said, "She's not a baby; she's a little mutt." And Mutt has been my nickname ever since. I carry that name with pride because I recognize what Mrs. Johnson meant was that I wasn't the passive, helpless little girl who was typical for my generation.

That's why my special name to myself is Mutt the Maverick because to me *mutt* means maverick, one who refuses to conform to the stereotype. My special name reminds me that I'm a self-protective person who is independent and self-thinking. It tells me that I am walking to my own African drumbeat. There are times when I've lost that feeling, but I've always been fortunate enough to have it restored and reset, and it has served me in good stead.

Once you've found your special name, use it to remind yourself of who you are. Then whenever you're feeling that a relationship with a man (or anybody else, for that matter) is wearing you down, you can think about that name and remember what the best parts of you stand for. Your special name will help you protect and keep those parts safe. Let your "name" be your little word association to remind you that you are too special to be downtrodden in any relationship. Remember that a relationship is not all of who you are.

I truly believe that if you focus on who you are and what you stand for, you can keep yourself in what I call *divine order*. If you're in divine order, you'll be better able to handle all the things that go wrong with men without losing your equilibrium and your essential sense of self. If you know what you stand for, no argument, no disappointment, no romantic loss is ever going to knock you over because divine order makes us emotionally resilient.

## Don't Let the Hot-and-Heavy Issues Wear You Down

When the man you love is giving you a hard time, don't let yourself fall into the victim trap. Carry this thought with you whatever you do: You are in charge of your life. Don't waste precious energy trying to change a man because you can't do it. But you *can* change the way you think, you *can* alter your perception of what happens, and you *can* change the way you react. If *you* change enough, your life will change accordingly. That's the truth.

Realize that no one can hurt you if you don't let it happen. If somebody is calling you names, for example, you don't have to absorb it or internalize what is being said. This other person isn't the one who is hurting you. This man or woman may be doing the talking, but you are the one who is doing the hurting because you are the one who is letting those names enter your heart. I want you to think about building a self-protective system that is based on what is going on *inside* you, not on the outside. Once you've done that you'll be protected no matter what's going wrong. Having said that, let's think about some of the issues that cause problems in relationships.

# When You Can't Believe Everything He Says

"I don't know what kind of fool my boyfriend thinks I am. He's supposed to pick me up at seven-thirty, and at eight-thirty, I'm still sitting there waiting, when the phone rings. He called to tell me he was stuck in the office. I could hear the music from a jukebox and people talking. He was at some kind of damn party! Why did he have to make a plan with me if he couldn't keep it? He's always lying to me because he wants me to hold still until he's finished playing."

—JUANITA, 33

Not that long ago, I read a *Vanity Fair* interview with the actor Jack Nicholson. When Nicholson was asked if he ever lied to the woman who was known as his girlfriend for many years, he said, "Of course I lied to her. It's the other woman I would never lie to. You only lie to two people in your whole life. Your girlfriend and the police. Everyone else you tell the truth to."

When sisters complain about brothers who can't always be counted on to tell the truth, the whole truth, and nothing but the truth, they make it sound like it's only Black men who mislead women. As the quote from Nicholson shows, white men can be just as guilty. Black men don't have a patent on lying. From where I sit, there's this exclusive men's club mentality that allows men to fool around with the truth. The only requirement for joining this club is that you've got to have balls.

Of course, there are many categories of deception. Some seem minor and reflect unreliability without ill intent: For example, I know a woman who frequently complains about her fiancé. She says he has promised to take her on a vacation to Jamaica, but whenever she brings it up, he kind of floats away, and the whole issue goes up in smoke and never gets firmed up. In this case, it's apparent that her fiancé doesn't take her on vacation because he doesn't have the money. Other kinds of deceptions indicate deeper issues. For instance, Brenda says her boyfriend lies about everything and then tries to camouflage what's going on by blaming her or, in her words, "He tries to piss in my face and tell me it's raining." Other examples of undependable behavior are these:

- He never calls when he says he will.
- He never is where he says he's going to be.
- He never does what he says he's going to do.
- He says things he doesn't mean just to get you to do what he wants.

- He's all talk and no follow-through. He makes promises, promises, promises.
- He lies about money and creates chaos in your life.
- He lies about other women.

When a man lies to a woman and she continues to let it happen, she usually puts part of her life on hold. She's expecting him to show up when he says he will, so she's holding up dinner; she's waiting to go to the movie with him, so she never sees it; or she's counting on him to fix the lamp, so it stays broken. Sometimes the situation is more serious like when she builds her life and her plans around his fidelity and trustworthiness, and he disappoints her.

Here are some common reasons for his lying: He's trying to control you and keep you where he wants you; he's trying to protect himself from your anger if you find out the truth; he's trying to save face because he can't give you something you deserve. Men have many rationalizations for this behavior. One brother told me: "She's the one who kept making excuses for me; I figured she really wanted me to run a game on her, so I did. My motto is, Give the sister what she wants." Here are some other rationalizations:

- "It makes her happy when I say I'm going to call, but I don't always have the time to do it."
- "I don't know why she's always asking me where I'm going to be. If she didn't ask me, I wouldn't have to lie."
- "What I'm doing has nothing to do with her. Besides, what she doesn't know can't hurt her."
- "I'm only telling her what she wants to hear."
- "If I told her the whole truth, we'd have a big fight about it. This way it's more peaceful."

Often a man believes he can operate as an individual in a committed situation. He thinks: "She's committed and she's right where I can find her; I'm committed, but I'm a damn free agent, and I can move through the world like I want to move making the choices I want to make." I call that way of thinking "committed with a single flair." A man like this wants to know that the woman in his life is one hundred percent reliable, truthful, and committed. She should always be right where he can find her. But for himself it's different.

As far as this kind of man is concerned, there's a world of difference between altering the truth to make it more acceptable to the woman in his life and telling a bold-faced lie.

## A Sweet-Talking Tradition

Him: "Hey girl, where you been all my life?"

Her: "Maybe I've been places you haven't thought of being."

Him: "Well, I sure should have been there."

Her: "Well, you're here now, what have you got to say for yourself?"

Him: "Well, I'm sayin' it. You're one fine brown frame."

Sometimes as Black Americans we communicate in special ways. Take the foregoing exchange—light superficial banter between two people who may or may not ever speak to each other again. The man is sweet talking; the woman recognizes it for what it is, and although she may appreciate the masculine attention, she's not giving the brother any ground. It's fun, it's easy.

Problems arise when a brother uses and abuses sweet talk to get a sister to do what he wants. Sometimes we don't know how to tell the difference between a man who is serious and a man who is just talking. Sometimes we don't know how to tell the difference between a man who is telling the truth and a man who doesn't want to get caught.

Traditionally, brothers have been indoctrinated to believe they have few things they can treat a woman with except their words. They often believe sweet talk is what a sister wants to hear, so they'll say whatever seems to work for the moment. Many of them are honestly shocked when a woman internalizes their words and takes them as gospel.

Although sweet talking is different from lying, a sister can react to it in the same way. She hears the words, and she responds to the promise implied in what is said. She listens to the words and ignores the action—or absence of action. When a man is sweet-talking, some sisters can't see that he is either just trying to please them for the moment or trying to make them more pliable so he can set up his play for future action.

When does a brother sweet-talk? (1) When he's trying to jump-start a relationship and get a sister to respond to him quickly, (2) when he's trying to gloss over problems and avoid an argument, and (3) when he's trying to avoid intimacy and keep you from talking about anything real. Through it all, there is a good chance that the brother is priding himself on his Mr. Hollywood, Omar Khayyám, love-talk style.

## Why Lying Bothers You So Much

"One falsehood spoils a thousand truths."

—ASHANTI PROVERB

Whether you call it sweet talk or lying, sisters hate being deceived. What they hate most are brothers who are so good at lying that it becomes a routine that they fall into at the slightest provocation. At some point, a brother who is honest with himself should be able to see what's happening. But sometimes the behavior has gone so far that he doesn't know how to be any different. And that's very bothersome.

Any sister who has ever tried to have a relationship with an unreliable man knows how difficult it is to sustain intimacy and trust without honesty. What you have to understand is that some men seem chronically incapable of intimacy. For them, lying and cheating are as much a way of putting emotional distance into a relationship as anything else. They find intimacy threatening and scary. What you're trying to achieve, they are working to destroy. Controlling you with a smoke screen of unreliable words is a way of keeping you at a manipulated distance.

Typically, when a sister is upset about a man's lying, what

she's really complaining about is the undependable behavior that causes the lie. For example, if he doesn't show up when he says he will, she wonders what he doesn't want her to find out about where he's been. She immediately assumes he is doing something that would get her even angrier, like fooling around with another woman or hanging out with friends she doesn't approve of.

When her partner makes promises he can't keep, a sister doesn't see just a broken promise. In her head, she sees a man she fears is never going to be the dependable rock she needs. She looks at him and worries that he will never be able to give her a sense of security. And, most important, she sees a man she feels she can't trust. She wants to be able to look at the man she loves and say, "I trust you not to hurt me, at least not on purpose." She can't understand why her pain in the face of his behavior isn't enough to make him change. She's got to understand that changing his behavior is his concern, not hers.

## Handling Yourself and the "Lying" Issue

If a brother is giving you unreliable information, what should you do and what shouldn't you do? Here are some common traps to avoid and some special techniques to help you handle what's happening.

1. *Be clear in your own head that you want to know the truth.* Often sisters believe what they are told because they want so badly to believe and trust the man they care about. If that's the case with you, it's easy for someone to take advantage of your goodwill. You have to decide that you *want* to hear and see the truth. If a man is telling you stories that don't make sense, open your eyes and admit what's happening. Looking at the man you love and seeing his faults doesn't make you into a suspicious woman. It just makes you a woman who is aware enough to see what's going on.

2. *Examine your own behavior.* Are any of your expectations causing him to lie? If he's promising you vacations or pre-

sents he can't afford, you have to question yourself about the messages you are conveying and the pressure you are placing on him.

3. *Recognize that nagging almost never works.* He just gets used to hearing it and turns off the sound of your voice.

4. *Don't stoop to spying or snooping to find out the truth.* If you do this, you're only going to get yourself all caught up in a potentially self-destructive pattern.

5. *Don't expect your tears to make him change.* Men build up an immunity to crying.

6. *Identify "camouflage" behavior when you see it.* Men who are adept at lying sometimes set you up so their behavior is camouflaged. Here's how this works: Instead of waiting for you to confront him, he starts an argument about something else and blames you or makes you feel guilty. A man who is skillful at camouflage can get off the hook and have you apologizing at the same time. Don't fall for it. Without raising your voice, let him know that you know what he's doing. Don't feed into his need for an argument, which may give him the excuse he's looking for to slam out the door or blame your attitude.

7. *Don't give him a chance to lie.* Don't ask him when he's coming home or when he's going to call; don't ask him any questions that make him feel that you're pinning him down to a schedule or a promise that he may not want to keep. In other words, don't create more lies by asking questions that will make him lie more.

8. *Don't blame yourself for his prevaricating ways.* A sister may worry that the man is lying because he thinks so little of her. Lying is his way of handling intimacy. It's not that he thinks so little of you; it's that he wants to control you and

keep you at an emotional distance. Understand that lying is part of his "control center."

9. *Try to have a nonconfrontational honest conversation with him.* Without whining or fighting, tell him how you are feeling. Stick to the facts and stay away from blame. Even though this technique may not give you the results you hope for, it can start a constructive dialogue. See if you can use this conversation to set up the dynamics for further communication. Don't press for promises that he may not be able to keep, but do try to open the door for some kind of negotiation.

## Leading Your Own Life Discourages Undependable Behavior

Here's the problem: You feel as though you can't live with him, but you can't live without him. What should you do? My advice is always the same no matter what the provocation: Stop trying to have a relationship with him and start having one with yourself. Can you lead your life comfortably and focus on you and your growth while he is still around? That's what you ultimately have to decide. In the meantime, you have to find ways of emotionally separating from him and his chaos, even when he's in the same room. That means you have to create some psychological distance, so you can, as my grandmother used to say, get a grip on yourself. Enough distance can help you become a better problem solver and decision maker. The fact is that sometimes up close creates uptight. So keep that idea in mind and start making your own distance. Here are some suggestions for doing just that.

1. *Lead your life as though your partner complements it and not as if he controls it.* That means you can't breathe his breath; you've got to breathe your own. If he's there to enjoy

the same summer breeze you're enjoying, fine, but even if he's not, the sun is still shining, and you're still breathing.

2. *Don't wait for him to follow through on his words.* Don't hold dinner; don't wait for him to come home; don't wait for him to call even if he said he would. Go about your own business. And try to have a nice time while you're doing it.

3. *Don't burden him with too much responsibility for your joy and happiness.* Sometimes a brother will become unreliable simply because the woman in his life is acting like he's the sun, and it's too much responsibility. You know in your heart if that's what you're doing.

4. *Change your attitude toward men in general.* As I said before, and I'll probably say again: Don't expect any one man to be the answer man for your life. He's not some kind of deity; he's just a fallible human being. Sometimes men are set up as supermen, and they have a hard time living up to that image.

## When Lying Becomes Abusive

If you're involved with somebody who's always doing things he has to lie about, an honest conversation is almost impossible. You need to recognize that you are in an abusive situation, and you have to behave accordingly. You need a support system to help you deal with this. If you can afford it, see about some counseling. Your local community mental health facility may be able to suggest inexpensive alternatives; the facility may even have a women's self-help group. Talk to your friends and family honestly. Ask them for support. And don't forget to speak to your religious adviser. When you're dealing with any kind of abusive behavior, it's essential that you stay connected to your family and friends and do not allow yourself to be isolated from the system that gives you support.

# Infidelity and Jealousy

"I found out my husband was seeing this other woman because this low-life woman just came up to me and told me. She told me he loved her, and I should get out of the way. At first, she said she was telling me for my own good because she was pregnant and didn't want anybody else telling me first. Then when I questioned her and insisted on talking to her and my husband together, she got really nasty and started calling me names. She began to insult everything about me, from the way I looked to the way I cooked. I told her she looked like a dried-up prune even if she was pregnant.

"That's when the garbage war began. She brought a big pail of garbage and dumped it in front of my door. Then I took a big bag of garbage and dumped it in front of her door. We just did this, back and forth, and it kept escalating. She would come to my door and call me names and dump things. It got worse and worse. She would come and play a radio in front of my window, so I got my brother to go and start banging on things in front of her window. Finally, all the neighbors complained, so we had to slow things down."

## *Some Ground Rules*

The stories I've heard. The stories we've all heard. The things we've all done. The ways we've acted on our jealous feelings are often ingenious as well as hurtful. The trouble is that the one you are hurting most usually is yourself. Here are some ground rules to follow if your partner is making you jealous or if you suspect that he is unfaithful.

1. *Ask yourself whether your suspicions are grounded in reality or whether you are unconsciously trying to put more drama into your relationship.*

2. *Try to assess the situation accurately.* Don't start snooping through his things, but think about what's going on. Does he

have a history of infidelity or promiscuity? (If this has been his pattern, it increases the possibility that he is being unfaithful now.) Is he spending more time away from you? Is there a difference in the way he behaves sexually? Does he act differently toward you in general? (Some men become irritable, but others can go to the other extreme and seem oversolicitous.) Is he unaccountable for too many hours? Is he spending more time on the way he looks (exercising excessively or buying new shirts)? Is he giving you outright clues (not coming home until all hours and giving you implausible excuses or bold-faced lies)?

3. *If you believe there may be a basis for your suspicions, discuss them honestly and openly.* Hear what he has to say, but be prepared to hear the worst and also be prepared to have him lie.

4. *Don't get into any garbage wars, symbolically or otherwise.* By garbage wars, I mean going through his things, his wastebaskets, his phone book. Don't get involved with name-calling, spying, and any kind of confrontation with the other woman. Absolutely never, ever, get into a woman-to-woman fight over a man. Think about all these activities as garbage, and don't mess yourself up with them. Recycled garbage improves the environment, not relationships. Yes, there are people who throw trash and talk trash, but don't you become a garbage collector.

5. *If he is fooling around, try not to spend too much time thinking about "the other woman."* Doing so gives this woman more power than she deserves. Don't give her a place in your life or in your thoughts. Thinking about what "he" may or may not be doing with "her" can trigger all kinds of other thoughts. If you have any unresolved issues (old business) with your family, thinking about the other woman will push those buttons. Family-induced insecurities, sibling rivalries, and competitiveness will come into play, and you can be thrown into a state of anxiety, depression, and anger that you may think has to do with *"her"* and *"him."* In truth,

what you will be dealing with are all your *own* emotional hot spots.

6. *Don't lay all the blame on the other woman because the man always plays an essential part in what's going on, and besides, you don't know what he told her.*

7. *If you're living with a man, take the power position concerning infidelity.* The other woman is seeking your position. You are in the driver's seat; she's just thumbing a ride.

8. *Keep reminding yourself that you are the most important woman in your own universe.* Think about your special name for yourself. Don't let negative thoughts enter your brain, and focus on finding positive ways you can be good to yourself.

## What Kind of Infidelity Are We Talking About?

If you are convinced your partner is being unfaithful, you really need to know what kind of infidelity is involved. From where I sit, there are at least three different kinds of infidelity, as in the following list:

- Is your partner chronically unfaithful, and does he see it as a physical exercise that, from his point of view, doesn't threaten the relationship?
- Is he involved in a love affair that is actually threatening the relationship?
- Was his infidelity a onetime occurrence that he acknowledges was a mistake?

These three different types of infidelity have different implications for your relationship. With all three types, however, it would be ideal if you could go into some kind of counseling together. If he is compulsively promiscuous, he has a sexual addiction that needs to be addressed; if he is involved in a love affair, you both have to come to terms with priorities and choices for the future; if his infidelity was a onetime occurrence, you need to find ways to heal your relationship and resolve the problems between the two of you that may have contributed to his straying. Even if he won't go with you, get counseling for yourself. Once again, check with your religious adviser or local mental health facility for referrals and inexpensive alternatives.

## When Do You Forgive a Man for Infidelity?

The first question is this: Is he sincerely asking for forgiveness? It's senseless to forgive a man who isn't repentant or a man who is just trying to sweet-talk you out of your anger. But if he is honestly sorry and you are convinced that he doesn't plan to repeat his infidelity, of course, you should forgive him. If you love your partner and want to work on the relationship, you have to find ways of being more sensitive to each other's needs and put some real effort into finding ways to communicate. People do make mistakes, people do have regrets, and often people do have trouble controlling their hormones. Don't throw away this opportunity for growth by letting everything slide back to the way it was. Turn this stressful situation into a learning experience by getting to know each other better and by improving your emotional negotiating skills.

## What About Sexually Transmitted Diseases?

In the inner city, infidelity is referred to as "peeping and hiding, slipping and sliding." It used to be considered an uncomplicated way of acting out frustrations. That's no longer the case. The fact is that STDs have changed the nature of sexuality. If your mate is not behaving in a monogamous fashion, stand firmly on your rights: You have the right to ask that he practice safe sex, and you have the right to ask him to take an AIDS test. You also have the right to ask him to become monogamous. Talk to a doctor to find out what you can do to prevent sexually transmitted diseases. And don't take chances. Be safe, not sorry.

## When a Woman You Know Is Trying to Steal Your Man

Let's admit it, for some women, a man doesn't seem worth noticing unless he's involved with another woman. Probably few women are consciously aware of their need for the drama that is involved in a love triangle, yet some sisters seem to go out of their way to fall in love with men who are already attached. All kinds of women fall into the "temptress" category. For example, I often hear stories of pious-appearing church women who are attempting to "get closer" to their religious leaders. Women who go after their best friends' husbands, women who keep seducing their sisters' boyfriends, and women who always fall in love with married men. We all know situations like this.

Although these women rarely realize their predicament, what they are usually doing is acting out a drama that has its roots in childhood events. Sometimes as children these women felt competitive with their mothers or their female siblings for the attention of their male parent figures. When they grow up, they don't lose this need to win out over other women. If you find that you are always attracted to other women's boyfriends or husbands, some counseling may help you understand the dynamics of your situation, so you can change your pattern. And if you are friendly with someone with this kind of pattern, watch out.

## For Yourself, Get a Handle on Jealousy

"I spent three precious years of my life wondering about what my so-called fiancé was doing with other women. Now, that I'm finally over him, I wonder how I could have wasted my time that way. There was so much else I could have been doing with my life."

—GALE, 29

Gale says it best. Uncontrolled jealousy can waste years of your own special life. Jealousy comes from underlying feelings of self-doubt and insufficient self-esteem. The more you doubt your self-worth in the world, the more jealous you will feel. Many times women will say, "I wouldn't mind losing him if I knew I could find someone else." Someone you love is moving away from you, and what you feel is not only the pain of the moment, but also the sense that you won't find anyone else and you will be lost in the world by yourself.

I've met quite a few sisters who are so worried about losing their partners that they are always jealous and on guard even when there's little reason. Their suspicious natures have them prying and spying and self-destructively invoking their jealousy response. Sometimes this attitude has been caused by their own life experiences. They may have been involved with cheating men before, or they may have grown up with fathers who were unfaithful or who in some way failed to help their daughters feel secure. These women need to resolve old feelings before they destroy future happiness.

Too often, a woman will inappropriately derive much of her self-esteem and sense of value from the man she loves. When he is good to her, he makes her feel sexy, attractive, and worthy. When he is not good to her, she reacts as if he is taking that feeling away—forever. The idea that her special man, who made her feel so special, can now be doing the same thing with another woman is more than she can bear.

Every woman needs to build and maintain her own sense of self-worth, with or without a man. You need to keep your sense of your own self, your own desirability, and your own specialness so strong and secure that you always know that you can live alone without a man and can be happy doing so. Knowing that you can, and will, walk away from a man who is hurting you will protect you in all your relationships. This ability is something that men sense as well, and it makes them think twice before they risk causing you pain.

## *Jealousy—His*

Another problem that almost every sister will have to deal with at one time or another is a jealous man. What you have to ask yourself is whether there is any foundation to his jealousy. Some women like the feeling of having a man express jealousy; they see it as a sign of caring. Because of this, they may provoke him by flirting with other men. This has been known to turn into a dangerous game, and you have to be careful with this kind of behavior.

Probably the most upsetting form of jealousy is the man who is obsessively jealous even though he has nothing to be jealous about. Jealousy like this has a psychological basis that really can't be handled within the framework of a relationship without professional guidance and counseling. It's scary, and it can turn abusive. There is no way for you to assure someone like this of your love and fidelity. It's his problem, and he needs help.

# A Triangle That's as Old as Time

"My wife and my girlfriend are giving me a hard time right now. I realize this situation isn't fair to either one of them, but what am I supposed to do?"

—A 42-YEAR-OLD BROTHER DESCRIBING HIS ROMANTIC LIFE

Danisha has been head over heels in love with Wesley since the first time they met at a social work convention. She was with a group of people in a dining hall, and she couldn't help noticing the good-looking brother sitting across the table. She was thinking about more coffee, when, as though he had read her thoughts, Wesley moved to the empty seat near her, handing her a steaming cup. Let's see, he said, that was milk and no sugar, right? When she asked him how he noticed what she took in her coffee, he said that he was noticing everything she did. That was the beginning, and for three incredibly romantic days, Wesley made Danisha feel like the star in his show. Then, on the plane back home,

Wesley made his confession. He told her he was married and that although he was trying to work it out, he wouldn't be able to see her as much as he would like.

That was a year ago, and although Danisha still thinks she is head over heels in love, she's upset because she doesn't see enough of Wesley, and she doesn't want to share him with his wife. When he is with her, Wesley seems so turned on that she can't believe he doesn't want their relationship to go on forever. But he's only seeing her once a week for a few hours, and they never go anywhere because he's worried about his wife finding out. He used to phone her every few days, but he is even doing less of that. All Danisha wants for her life is to have Wesley be the way he was when they first met and he put milk in her coffee. This is what I call the coffee-light feeling, i.e., uncomplicated.

Danisha knows from people who work with him that Wesley had an affair with another woman before he met her. Danisha believes that this former affair proves that Wesley isn't getting what he needs from his wife. She believes that if she could only figure out a way to get him to leave his wife, then she and Wesley could marry and live happily ever after. Sometimes Danisha blames herself for the relationship, saying that she shouldn't be involved with a married man, but she usually manages to rationalize that feeling away by telling herself that if Wesley were happy at home, he wouldn't be with her. Whether she fantasizes or rationalizes, it's all the same fairy tale.

Trina is Wesley's wife, and she's also fed up and annoyed. Wesley always has a million and one excuses why he's coming home late or why he can't help her shop or clean. Although he does spend time with their two boys on the weekend, he does so only *after* he plays golf. Trina complains that Wesley treats his sons like buddies and doesn't act like a father figure. She's demoralized by this situation, but she feels helpless to change what's happening.

What is even more stressful for Trina is that she heard through the grapevine that when Wesley goes to conferences or on business trips, he fools around with other women. She doesn't really want to think about it too much, but her sister works with someone who told her that Wesley is seeing a woman he met last year. When Trina thinks about this woman, she pictures a seductress with no morals and no sense of family. The truth is that Trina feels as though she has been in combat with other women throughout her marriage. She believes that Wesley fools around because he has a need to prove something, and she worries that she may not be satisfying all his needs. Nevertheless, she thinks that none of these affairs would have occurred if there weren't so many man-hungry sisters out to steal her husband.

## Sisters in Common

Danisha and Trina need to recognize that they share an attitude that allows them to compensate for and excuse male behavior by blaming other women. This attitude is compounding their problems and helping them maintain unrealistic views about what's going on. They both need to come to grips with the fact that they are playing parts in a triangle that is being directed and produced by Wesley. Wesley is the person who set the stage for the chaos, and is reaping the best of two worlds. However, they are both contributing to this situation.

If, like Trina, you are married to a man who is fooling around, the first thing to do is to stop sitting home. Don't go out with other men, but you can keep busy. Put out your clothes, so he can see that you are a person with places to go, dress yourself up, and let him see you enjoying yourself. Get a baby-sitter for the kids, or better yet, set up a schedule, so he can baby-sit while you go out with friends. Try to keep him busier around the house, so he doesn't have so much free time, and find more free time for yourself.

If, like Danisha, you are involved with a married man, realize that the statistics are very much against his leaving his wife. And of the men who do leave their wives, few settle down with the first woman they meet. Men who find it extremely stressful to maintain relationships with two women and experience serious guilt and pain from this kind of situation are typically the ones who end one of their relationships quickly. In contrast, men who go back and forth between two women rarely end their marriages quickly. A man who is able to turn off and tune out the complaints of two—or more—women sometimes has such strong defense systems that nothing you say or do will make a real difference in his plans.

With that point in mind, don't arrange your life around a married man. Don't try to prove that you're sexier or smarter than his wife. Instead, use those smarts and that sex appeal to figure out a way to have a fuller life for yourself.

Both Danisha and Trina need to make some decisions about their future. If you are involved in a similar triangle, here's a way to start:

1. *Look at the situation realistically.* Whether you are the wife or the girlfriend, understand and accept that you are involved with a man who cheats. This is *his* problem.

2. *Stop blaming yourself.* Men who cheat are men who cheat. They cheat out of habit, they cheat out of convenience, they cheat out of ego, they cheat out of curiosity, and they cheat because they think they can get away with it. It's not because of something that's wrong with you.

3. *Stop blaming "her."* If he really wanted to leave his wife, he would make moves in that direction. If he really wanted to end his affair, ditto. He's probably doing exactly what he wants to do. He's got it going his way, so why should he stop?

4. *Stop thinking he's different with her than he is with you.* A man rarely changes from situation to situation. The woman may be different, but he's the same. He may even be using

the same pet names for both of you. That way he doesn't even have to bother remembering which woman he's with. I call this the same woman–different body syndrome.

5. *Stop thinking he's not getting something from her that he's getting from you.* Women typically assume that the man isn't having good sex with his wife, good conversations with the other woman, or good understanding from either one of them. If he's a man who likes good sex, good conversation, and understanding, he's probably getting both from both of you.

6. *Stop waiting for the man to make up his mind.* Sisters who are involved in triangles often waste precious time because they are waiting for the man to decide which woman he wants. But he has already made a decision: He wants them both—like a child with a lollipop in each hand, loving every lick.

7. *Stop allowing sister mistrust to dominate your life.* Remember these feelings are often linked to our past slave history when sisters were encouraged to compete against one another for "the favors of the menfolk."

8. *Start leading your life as though you are the focus person.* Instead of wasting precious emotions feeling excluded from his plans, start making plans of your own. Get off the old avenue you're walking on and walk down a new boulevard with a new attitude: "Me first—everybody else line up behind me."

9. *Refocus your energy—on yourself.* Think about all the good energy you've wasted trying to figure out what some man is doing. All this spiritual and emotional energy going outward worrying about a man, no matter how much you may think you love him, means only one thing: You don't have enough energy left for yourself. Start transferring all

that positive emotional energy back to you—right where it belongs. Forget about worrying about your partner; forget about worrying about any woman he may be with; and stop thinking about what they may be doing together. There is only one way to correct this kind of misdirected thinking: Start thinking, *full time*, about yourself, and refocus positive attention and love on the most important person in your world—you.

**6**

# Getting a
# New Attitude
# Toward
# Breadwinning
# and Sex

Desiree, an attractive 38-year-old lawyer with two school-age children, is successful by anybody's standards. She drives an Audi, and she wears designer labels. As a member of an all-Black law firm, she earns a solid income. She has worked hard to get where she is, and she deserves every bit of her success.

For the past year, Desiree has been going out with Joseph, a 35-year-old physical therapist who seems to be very much in love with her. Joseph is very solid and, better yet, he thinks Desiree is the sexiest woman he has ever seen and he thinks her kids are great. He says he is ready and willing to devote himself to keeping her and her family happy.

But lately, they have been fighting about money. You see,

Joseph doesn't make as much as Desiree does, and he can't afford to take her to the places she wants to go. Desiree worries about this. She doesn't want to have to go out Dutch. It makes her feel embarrassed and as though her self-worth is being attacked. As much as she cares for Joseph, a part of Desiree feels ashamed that she hasn't been able to attract a more successful man, and she feels as though she has less value as a woman because of it.

Joseph loves Desiree, but he can't afford to keep picking up all the bills. Even a simple dinner at McDonald's with Desiree and the children can cost him thirty dollars or more. On his salary, that kind of expenditure keeps adding up. Besides, he doesn't understand why Desiree, who makes almost three times as much money as he does, is so rigid about the man always paying. He thinks that if she really loved him, she would understand that he is in a lower-paying profession than she is.

Within African American relationships, Desiree and Joseph represent but one of several conflicts that revolve around money. Money is a potentially explosive issue in all male-female relationships, but it seems to take on even more significance in the African American community. All too often, money is the main reason for disagreements in our households. This state of affairs is particularly sad because Black people share a common economic history. This claim can be made by no other ethnic group.

No matter how much or how little you have in the bank today, when you look at every other brother and sister, your chances of finding someone whose family was able to secure financial assets is practically nil. As hard as you try, you're not going to find anybody who is substantially removed from the economic disenfranchisement that was visited on Black men and women in this country. When I was in school and studying about the Great Depression of 1929, I remember asking my father how come no Black people were jumping out of windows from losing their money. He replied, "That's because none of us had a damned dime to lose."

There is no old money like Rockefeller money in our

communities and, nothing in our common history has given us expectations of financial stability or asset ownership. Chronic unemployment is one of the most urgent problems in African American families, and the feeling of failure that often acompanies career underachievement or underemployment is one of the most common emotional problems even among middle-class Black families.

Because of what we've shared, we should be sensitive to the anxieties that each of us, male and female, feel about economic status. We should all be aware of each other's struggles to get ahead. When you look at a brother or a sister, you should automatically be aware of his or her financial dreams and goals, but with most of us, that's not what happens.

# The Shame-and-Blame Reaction

Why is it when you don't have money to buy nice things or to go to nice places you feel a sense of shame, particularly if the people you know are living it up? This is a very common reaction. We don't want others to see us not being able to join in with everyone else. We can't have a nice house or a big apartment, and we feel ashamed. We can't wear good clothes, and we feel ashamed. We can't take trips, and we feel ashamed.

There are two common ways of covering up this sense of shame, and they are connected to each other. The first is to use plastic money. If you can't afford to live large, but you want to look as though you are a high liver, charge it up and worry about it later. If you and your partner run up debts, you're both going to be anxious and nervous. You'll probably fall into roles—one of you will become the "bad" person who spends too much; the other will become the "parental" person who's always nagging.

The second way of feeling less ashamed of not having as much money as you would like is to blame your partner, saying, "It's all your fault; if you hadn't wasted that money, we wouldn't be in this kind of trouble" or "It's all your fault, if you made more money, we wouldn't be in this kind of trouble.

African Americans were conditioned to feel *shame* about not having as much as the rest of the country, even though it was no fault of our own. We were conditioned to believe that the only way we could eradicate this foolish sense of shame was through money. We were conditioned to *blame* each other for insufficient financial security and the feelings this situation engendered. As a result, more than anything else, brothers and sisters seem to be fighting over material things. What can you do to stop the shame and the blame in your own life?

## Understand the Messages You've Received as a Black Woman

If you are a typical sister, you grew up with two conflicting messages about money and love.

1. *Because you are a Black woman, you will not be able to rely on a man, and you will have to take care of yourself.* In all likelihood, this message made you envious of women who had an easier time of it. If your mother was overworked and overburdened financially, you may have thought about ways of not repeating her patterns. You may have resented your male parent figure for failing to give you the economic base you wanted. Or you may have become depressed and unhappy from watching your father struggling to the best of his ability and still not achieving at his full potential.

2. *You have little value until you find a Black man who will take care of you in style.* Even though you had little concrete evidence of this happening, you were told that when a man loves a woman, he takes care of her, and he gives her things—nice things. The messages you received all around you may have convinced you that your worth as a woman was dependent on having a man spend money on you. These are your "money prints." Even today, women receive this kind of

message. Recently on BET, a funny sister comedienne named Edwanda White said that sisters ought to demand two things from men—"a negative HIV and a positive cash flow."

Conflicting messages have left Black women confused and at a loss about how to handle money issues. We all know about the materialistic stereotypes attached to sisters, and we struggle against them. Yet, when a man doesn't treat us well financially, we feel foolish and, here's that word again, ashamed. We often honestly believe that people will think more of us if we are with a generous well-to-do man. However, the reality is that few men in our communities can afford to be generous, and when they are, they are often running up debt.

## Stop Indulging in Victim-to-Victim Thinking

Victim-to-victim thinking is another way that plantation psychology can enter your relationships. So many marital arguments, particularly those about money, come about because both partners are frustrated by an oppressive system that keeps them from doing what they want. Instead of focusing on the system and figuring out how to achieve a mutual goal, the partners tend to fight and compete with each other. Psychology teaches us that when one feels powerless against the larger system, one tends to vent anger and rage against those who are close to us.

Since the brother you care about isn't living next door to Princess Di, guess who gets to experience his frustration firsthand? Here's an example of how this works: Vernita is going to school to get a better job; her live-in boyfriend, Jason, is not being emotionally supportive of her. He's worried that if she gets more education and starts making more money, she will have even "bigger ideas." Instead of being happy for her, he has started picking fights and competing with her about small things. He argues with her about the best way to do things and indicates that just because she has so much education, she shouldn't think she is so smart.

Jason's insecurities are at the base of his thinking. He needs to be reassured that Vernita doesn't want to compete with him and doesn't want to take over or prove that she's better than he is. He needs to learn that supporting her efforts will help both of them, as well as their relationship.

If your partner believes that your success is taking away from him, you've got to sit down and talk with him about mutual goals. The two of you need to develop a "we" focus. Perhaps you can help him with things that *he* wants to accomplish. Let him know that the two of you have a mutual support group of your own and that working together will help you both get what you want.

## *Expect to Have Money Issues in Your Relationships*

Everyone has disagreements about money. People who want to save, save, save marry people who want to spend, spend, spend. Naturally disagreements occur. Just about everyone has different ideas about what to spend on rent, food, and entertainment.

As a sister, you have an additional financial-romantic burden: *All Black people have money issues.* How could we not?

Not having money or assets is symbolic of the Black experience. We carry that knowledge with us. No matter what our current income, we always carry the anxiety of not having enough or losing what we already have. Each of us, in some way, has been falsely programmed to believe that having more money will bring us to a nirvanalike state where our problems will disappear.

All Black couples need to learn to talk about their feelings about money early in the relationships. We need to bring our thoughts and our insecurities out in the open so we can learn more about each other and put money into perspective. We need to make money into a less-loaded issue. We can do this by becoming less reactive and more communicative about what money means.

Here are some suggestions for money conversations you

and your partner should have. Start by exploring what money means to each of you. For example, do you think you have more value when you have money, and, if so, why is that the case? What happened in your childhood to make you insecure about your place in the world? What kinds of judgments have you heard about Black people's finances, and have you internalized any of these judgments? What kind of judgments may have been cast on you by your community because you didn't have enough money? What kind of judgments were cast on you because you had more money than the people around you? Discuss attitudes of envy, jealousy, and competitiveness that you've witnessed or experienced. Have either of you been in a situation in which friends or acquaintances resented you because of some material good fortune? Have you ever felt that way about someone else? Do you have any guilt about money when you have it? Do you subconsciously believe that having more expensive equipment, cars, and so on will make you feel like more of a person? Do you want to go back to your roots and show people how well you've done? If you've ever had the chance to do so, have you discovered that you feel guilty about your achievement and ownership of assets? Do you worry that because you have a job, you minimize another Black person's chances? Are you embarrassed to be seen in your good car wearing your good clothes? Has anybody made you feel less Black because you've achieved financially? What kind of labels have been slammed on you because of money issues? What kind of labels have you slammed on others?

Try to talk about the pride or shame you connect to having or not having money. Talk about how your "shame-and-blame" reactions affect your relationship. Talk about your fears of acting out financial stereotypes. Talk about your fears of being taken advantage of financially by your nearest and dearest. What can you do to reassure each other about these fears?

These kinds of discussions will help you as a couple to open up new ways of talking about your financial issues. They will bring you closer and help alleviate the money pressures you feel. Make your money issues more human before they turn catastrophic. Decode and unravel what you think about yourself and your material worth. Don't argue during these conversations. This is about exploration and communication. This is serious stuff. Nonetheless, together try to see the humor and silliness in the agony we've perpetuated in our money issues.

## *Develop a No-Fault Money Approach*

There is a theory that 20 percent of the population own 80 percent of the wealth, which leaves the rest of us—Black, white, Asian, and Latino—to scrap over what's left. The people who control the economy try to make the "have-nots" believe that the fight over money is between Black and white, when the real color they control is green. I'm saying this because it's a mistake to believe that only Black people are caught in this economic confusion. The difference is that we carry this memory of the slavery experience. This disenfranchised history makes us less experienced and a little more unrealistic about what's really happening economically. Nonetheless, as the late Whitney Young, Jr., of the Urban League, once said, "We may have all come over on different ships, but we're in the same boat now."

Frequently, this attitude of blame carries over into our relationships. This is foolish and counterproductive. It's not your problem, it's not his problem; it's our problem. When you're not in control of the economy, you must become philosophical and take a no-fault attitude toward money. Here are some easy rules to follow.

- Don't allow money to assume top priority in your intimate relationships.
- Never demean a brother—or a sister, for that matter—because of a low cash flow.
- Depersonalize money. Instead of saying "my" money or "your" money, make it "the" money.
- Realize that when one family member is unemployed,

it's a family problem and practice share-the-load economics.

- Whenever you have money troubles, make a special effort to be loving and affectionate to each other.
- Reset your personal goals so that money and the acquisition of material goods assume less importance.
- Don't let your self-esteem be lowered because of insufficient assets.
- Don't let your emphasis on material goods pressure a brother to spend more money than he really has.
- Don't run up your own debts with credit cards because you believe that spending enhances your self-esteem.

## Finally, Practice Cooperative Economics

In our families and in our relationships, it's essential that we do not compete with each other about who has more or less, or who is giving more or less. Forget about one-upmanship and cooperate toward couple strength. Realize that as a couple, your strength is in your capacity to share and grow in a mutual team effort. Washington, D.C.-based psychiatrist, Frances Cress Welsing, calls this "like-minded focus." She says that people grow closer as long as they stay focused in the same direction. Sometimes sisters and brothers are concerned that those they love will take advantage of them financially. What you have to do with each other is make a commitment not to do this. If that commitment is broken, you need to reassess the relationship and have a calm talk about what's happening. You need to establish ground rules of behavior that allow you to build trust in each other without threatening your individual sense of financial security.

Those of you who have attended Kwanzaa celebrations know that Kwanzaa is based on the *Nguzo Saba*, or the Seven Principles of Blackness. The fourth principle is *Ujamaa*, or cooperative economics. That is about sharing work and wealth to build a society that offers an ocean of human possibilities. It is Ujamaa that we need to stress in our romantic partnerships.

# Sexual Concerns

Even today, with all our so-called sexual advancement and up-to-date information sources, men and women have two different perceptions about sexuality and sexual conduct. We simply don't always understand each other. Men are goal oriented; when they think of sex, they think of action as soon as possible. Many brothers consider an erection to be some kind of emergency. They actually say things like "There's a fire in the cellar." That means they want somebody to put it out—as soon as possible because the alarm has sounded. My first message about sex is to tell you as a sister that you are not a sprinkler system.

Women are different. It's clear to me that, by and large, sisters believe that sexuality is an overall feeling. The typical woman doesn't think things like "My clitoris is erect" or "My vagina is throbbing." She tends to enjoy a more holistic view. I once heard a sister say, "No, I didn't have an orgasm like they describe in those books, but I was kicking 'em high and hollering loud because I had that all-over feeling. The more I moved my body to that feeling, the better the feeling got. I was feeling it all over, even in my head."

To a sister, sexuality usually suggests intimacy. She wants to communicate with her man through the language of her mind, body, and spirit; she wants to bond with him in the deepest, most sacred part of herself. In the meantime, all he may be thinking about is thrusting into the deepest corners of her vagina. These two opposing views give a good picture of why men and women have such a hard time understanding each other.

For example, men tend to see women in parts; they seem to be programmed that way. A man might say something like "I'm an ass man" (or "a breast man," or "a leg man"). I call this Kentucky Fried Chicken sex. You know that word *intimacy*? A brother who is seeing a woman in parts only understands the first two letters of that word—*in*. He just wants to get it in, preferably while he's nibbling away on a breast. That's his problem with the word you love so much.

## Sexual Power Games Also Inhibit Intimacy

Too many men, of all races, derive a sense of power from controlling women. I call this "penis power." For Black men, it is even more complicated. For one thing, we can't really ignore the years under slavery when our sexuality was controlled, and some brothers were turned into studs and were rewarded accordingly, while others were kept from the women they wanted. We can't really forget all those years when families were sold apart and insensitivity was a desirable trait insofar as it made it easier for men to handle being separated from their children and other loved ones.

We also need to remember that the predominantly white society has a sexist attitude toward women that Black men have internalized as well. It stands to reason that some brothers, frustrated at not being able to achieve enough power through political, economic, or social means, try to get some power by lording it over the women they deal with. But even brothers who *have* power may not be immune to these techniques. We've all met men who use sex to play power games. Here are some classic types:

*The Stud.* This brother gets a sense of power (which may or may not be lacking in other areas of his life) from being able to "handle" women sexually. Black men typically take their sexual abilities very seriously; they have been told they are good lovers, and they work at it. But the Stud is even more committed. To him, every act of lovemaking is like some kind of heavyweight championship. He's defending his title, and he wants each bout to be a knockout.

The Stud always believes that he knows what a woman really needs, but often he really doesn't. Because studs are big on performance, they don't always take women's whole-person sexual needs into account. Who the woman is, what she feels, and what she really wants are left by the wayside because the Stud focuses on skill, not on emotional contact.

If you're involved with a Stud, here's a situation you probably know all too well: You're tired, you want a hug, a kiss, some cuddling, and some sleep. The Stud, however, is convinced that he knows what you really want and need, and he's intent on making his case. And he wants you involved and playing your part. You're supposed to moan and carry on like he's the greatest thing in the universe because that makes him feel more powerful.

For a Stud, there is also—pardon the expression—a downside. He may not always be in the mood to live up to his sexual reputation, but he doesn't know how to do anything else. Unfortunately, like all of us, the Stud will eventually get older, and if his sense of manhood is all arranged around his genitals, he's going to have a difficult time finding something else to give him the same kind of satisfaction.

*The Baby Maker.* Sisters of all ages need to be clear about the difference between a Baby Maker and a family man. Yes, it's true that the Baby Maker is frequently a victim of *his* history, but at this point in *our* history, that's no real excuse. The Baby Maker is misusing African fertility rights, impregnating women without assuming the true responsibilities attached to fatherhood. Sometimes you hear a Baby Maker bragging about his children; sometimes you may even see him going to visit one of them for a bit, but he doesn't love them the way their mother does. To him, they are just "showcase" babies for him to show off and prove his manhood.

Sisters have to understand how easy it is for young men to fall into the Baby Maker frame of mind. These men are using this as a manhood thing, and when you go along with it, you're making a big mistake. Sometimes a sister keeps holding on to the idea that eventually babies will win their father over and make him into a family man, but it doesn't work that way.

In the meantime, the Baby Maker is on a power trip with women that isn't good for either one of you. Tell your daughters, tell your nieces, tell the young girls in your neighborhood, pass it on: Don't let some guy who doesn't want to be inconvenienced with safe sex or birth control convince you to have his baby just because it seems like the thing to do. Don't help some irresponsible guy shore up his manhood that way. It's not good for you, and it's not good for him either because eventually his inability to fulfill his parenting duties adequately will only make him feel like more of a failure.

*The Sexual Ruler.* This brother acts like he's Dr. Feelgood and only he can write the prescriptions. Clearly, he's into sexual control. Typically, he appears to become unduly threatened when a women assumes any sexual responsibility. He decides where, when, and how and may perceive even affection as a demand for sex, which is a no-no because he doesn't want you to initiate anything.

For the Sexual Ruler, even sexual positions can become controversial. He may, for example, have strong feelings against having a women on top because to him, that's the power position, and he's not about to relinquish it. He may encourage only those sexual acts that make him feel as though he is the king and the woman is there to serve him. He may, for example, feel strongly that it's a woman's duty to perform nonreciprocal oral sex whenever *he* is in the mood— and with few preliminaries.

*The Precious Object.* This brother represents a recent phenomenon. Instead of chasing after women, he is convinced that all women are chasing after him. He thinks he is hot stuff and says things like, "Black women always want sex." Sometimes this brother is living large and is convinced that he has so much flash that no woman could resist him. Other times, he's just a street-corner man with good looks, a better line, and his hand on his manhood. Other times, he's a man who chases you until he catches you and then acts like you were chasing him. He thinks he's doing you "a big favor" just by being on the scene. The Precious Object is excellent at making women insecure, and you have to be careful not to buy in to his version of his sex appeal. The bottom line: Precious Object is no Precious Lord.

All these sexual power roles keep a brother from behaving as though both you and he are whole people with many sets of complicated emotional and physical needs. The question is, What can you do for yourself to put more sensuality in your life?

## Start Enjoying Whole-Person Sexuality

A sister can talk about her desire for intimacy, but still not do much to introduce the concept into her own life. She may want the spiritual nourishment that comes with embracing, touching, talking, and bonding in an intimate way, but never move in that direction. She may say she wants to commune through the language of the body, mind, and spirit, but may never convey that wish to a man. All too often, she lets the man rush her into sexual intercourse, often before either of them is ready.

*The Golden Rule of Sex:* Stop moving into intercourse so fast. This is true with a man you've just met, but it's also true with the man you may have been married to for a dozen or more years. Men think it's their prerogative to set the pace for sex. Try changing that and set your own pace. Slow it down. Get to know each other better and at a more intimate level before you move into intercourse. One way of slowing things down with a sense of humor is to offer him what sister comedienne Montana Taylor, of Houston, Texas, calls a Coochie coupon, to be redeemed at a later date. Don't be afraid to use humor to reduce sexual urgency as long as it's not demoralizing.

Whole-person sexuality is more than just an erect penis and a pulsating vagina. Whole-person sexuality requires intimacy; this takes time and a lot of sharing and support. Intimacy suggests that you are attempting to share the deepest, most sacred parts of yourself. This is not a sexual response; this is a depth response. This kind of closeness is the place where we build the foundation for trust. Why is intimacy important? I believe that the closer I get to YOU, the more I learn about ME. This feeling is scary, but it's worth investigating.

Get closer to a man before you move forward to sex. For example, before you get into the tactile stuff, talk about sex to describe sexuality as a part of life. I don't mean that you should start talking about the sexual act or any previous experience you've had. That is specifically *not* what I mean. What I want you to do is to show him through words that you think sex is a beautiful, sacred, appropriate human response. Give sex the respect it deserves, so you can get the respect you deserve. In your conversations, make it clear that you see sex as the profound human rite it is. Sex can be a spiritual manifestation of a human response. Let the man in your life know that's what you want.

Before you can fully explain this sexual attitude, you should explain other things about yourself. Show him through your words who you are, what you believe, and what you want for yourself. Discuss your spiritual side. I call this type of conversation "gender forerunner talk." Before you approach a sexual connection, you have set up the atmosphere to discuss your essential self. Find out about him as well. This is going to make him take you more seriously, and if this level of seriousness isn't what he wants and he moves on, it's his problem. This exercise, by the way, is a perfect way to find out where his head is at.

## Sisters Need More Sexual Information

Many sisters were raised in conservative sexual environments or were raised to be body denying. Keep your skirt down and your hands away from your genitals was frequently the only sexual education a young Black girl received. Mothers who were struggling against the Miss Loosey stereotype were often afraid that giving their daughters more information would make them more likely to become sexually active.

Today young sisters have a lot more experience than women in earlier generations did, but their knowledge hasn't improved all that much. The proof of this sad state is our high rate of teenage pregnancy and sexually transmitted diseases. Statistics show that nationwide Black women have the fastest-growing number of reported AIDS cases among any racial or gender group.

Sexually, sisters need to be less trusting of their partners. Often men and women practice safe sex only the first few times they make love. Then they assume that because they know their partners, the danger of getting a sexually transmitted disease has passed. This is a foolish idea. You can't see sexually transmitted diseases. Before you start a sexual relationship with a new man, it is advisable for both of you to be tested for HIV and then practice safe sex for at least six months, when you can be tested again. If you both test negative both times and you have both been monogamous, then you should discuss it further to make sure that your clean bill of health is going to be part of a long-range commitment to each other. To minimize the risk of a condom breaking, some couples use a condom for the man, a diaphragm for the woman, and a contraceptive jelly that includes nonoxydol 9. This may seem like a great deal of effort, but it's less work than getting a sexual disease. And don't forget the female condom, a barrier device for the vagina made of polyurethane, which gives a sister more control in situations in which a brother refuses to wear a condom. You can get more information about this at women's health centers, doctors' offices, and Planned Parenthood.

## Learn Some Penis Facts

Men typically intimidate women with their erections. They try to encourage a penis-pacifier approach to sex, that is, using sexual intercourse as a problem solver. When it comes to women and sex, brothers typically take an "I know what you need" approach. What you have to do is reject the penis-pacifier approach and learn more about what a penis can and can't do. Here are some facts you need to know.

1. An erect penis does not a man make. Don't assume a man needs an erection to be sexual. This is an important point because men are so focused on their erections that as they get older and run into physical difficulties, they don't know how to continue to be sexual. Yet most men will expe-

rience sexual difficulties some time during their lives. We all need to make less of a fuss about the rigid shaft.

2. The size of a penis has nothing to do with giving a woman pleasure. Black men have this big penis mythology that they have to deal with, and if they don't "measure up" to the myth, they think less of themselves as dynamic sexual partners. Put away the measuring stick and stick to the facts. Penis size and pleasure have no correlation.

3. Young men need to learn that a man can have erections and do a lot of sexually pleasurable things without having intercourse. If your partner learns this fact when he's young, he will avoid many of the emotional conflicts men have about their erections when they get older.

4. Older men need to learn that if they have difficulties getting an erection or even if they can't get an erection at all, they can do lots of sexually pleasurable things without an erect penis. There are two whole bodies that need to be explored.

Your knowledge can help the man you love get over those classical male fixations about his sexuality. It is particularly important for him to do so as he gets older and his sexual reactions and capacities change.

## Understand and Satisfy Your Own Skin Hunger

"What I really needed was just a hug, but I ended up getting pregnant."

—LILAH, 19

This is a common situation. Too many sisters have ended up having sex when all they wanted was affection. Everyone needs to be touched. Scientific studies have found that children who are not touched from infancy tend to suffer from mental disorders and physical problems. We all need to be nourished on a tactile level. If we don't get it, our skin feels as though it's starving to be touched. This can be an even greater need than the need for genital stimulation. Unfortunately, sisters sometimes confuse this need to be touched with a need for intercourse. It's not unusual for sisters to trade off this need to be touched by giving into intercourse, even when what they really want is more hugging and kissing.

Sometimes when I conduct seminars, I engage the room in an exercise to relieve skin hunger. It's a simple hugging exercise in which each person hugs other people of both sexes. Men learn to hug men, women learn to hug women. This is a specifically nonsexual exercise for nonsexual touch, and it's an excellent way to help people get over their homophobia and fear of same-sex touching. I tell people that while they are hugging, they should specifically keep themselves from thinking about their genitals. This exercise reminds us that although only those partners you desire can address your need for sexual intercourse, just about anybody can nourish your skin hunger. When I do this exercise with a room full of people, I'm always amazed at the way the room seems to change after people touch one another. The room warms up, and suddenly it's filled with friends who have given something to each other.

I firmly believe that all sisters need to get into some nonsexual hugging and touching. Doing so will help keep your life balanced. It will help relieve skin hunger, which, in turn, relieves your feeling of loneliness and the sense that only your man can make you feel good about yourself.

The Black community used to be filled with people who expressed affection easily. If you need to feel some warmth and need a hug, get yourself to a local Black church, where people still touch each other and sweet-talk each other, no matter what their sex and with no intention of engaging in sexual intercourse. And don't forget to hug friends and family members as well.

# Learn the Art of Self-Pleasuring

Gail Elizabeth Wyatt, Ph.D., of the University of California at Los Angeles, is a sister who conducted a study of Black women's sexuality. One of her most astonishing findings concerned masturbation: Only about 50 percent of the Black women, compared to 80 percent of the white women, in her study had masturbated. The explanation for this finding is directly connected to the conservative nature of the sexual upbringing of young Black females. But it clearly points up the fact that Black women need to know more about how to satisfy themselves sexually.

I don't like to use the word *masturbation* because it suggests that your sexual focus is only between your legs. I prefer the term *self-pleasuring* because I believe that you should treat sexuality as though it is a whole-body experience. I think every sister needs to get to know and pleasure her own body.

The first thing I would suggest you do is to get a full-length mirror and take pleasure in your sensuality. Take a good look at yourself. Think of yourself as a sexual explorer of your own body and run your hands over you. Look at all your curves and feel your roundness and your bones and your muscles. You're a map, and chances are, you haven't explored your own map. How can you know the world if you don't know the world of your own body? Body knowledge is also important to a woman's health. It allows you to monitor your health because you'll notice any significant changes.

The second thing you need is a hand mirror, so you can locate your gender identity and take a look at your genitals. Many women have never looked at their own genitals. They think of their genitals as some dark forbidden nasty place. You need to take a good look at them, examine the creases and folds, and find new ways to glorify what you see.

Learn how to give yourself pleasure. Massage your own hands, feet, arms, and legs. Learn how to touch yourself so that you can reach orgasm. This is essential for any woman who has a difficult time climaxing. If you can learn to achieve orgasm by yourself, it will make it much easier to explain to a man what he needs to do. Knowing your own body allows you to help someone else explore it. Women are always waiting for men to wake them up sexually. Wake *yourself* up, Sleeping Beauty.

# 7

# Overdoing Your Part: When a Relationship Gets Out of Balance

"I loved my husband so much sometimes. Before he would come home, all I could think about were things to make him happy. I would be running all over, buying and preparing his special dishes . . . trying to make things just so for him. Then he would walk through the door, and we would start fighting about where he had been, and I would hate him so much I didn't know what to do. I was always making it too easy for him and then getting angry because of it. There was too much give and not enough take."

—MONIQUE

Too much give and not enough take. I'll bet many of you have experienced these feelings. When you first fall in love, it doesn't seem possible that you could end up in a relationship that's so unbalanced. In fact, when the two of you first started going out, he probably seemed ultra anxious to please you. Later, you were doing most of the pleasing. How did the scales get tipped so far to his advantage? When you end up giving more than you're getting, typically, insecurity and a poor sense of self-confidence are the major contributing factors. You're not sure of your value and want to be liked and loved, so you try to be more likable and lovable by being more giving. The next thing you know, you've established a pattern where you're always giving more.

Equality is an essential ingredient in a satisfying relationship. When the interchange between two people loses its balance, it feels emotionally abusive to the partner who is giving more. Usually, the "giver" feels taken advantage of and starts to resent what's happening while the "taker" becomes less respectful of the "giver's" needs and humanity. That's when the relationship starts to disintegrate.

# Playing a Part and Not Knowing How to Act

When I say a sister is overdoing her part, what I mean is that she has turned into too much of a good thing. For example, she's catering *too* much, she's accepting *too* much, or she's expecting *too* little. Some of us grew up with messages from the mass media and from those around us that this is how a woman is supposed to behave. After all, isn't a sister supposed to "take care of her man?" Isn't she supposed to be cozy and comforting, sexual and satisfying? Isn't that what we've been told? Black women, who have so often been accused of being controlling and just plain bossy, are particularly sensitive to these messages. They often start out their relationships by bending over backward to let their men assume what they think is a more traditional macho role.

Typically the issues played out in African American relationships get more complicated when the sister starts out assuming a role that she ultimately doesn't want any part of. Sometimes she's playing "lady in waiting," waiting for the man to make up his mind, make a commitment, or just come home when he says he will. Or she finds herself acting out a stereotypical mama role, even though she doesn't feel a bit like his mama. Monique, who is now separated from her husband, is a good example of a sister who played out a variety of roles that she didn't want because she didn't know what else to do. She says that while she was playing these roles, she kept expecting him to change into the man she thought he could be. All the while, she was getting angrier and angrier.

## A Sister Who Made It Too Easy for the Man She Loved

Monique, 36, is a tall, elegant full-bodied woman who always looks as though she stepped out of the pages of a fashion magazine. She firmly believes that no matter what's going on in your life, it's important to look nice. Otherwise you feel even worse.

Monique is a teller at a large bank. She has held this job, which offers a steady salary and good benefits, for more than ten years, during which her life has been a roller coaster of emotional ups and downs. Right now, most of her personal focus is directed toward her three teenage children. She is concerned that they grow up right and have a chance for a happy life. Although she doesn't have a formal divorce, Monique hasn't lived with the children's father for over a year. She says: "The story of my life is no money and no sense of security. My husband's a musician, a drummer, who doesn't always find work. His problem is that he thinks he's above having a normal job . . . or a normal life. The first years we were together, I would go out with him to the clubs whether he had a gig or not, and it was all just fine. But once we started to have kids, I couldn't do that no more. But he didn't stop. It felt like he didn't want to grow up. Even when I was in the hospital giving birth, he wasn't worrying about me. He was worrying that he was missing some action with his friends."

Monique told me that her husband would sometimes find

straight jobs, but he would hold them only for a few weeks, and then something would always go wrong. Mostly with him. From his point of view, he seemed to equate having a job with failure. If he got a menial job or a job with no real status, he thought it meant giving up his dream of becoming a famous drummer. Monique said that she didn't want to hurt his dreams by forcing him to go to work. A bigger issue to her was that because of his lifestyle, he came into daily contact with drugs and booze. Monique complained most about the liquor.

"Although he may have used some drugs, my husband said he never paid for them, and I believe him. The drinking was something else. It seemed like it was more of a problem because of the money it cost than because of his behavior. That man could hold his liquor. But a couple of drinks here and a couple of drinks there, and the money adds up. I always felt as though I was out working while he was out playing Mr. Big-Time Spender, treating somebody else. That money was coming out of *my* pocket. You know the old saying—'I had no sense, so now I got no cents.'"

Monique says that when she tries to figure out how she could have worked so many years and have so little to show for it, she remembers all the money she gave her husband. It makes her feel stupid and used. She says she'll never do that again. Nor will she ever work so hard to please a man. Monique's behavior in her marriage reflects what I see as a characteristic caretaker response, a clear-cut picture of when giving all ends up with having nothing at all. Monique describes her marriage as being completely lopsided:

"I really loved that man, and I wanted to please him. I tried to keep a nice house—not fancy, but comfortable and attractive. I was always cleaning up or washing and ironing his shirts. I'd come home from work every day and make dinner for everybody. I'd try to make things he liked, and I tried to look good, but he was no sooner finished eating than he'd be ready to go out. He never wanted to stay home, watch television, and be a regular family. If I tried to force him to stay, he would get mad and abusive. He was like a big child when he didn't get his way. It was easier to let him go and do what he wanted.

"By the time he left the clubs and got home, I'd be sound asleep, often for hours. Very sound asleep. That's how I got pregnant—twice. I was too tired to even notice what was happening until after he ejaculated. I've got no one to blame but myself—I made this kind of life too easy for him. I had to get up for work, and he could sleep till noon."

Monique says she might still be married to this man except that he started playing around with other women and, even though he had a million and one excuses for staying out, many nights he stopped coming home altogether.

"I guess I put up with a lot. I don't really think it's because of low self-esteem or anything like that. I was just raised to believe in God and Jesus Christ and to give everybody a chance. My husband is a good-looking man, and women threw themselves at him. Whenever I confronted him about other women, he would apologize and say it wasn't his fault. He kept apologizing, and I kept giving him chances. I would see him flirting with somebody or hear that he was with another woman, and I would get mad, but I didn't do anything about it. At first, he would start crying to me about how I was 'his woman' and ask why I was believing somebody else!

"We would fight and make up and fight and make up. But each time took something out of me. I just had less and less trust and was less and less interested in him. When my brother started seeing him coming out of this woman's house two or three times a week, he told me about it. Then my brother took me by the hand and made me see it, too.

"Even so, I couldn't throw my husband out of the house. I was too emotionally dependent even though he was nobody you could depend on. Eventually, I stopped giving him sex and made him sleep on the couch . . . at first for a week or two and then for longer. We both got used to it, and we just drifted apart. For a while, he used the house as a place to throw his hat. Then he stopped coming home, although a lot of his clothes are still here.

"In many ways I blame myself for what happened. We got into bad patterns, and I didn't know how to change them. There was a lot of love between us, but not enough sharing. He didn't know how to be a husband, and I acted in a way that made it worse. Sometimes I wonder what would have happened if when we were first married I had insisted that he behave more responsibly. But I was afraid that I would lose him, and I also didn't want to make things harder for him than they already were. Instead, I would make excuses for him until I couldn't stand it any more and then I would explode. Nothing ever got resolved."

# Acting Like He's the Best *or* the Worst Doesn't Work

Here's something to think about: As a Black woman, you've been conditioned to think about a man as being one of two things—a prince or a "dog"—and typically you were raised to relate to men as though they are one or the other. Much of the time Monique treated her husband like a prince she was terrified of losing. Then, when he didn't act like a prince, in her head he became a dog who didn't even know how to do any cute tricks. The typical sister has little experience relating to a man as a human being—nothing more, nothing less.

Sisters tend to get into what I call the protection–put-down confusion. These two contradictory extremes are easy to understand. As a Black woman, you were probably raised with the knowledge that Black men are at risk in this society. Growing up, you were taught that Black boys were special and needed special protection, from the community, from their mamas, and from you. But at the same time, everywhere you went, you also heard women complaining about men. You heard that Black men were difficult, you heard that Black men were controlling, and you heard a lot about BMT (Black man's time). From all you heard, it sounded as though you needed to be very careful whenever you had dealings with a brother.

In all likelihood, you were still a young girl when you first became aware of one of the primary contradictions in our relationships: Black women are trained to protect men from the outside world as much as they find fault with them among themselves. And, as much as they may resent it, Black men are conditioned to expect protection from the women around them.

Look at the furor Anita Hill created by presenting her charges against Clarence Thomas. For many Black Americans, it didn't matter what Thomas did or didn't do or say. All that mattered was that an African American woman had turned him in. This the fine line of history that Black women have had to walk for a very long time, and it's unfair. In an interview with Anita Hill in the March 1992 issue of *Essence*, Hill says:

> . . . as African-American women, we are always trained to value our community even at the expense of ourselves, and so we attempt to protect the African-American community. We don't want to say things that will reflect negatively on it. We are constrained from expressing our negative experiences, because they are perceived in the larger community as a bad reflection on African-Americans.

Those who promote this point of view believe that whatever faults Black men may exhibit, exposing them to the rest of the world can only add to the already large list of injustices. Because this kind of reaction permeates our communities, no matter how resentful she may be, the typical sister knows she should think twice before venting her feelings in the world. Sisters recognize this unfairness, and it can't help but affect the way they behave. As a sister I met in Detroit complained, "If my man do me wrong and I sing a sad song about it, then I'm called a bitch. Ain't that a switch! He runs a game on me, and I end up being called 'Ms. Black and Evil.'"

Brothers often recognize our tendency to protect and shield them. Some are resentful and complain that all this worry makes them feel and behave like adolescents with overprotective mothers. Others have been conditioned to use our fears about their well-being and safety to their own advantage. They get away with a lot because we care about them, and they know it. Because they have honestly been at risk in the world, they don't necessarily feel guilty about manipulating our compassion and our concerns to their own ends. This all sets up an amazing number of contradictions in our relationships. Recognize this fact and realize that brothers also need reeducating. Let's look at some of the wrong parts that Black men and women act out, and let's see if we can find ways of changing our patterns.

# Overdoing the "Mama" Part

Babying the one you love is part of our culture, and we've developed a whole special way of talking to one another that confirms this. Black psychiatrist Frances Cress Welsing talks about this phenomenon in her book *The Isis Papers*, saying:

> In addition to Black males frequently referring to one another as "baby," many Black females often refer to their Black male peers and companions as "baby." While Black adult females refer to Black adult males as "baby," Black adult males often refer to Black adult female peers and companions as "mama," often expecting those "mamas" to provide food, clothes and shelter for them.

Although sisters may complain that they are being forced to play mama roles to men who won't grow up and stand on their own two feet, the truth is that many women have been conditioned to believe that acting like a man's mama is the best and sometimes the only way to express their love. A sister who is acting this way frames her actions so they will appeal to the little boy in her partner. In a symbolic sense, she is cradling him, protecting him as much as she possibly can from the harsh elements of the world.

There are different ways of overdoing a mama part. If you don't want to set yourself up to act like his mama, here are some behaviors to avoid:

1. *Don't assume primary responsibility for household expenses and chores.* Many households are run as though the man is a helpless impractical child while the woman is doing all the adult thinking and worrying. This imbalance sets up a burdensome situation. She resents him because she's working too hard; he resents her because she's turned into a supervisor who doesn't know how to lighten up and have any fun. In other words, the sister gets chored, and the brother gets bored.

2. *Don't overinvolve yourself with what a man wears.* Sisters baby men by choosing and color coordinating their jackets, shirts, and suits as well as taking care of their laundry and dry cleaning. Sometimes sisters even help men buy expensive clothes when they can't afford them for themselves. In such a situation, the man becomes the sex-symbol stud, and the woman becomes the doting mama. The risk: Not only may he turn into "Superfly," he may even sprout wings and take off.

3. *Don't act as though only you can cook or clean.* Obviously, every time you make a cake, you don't want to be accused of mothering the man you love. However, when you are always doing for a man as though he is a child, it can make him feel as though he can't take care of himself. Encourage him to cook for you, even if all he can do is open a can of tuna fish and stick it on a plate next to a tomato. If you're both working, share chores. For example, ask him to do all or some of the food shopping or make a date to go food shopping together. Encourage the team effort.

4. *Don't make excuses for him.* Everyone is more tolerant of male children. "Boys will be boys" is an old expression. A sister who is mothering a man will even make excuses for his

infidelity, telling herself, "He can't help himself—that's just the way men are." She'll blame the other woman, saying, "These women just won't let him alone." Sometimes she even blames herself! This attitude can't help but weaken a man and make him more irresponsible. Treat him like the adult he is, and act as though you expect responsible adult behavior.

5. *Don't assume full financial support for the household.* No sister starts out *wanting* to find a man who doesn't contribute to household expenses, all the while eating her out of house and home. However, many sisters end up living this kind of burdensome life. Couples should put together a budget and talk about ways of balancing it. Everyone needs to be contributing to the best of his or her ability.

If you're with a man who is accustomed to having you shoulder most of the financial responsibility for food and shelter while he spends his money on himself, you need to put more balance into your relationship. You can do this by changing your behavior and your attitude one step at a time. Gentle action is what counts here, not nagging words. Encourage him to assume more responsibility, and don't keep taking up his financial slack. When you take him grocery shopping with you, don't carry money. Let him get rid of the image of you as the powerful woman who will always take care of him. Don't ever say, "How am *I* going to pay the rent?" or anything else, for that matter. Remember you are a couple, and the correct question is: "How are *we* going to pay for it?"

6. *Don't get involved in all his business.* Where are you going? How are you feeling? What were you doing? Don't always be checking up on him, and don't try to crawl up into a man and become part of who he is. We're all independent people who need emotional and physical space.

7. *Don't worry that the minute he's out of sight, he's going to get into trouble.* Keep repeating to yourself, "He's not my

child. . . . He's not my child. . . . " Then go on about the business of leading your own life. Fill your life with other things and stop concentrating on him. Try to have a nice time doing this.

## Why Mothering Causes Resentment

"Baby, cut me some slack here. You're always on top of me. I know you want to do what's good for me, but I can run my own bath. I'm not helpless."

—AN OVERLOVED BROTHER

There's no way around it, a grown man doesn't appreciate feeling dependent; all that care and instruction giving feels controlling and oppressive. It feels demeaning because to him, it seems as though he's not getting the respect a man deserves. It may remind him of all the things about childhood that he wanted to escape; too much mothering makes him want to get out from under the comforter of caring and breathe on his own.

Acting like your partner's mama gives him a loud message: You want him to feel happy because of what you are giving; you want him to be satisfied because of what you are providing; you want him to feel comfortable because of what you are doing. In other words, you want to be his whole world, much as a mother is a baby's whole world. The attitude you are conveying as a woman is, "I'm everything to you. How can anyone else be anything?"

The bond this attitude sets up is spelled *dependency*, and ultimately extreme dependency creates extreme resentment. In some relationships, dependency is the primary connection; we've all seen men and women who are dependent on one another long after the love and caring are gone. Some women spend much of their time creating an environment that encourages dependency and provides a comfort zone for a man. My mother used to call it, "setting up the soap and soup thing." What she meant was that some women had houses that were abundantly aromatic, with the smell of cleanliness and food. These smells can make a man feel as though he is in a kitchen with the perfect mother: secure, loved, and comfortable. These are the smells that can spell *mama* and encourage dependency.

Although we all need some of this comfort in our lives, if you overplay this part, your partner may just sink into the environment you create and allow you to take care of him. He may get angry because of the respect issue. Too much of this, and you could end up with a man who acts like a rebellious teenager. If he feels he's not doing his adult share, yes, he may feel guilty, but he doesn't like the feeling, and he doesn't like what you've done to promote the feeling inside him. Besides, guilt rarely makes a man change.

## When Mama Gets Fed Up

"If I wanted another baby around here, I'd go out and have one."

—AN OVERWORKED SISTER

What woman hasn't felt like saying something like this. Mothers are human, too. They get angry, hurt, disgusted, defensive, and needy. They even get spiteful. When a maternal woman is fed up, the "soap and soup thing" typically becomes the "fire and brimstone thing." Then, in a man's head, she becomes the bad mama straight from hell. If you don't want to be seen as a "bad mama," here are some behaviors to avoid:

1. *Don't make him feel as though he has to prove himself.* Some sisters talk as though they are giving out marks, and the marks are often failing. Failing grades downgrade a person. If you want positive responses, send positive messages.

2. *Don't demoralize him by pointing out all his shortcomings— even when you have his best interests at heart.* A woman sometimes believes that pointing out what a man does wrong— like a mother does—will bring him up to snuff. What she does is bring him up to resentment—fast.

3. *Don't bad-mouth him, especially to other people.* The minute any woman starts saying critical things about the man she loves, in his head she becomes an out-of-control hurtful mother. If you continue, eventually none of your words—no matter how constructive—will have any effect.

4. *Don't worry more about how he looks than you do about his feelings.* African Americans tend to spend an unnecessary amount of energy thinking about what other people are going to say. When a sister criticizes a man's appearance, it's negative mothering. For example, she may say: "You think you're going to just walk out there like that, with your pants around your shoes. You're just a sorry excuse for a man." The sister thinks she is protecting the man and herself from the judgments of the outside world. The man feels diminished and self-conscious.

5. *Don't "signify" when you want to communicate.* In our communities, the word *signifying* has come to have special meaning. A "signifying sister" is always spelling out a worst-case scenario that befell somebody else. She uses this technique as an indirect way of warning a man that he shouldn't behave a certain way. The implied threat is that if he does, "fate is going to catch up with his behind." This is something mothers do with children. For example, when a mother says to her 14-year-old son, "Did you hear what happened to Johnny up on the next block when he started to mess around with those boys who are taking cars?" what she is telling him is that if he gets involved with something so stupid, he might meet the same terrible fate. When a woman signifies, a brother typically regards it as an attempt to get involved in his business. Signifying tends to magnify the problem.

6. *Don't take up his slack.* Compensating for what a man doesn't do right removes all his challenges and places him at your mercy. This is a self-esteem destroyer. Here's a rule: Taking up a man's slack will make him slack.

# When He Fell in Love with You, He Was Thinking of Romance, Not Strained Baby Food

Believe me, no man starts out with a woman feeling like he wants pablum and pacifiers. This kind of dependent connection evolves over time, but while it's evolving, the relationship is suffering because there is less and less romantic sharing between two equals. Dependence produces the wrong kind of intimacy, and it takes the life and the romance out of the relationship. If you're a woman with excellent maternal skills, you should feel proud of this ability, but don't use them on a man. Use them on any children you may have. Another person to use maternal skills on is yourself. Raise yourself up to be the person you want to be. Dress yourself up to look the way you want. Treat yourself as though you're the brightest, most beautiful child in the whole world. Cherish the child, but love the woman in you.

As far as your romantic life is concerned, work on developing different skills. Learn how to approach your relationship like an equal partnership with lots of communication and love. Sure, it's fun to take care of the one you love every now and then. But make sure he's taking care of you, too. This shared caring is sexy and satisfying, and that's what you want in your life. Believe me, *the best kind of loving* takes place on a two-way street.

# Looking for a Daddy Figure

There are sisters who wouldn't dream of mothering a man. These women are too busy turning their romantic partners into father figures. Every little girl grows up wanting a loving daddy. To a female child, a loving daddy means she has someone who is big and strong and will take care of her and protect her from the cruelties of the world. Some sisters were fortunate enough to grow up with this kind of male parental figure. Others weren't so lucky, and they spend their entire lives looking for men who will make them feel safe in the way a good daddy makes a child feel safe. Some of these women have so internalized their need for protective fathers that the only way they know how to relate to men is as a little girl would to a strong father figure.

There is another reason why sisters sometimes encourage their romantic partners to behave in a more parental fashion: Historically, Black women have been accused of usurping authority from men. As a response to this accusation, sisters may want to create a place where the men they love will feel more in control. As much as possible, these women will submit to a man's opinion.

There are at least two major reasons why you don't want to set up a relationship in which you play the child and he plays the parent. First, although he may think it's cute at the beginning of a relationship, the typical man grows tired of a grown woman's little-girl games. He can end up losing respect for any woman who plays too hard at being a child. Second, he may believe the setup and become accustomed to talking and behaving in a controlling fashion. It may seem attractive and masculine at the beginning of a relationship, but over the long haul, it's no fun living with a controlling man.

If you don't want to be treated like a child, here are some behaviors to avoid:

1. *Don't ask him for permission before you go anywhere or do anything.* "Do you mind if I go to the store?" "Is it OK if I go to the movies with the girls?" Sisters who talk this way are encouraging inequality in their relationships.

2. *Don't expect him to assume responsibility for your debts.* If you run up your bills and credit cards and expect a man to pick up after your financial chaos, chances are that you're going to end up with one very resentful and angry man. Financial irresponsibility isn't attractive.

3. *Don't play coy and cute games.* Some sisters discovered early in life that boys find girlish behavior appealing. Unfortunately, in the long run, this behavior loses its charm and gets boring.

4. *Don't talk about him as though he's the warden.* We've all heard women say things like "My husband's going to kill me when he finds out about. . . ." "Robert is going to be full of questions when I get home. . . ." or "I'm on my best behavior 'cause I want a new bedroom set." If you don't want a man to turn into a control freak, don't act like he's your judge and jailer.

5. *Don't expect him to fix all your messes.* Whether it's something you said that got you into hot water or something you did that got your car stuck in the driveway, don't automatically expect a man to bail you out and make everything all right. Learn to do your own trouble shooting.

6. *Don't talk to him in a different way than you talk to everyone else.* Did you ever notice how some women seem intelligent and independent until they get around men and then turn into helpless-sounding, permission-asking strangers. When a woman behaves this way, I call her a "Boo-Hoo gal." "Boo-hoo, I can't do this. . . . Boo-hoo, I can't do that." If you fall into this routine, even a little bit, start practicing sounding more like your usual self whenever "he" is around. It's hard to break this pattern, but eventually, you'll both be happier with the real you, and you won't be seen as a childish woman.

## *Encouraging Him to Be Your Daddy Isn't Good for His Health*

Here is another issue to think about: Some brothers are so sensitive to the stereotypical views of irresponsibility in our communities that they have compensated by assuming too much responsibility for their own good. This kind of man feels as though he carries the weight and burden of the Black community on his shoulders. He builds his life in a way that he will always respect himself and he will always receive the respect he is due. Because he is so responsible, he is willing to assume superhuman responsibility for the people around him. Superhuman demands breed frustration and can lead to him taking it out on others.

If you're with a man who is quick to assume responsibility, it's easy to take advantage of his strength and turn him into the parental figure for everyone in the household, including you. The fact is, however, that it's not fair to him because it's not good for his well-being or his health. Let's not forget the statistics about hypertension, heart disease, and other stress-related ailments among Black men.

## Don't Act Like He's the Answer Man and You're the Lady in Waiting

Too often a sister is waiting for "Mr. Right Brother" to come along to answer her prayers and make everything perfect. Many women have been fed a lot of unrealistic information about finding one man who will be able to provide the connection that will make them feel whole and complete. When they finally do meet a man, they bring all these feelings and beliefs with them. In other words, they expect him to be able to make them feel good about life in general. They think he must have all the answers to all the questions they've been asking about life. In short, they act like he's the Answer Man.

The truth is that when you connect to men in this way, you are looking for confirmation of yourself and your role in the world. My great-grandmother used to say, "Some women don't just need assurance, they need blessed assurance, and only the Savior can give them that." She was a smart woman who knew that if you expect a man to save you or fulfill all your major needs, you are going to end up with a lot of disappointment.

We've all seen women behave in the following way. In fact, you may have even done so yourself: Sister Lady in Waiting is going along putting her life in order. She may have a good place to live, a nice car, good friends, and a number of interests. She's taking care of her children, her life, and her job. She's got a lot of responsibilities, but she's doing just fine. Then some man spins into her life and tries to recreate the whole thing to suit him and his tastes. Because he acts like he likes her, she figures he's the Answer Man she's been waiting for. So she not only lets him into her life, she lets him *take over* her life. And he makes a mess. More often than not, he then spins out of her life, just like he spun in.

In the meantime, she's so caught up by all that has happened that she's convinced he's taken her life with him. It was all there when he got there, but she doesn't see it. Some men practice this routine as a matter of style with every woman they meet. But the only women whom they can hurt are women who were sitting there waiting for the Answer Man.

Here's a major problem: While a woman is waiting for the Lord himself to come down and take her hand, she may not notice a good, decent mortal man who may be a good partner here on Earth. Also, as in anything, there are a lot of false gods out there who are prepared to act, for a brief time, as though they are Answer Men. They promise you the world and don't follow through. These men can cause you pain because they encourage you to believe in unrealistic fantasies. Every sister needs to know for herself that there are no Answer Men here on Earth. However, it doesn't mean that she can't find good men in her own neighborhood.

# Don't Cast Him as the Buffoon and Yourself as the "Straight Sister"

This past weekend, Kelli noticed a leak coming out of the faucet and she wanted to call the plumber. Her husband, Roy, said no; he would fix it himself. Well, he dragged all his tools up from the basement and he started in hitting and twisting. It took over an hour, and when he was finished, the drip was gone. In its place was a fountain of running water and a completely messed-up kitchen. By the time Roy literally threw in the towel and called the plumber, his mistakes were obvious to everyone.

Roy is a real man, and, you see, real-life men are far from perfect. They do foolish things and they say foolish things. They don't always have perfect bodies or perfect bank accounts either. But just because a brother isn't behaving like the Answer Man or the leading man on your favorite soap opera doesn't mean that you have the right to treat him as though he is a buffoon or a stereotype like a character on the old radio show *Amos & Andy*. The truth is, if you're always competing with a man to prove that you have better sense than he does, your life will be filled with nonsense. The thing to remember is that you're not his straight man, or straight sister, whose job in life is to point out the foolishness of her man to anybody who is willing to listen.

- Don't make fun of the way he talks, walks, chews, dresses, sings, or snores.
- Don't make fun of the way he spends his money, saves his money, or makes his money.
- Don't make fun of his mistakes, his interests, his pet projects, his human weaknesses, or his sports ability.

Here's your rule: If you want people to think your partner is attractive, smart, interesting, and desirable, treat him that way. Remember, what you say about him says a lot about you.

# Overdoing the Handmaiden Part

Did you ever know a woman who goes around with an "excuse me for living" attitude toward her partner? Keila is that kind of woman. She treats her live-in boyfriend like he's some kind of Oriental potentate sitting on a big throne. Only in this case, the throne is the couch in front of the television set in the living room. He says, "How about a beer," and she gets a beer. He asks, "What's happening about dinner?" and she rushes to make dinner. He wants to talk about his interests or his work, so she drops her own and sits at his feet. He says, "Come here, honey," and she feels loved and cared for.

The truth in this situation: Keila believes she gets more attention from Shawn when she's acting like his handmaiden than she does at any other time. When he's sitting around being waited on, it feels to Keila as if he is acknowledging the deep bond between the two of them, and it feels right and close.

Whenever she gets totally fed up with Shawn's behavior, Keila starts in nagging him. Shawn is usually sitting on the couch, minding his own business, reading the newspaper or watching the news on television, when suddenly Keila snaps. It all becomes too much—the amount of work she does for the family, the amount of work she does for him, the amount of work she does with no appreciation and no support. Then Keila typically starts by pointing out something small like the fact that Shawn hasn't bothered to pick up his jockey shorts off the bedroom floor. If he doesn't say or do anything to make it better, all her grievances starts coming out. When one is not emotionally nourished, negative memories always surface.

Keila remembers the way Shawn wasn't nice to her mother at her cousin's wedding, she remembers how he never bought her the birthday present he promised, she remembers how he didn't even bother to get home on time for their child's birthday, and she remembers all the times she's picked up his socks and underwear or his damn silver cigarette lighter that some other woman gave him years ago and that he just leaves around to make her jealous.

That's when Keila starts screaming and calling Shawn names. She tells him that she would be better off without him, that he never gave her anything that mattered or counted, and that life has been harder for her ever since she met him. Once Keila got so angry that she took all Shawn's underwear and threw it out their apartment window, all the while telling him that he was a no-good bum who didn't deserve to walk the face of this Earth. In these scenes, Keila usually keeps screaming until Shawn gets fed up. Then one of two things happens: Either Shawn starts yelling back, and Keila gets scared that he's really going to get mad at her or Shawn storms out of the house, and then Keila gets scared that he won't come back. Either way, it seems as though Keila is always the one who ends up apologizing, and Shawn ends up accepting her apology, sometimes saying something about how it must be near her 'time of the month.' Keila vows that she'll be better in the future; she makes an extra-special meal and sometimes she even buys him a present, something small like some new socks or underwear to replace the ones that ended up on the street or in the incinerator.

## Giving Up Your Handmaiden Ways

When you see a handmaiden at work, it's easy to recognize the major-league inequality that is taking place. All the time she's puffing up the man's ego, she feels more and more like a dishrag. The best way to avoid this role is never to take the part because once you've convinced a man he's the king, he doesn't want to go back to being a regular person. He's no fool, why should he? It's a lot of work to make that transition back to a more balanced relationship, but here are some ways to start the process:

1. *Don't put him up on a pedestal because you think he's going to share the space.* A woman sometimes erroneously believes that a man will so appreciate being treated like a king that he will automatically make her his queen. It doesn't work that way. If you want to be treated like a queen, act like a queen.

2. *Don't give him more than he needs.* A woman can turn a man into a king in hundreds of small ways. For example, don't talk to him differently from the way you talk to everyone else; don't rush to get things he wants; don't run all his

errands; don't make his desires your first priority; don't pick up after him; and don't be at his beck and call.

3. *Don't turn into his harem woman at the drop of a hat.* Often a handmaiden will pride herself on being sexy even while she is washing the floor and picking up a man's clothes. All the man has to do is indicate a little sexual interest, and she's prepared to do the Dance of the Seven Veils. Make him work just a little bit more to get your sexual attention.

4. *Don't give up your life to further his.* Handmaidens often put their own work and interests on a back burner, so they can focus on their partners. This is a big mistake.

5. *Modify your cheerleader approach to what he says and does.* It's great to be supportive, but don't jump on the bandwagon for everything he says and does. He's not the whole team; he's just one player.

6. *Don't be so nervous in the service.* Handmaidens often are worried that once they stop being perfect support systems, the men are going to take off. Relationships don't work that way. This is the old he says, "Jump," you say, "How high?" response.

7. *Don't encourage "macho" behavior.* What seems masculine and cute is sometimes just infantile. For example, men grow up and go from "Mama, I want my binky," to "Woman, get me my dinner." Don't act like you appreciate this kind of behavior because it makes you feel that you have a special place in the man's heart and mind.

## Keeping Notes—The Mark of a Handmaiden

Handmaidens usually have this very clear picture of how they want to be treated, but their ideas are often fantasies.

They want adoration—that's why they give it. If you have a tendency to fall into handmaiden roles—and what woman doesn't—what you've got to do is stop trying to fulfill all his needs. Then stop being resentful whenever you get frustrated because he's not giving you everything you need every time you need it.

The typical handmaiden has a tendency to keep mental notes on everything that occurs. Then when her resentment gets to be too much to handle, she pulls out the "record" and starts enumerating all the ways this man has failed her. In the meantime, her partner, the "king," can't understand why his subject is staging a revolution. He just wants to get back behind his castle walls. Instead of staging periodic revolts, the handmaiden has to bring the relationship back to an equal partnership.

Here's a simple rule: Don't reward any behavior you don't want repeated. Calmly, without making scenes, *you* have to find different ways of behaving. If he says, "I'm hungry," instead of rushing off to make something, you say, "I'm hungry, too, what can we eat?" or "Sugar babe, I'm a little bit tired, can you help me?" Give him simple tasks, such as tearing the lettuce for the salad. If he wants to watch television instead of helping you cook, say, "That's a good idea, we can both watch this show before we prepare dinner."

Learn a series of simple phrases like "While you're down there, could you put the clothes in the dryer?" "Can you please stop at the store on the way home?" and "Would you please finish vacuuming upstairs, while I clean the kitchen?" Tell him how much you love him for being nonsexist and having a cooperative contemporary attitude. Tell him how wonderful it is that he is able to get beyond the old-fashioned attitudes he inherited from men of an earlier generation.

A rule to keep in mind: Don't take sole possession of every chore in the house, as well as every room. The laundry is shared laundry—his and yours. It's a shared kitchen with shared responsibilities. It's shared food and shared garbage. Most important, if you have children, don't ask him to "baby-sit" his own children like he's doing something special or out of the ordinary. He's taking care of the children just like you do. Don't sell men short. Fathers can be good caregivers, too. Here's your signpost: Take the *we* road, not the *me* trail. *Ujima* is another of the Seven Principles of Blackness of the Nguzo Saba. *Ujima*, which means collective work and responsibility, is essential to our survival.

Here is an interesting historical note about Black families in America that you need to keep in mind: Traditionally, Black men were very involved in child care and household tasks because Black women have always worked. It's only within the past few decades that Black men have followed rigid roles that don't adapt to realistic lifestyles. They have apparently been influenced as much as white men by macho and Archie Bunker–type male behavior.

A final thought: *Being a woman means playing many different parts—mother, sister, lover, wife, friend. When you overdo any one of these parts, you never get what you need to satisfy the whole you.*

**8**

# Mate Selection: Mama Told Me to Pick You Out

> "What's the sense of my trying to meet a man? There's nobody out there for me."
>
> —JOYCE, 29

I strongly disagree with Joyce because I firmly believe there are many men out there for her to meet and love. However, I think she's got to start looking at the right men and stop paying attention to the wrong ones. I used to have a late-night radio talk show, and I was consistently amazed that even more men than women called in to talk about their romantic disappointments. These intelligent-sounding brothers kept telling me that they were having trouble meeting women.

Here's a fact: It may be true that there are not enough doctors, lawyers, MBAs, and professional sports figures to satisfy every unmarried sister, but there are plenty of good, kind, sincere, decent, loving men. The problem, let's face it, is that many of you don't want ordinary do-the-right-thing guys. At face value, these guys don't look exceptional enough. I call these men you're not appreciating "the overlooked brothers." You are overlooking these men in the same way that the basketball players or stockbrokers of your dreams are overlooking you.

You know how good and valuable you are even if you don't have handsome actors or rich doctors beating a path to your door. Well, trust me, many of these overlooked brothers are every bit as worthy of love and commitment as you are. Unfortunately, many of these brothers don't yet have the kind of bank account that you may be dreaming about; in fact, not noticing them may have much more to do with their material worth than their inner worth.

There's something I think the single Black woman has to realize: If she insists on judging Black men by their paychecks while she waits for her Mr. Right, she may always come up short or empty-handed. In a study published in *Essence* a few years ago, 37 percent of the respondents said they would have a relationship with someone of a different race, but only 32 percent said they would have a relationship with someone who makes less money than they do. Any sister with this attitude is going to have a real problem. The poor economic base in the African American community doesn't naturally support the traditional American family system typified by the husband providing the bulk of the income. This is a reality we have to deal with, and dreaming about rich men isn't going to change the situation.

Historically the African American community supported marriages in which the wife either earned more money or had a higher outside-world job status. Growing up, many of us witnessed marriages of the Pullman porter–schoolteacher variety. In the world, the wife had more job status, but at home everyone knew that her job status was just window dressing and that both partners were equals who were contributing to the best of their ability, given the social and economic realities. Only recently have we begun to put down men who, through no fault of their own, haven't yet been able to turn into heavy earners. Think about our African-based values and our history as an ethnic group. The Black family has a tradition of egalitarian attitudes. Women have worked; men have cooked and taken care of children. Everyone had to pitch in to survive. If we are going to continue to survive, we must remember these lessons and get rid of husband-searching methods based on media values rather than inner African-based values that worked for us before.

The primary reason why you're not noticing the overlooked brothers has everything to do with you and little to do with them. You see, as women, we are still conditioned to believe that men create "the life" and women follow along. Men set the pace, and women keep up. Men make the rules, and women adjust. Men make the money, and women spend it. This is the way things were in movies and television sitcoms made by white producers since the 1950s. It has nothing to do with the way things really are.

When you're looking for your Black Knight in Shining Armor, the man you can follow to the ends of the Earth, what you are really trying to find is someone who will both protect you and give you a life. This is the wrong plan. If you're going to find a romantic partner who is capable of the best kind of loving, you need new goals, a better plan, and a wise marketing strategy. You need a plan that revolves around one person finding her own life and her own self-protection, and that person is you. How you market yourself determines what kind of man you will attract. For example, "too needy" may attract an abuser; "too helpless" may attract a bossy, big daddy; and "too desperate" may attract a temporary brother who'll give you sex but withhold intimacy. Always remember, the best kind of marketing, like the best kind of loving, begins and ends with high self-esteem.

186 THE BEST KIND OF LOVING

# Developing the Right Kind of Attitude

Searching for a romantic partner is serious business. We are talking about your life and possibly a lifetime. This search takes time and thought, and you shouldn't rush into anything. You need to make good decisions and good choices. Here's an easy plan to keep you on track.

## • Find Yourself Before You Look for a Man

When I was a romantic teenager, I remember my mama telling me, "You didn't come onto this Earth with a man, and you're not going to die with a man." She was telling me to get my essential self in order before I worried about anything else. Women have been fed a bill of goods that tells them once they find a man to love, they will be "fulfilled." That's a lot of you know what!

The idea that you can find your one person, your own Black Knight in Shining Armor, is pure fantasy. Among other things, you place a tremendous burden on a man if you expect him to fulfill all your expectations. Remember the old expression, "Don't put all your eggs in one basket"? It's true when it comes to romance. Don't get me wrong, I'm not telling you to become a street runner going from man to man. Quite the opposite: I'm telling you to think about all the different parts of you that need nurturing and love. There's the part that wants to relax and go to movies; you can find friends to do that with even if you don't have a man in your life. There's the part of you that wants intellectual stimulation; you can easily have that even if you don't have a man in your life because you can always go back to school.

See if you can figure out a way to identify your needs and separate all the nonromantic parts of yourself that need support. Then find ways to give yourself what you need in nonromantic areas, so you'll be able to look at a man more realistically. Once you reach the place where you don't expect a man to be carrying your books or your whole world with him, then no matter whether he's there or whether he leaves, you'll pretty much still be in one piece.

### • Widen Your Options and Start Noticing Men You May Not Have Noticed Before

Don't sit around waiting for the right man to come along and sweep you off your feet. Sometimes the men who are doing all this sweeping are experienced womanizers who know exactly what to say and do to get your attention. These brothers have all the flash and dash, and they are easy to notice.

I'm asking you to start paying attention to the quieter, less obvious, brother. He might be working in a store; he might be sitting next to you at the library; he might be repairing cars at the local garage; he might be worshiping at a nearby church, mosque, or even a Black synagogue; he might be working in civil service or a nearby hospital; or he might own a small business in your neighborhood. Whatever he's doing, the chances are that he doesn't immediately know what to say to make you feel special. In other words, he doesn't have a well-practiced line.

When I say this, sometimes sisters get on my case because they think I'm telling them to lower their standards. I want to make it clear that this isn't about lowering your standards, it's about widening your options. Sometimes a sister will turn down a man because she thinks he's nothing special and then some other sister will see his worth. A few months later, this brother is shining like a new apple, and the original woman will discover that she's highly attracted to him. Here's something to think about: Any man starts looking more desirable when another woman desires him. My mama used to say, "One woman put lead in his pencil, and now another sister wants to write the story."

### • Don't Be a Last-Chance Woman

I can't tell you how many times a sister has told me that she has gotten involved with a man, even when she had serious reservations, because she thought he might be her last chance. Please, please, pretty please give up this kind of thinking. Don't let a man talk you into sex, a relationship, or marriage because you believe you have limited options based on your age, education, loneliness, ticking biological clock, or a mixed-up sense of feeling unattractive.

Take your chances and don't pity your circumstances. Taking your chances makes you a free agent; feeling self-pity turns you into a victim. If you feel as though you are the last person you know who is still single, remind yourself that last does not mean least. In fact, it often means saving the best for last.

Start every day saying to yourself, "Here I go again, taking a chance on love." But after you say it, recognize that love begins inside yourself, which means that you will always be your best bet. Don't let others set up your "last chance" timetable. If you operate from the love inside you, you'll always make good choices.

### • Stop Trying to Fall in Love

I hate the whole idea of a sister "falling in love." When I say this, women usually look at me funny. They think I don't understand how thrilling it is to feel the emotions of romance. I understand all too well about the emotions you want to feel, but I want you to give the term *falling in love* some more thought. This is really bad terminology. It implies that the person who falls in love is not thinking and not noticing where she is going. She's just stumbling and bumbling about and then she free-falls. When you free-fall, you can't think. Go into love with an open parachute and full survival gear and stay in control, so you can make flight corrections if necessary. In control and in love sounds like a good flight plan.

## • Keep Your Eyes Open

I want you to approach love very, very slowly with an emotional magnifying glass in your hand. Notice everything about the man. Don't comment on it, don't discuss it with your friends, don't have long conversations with your relatives. Just notice, so you can be in charge of your own life. Women think that if they try to stay clearheaded and careful, they are being disloyal to the magnificence of their love. Sometimes they don't want to expose their newfound love to the glare of daylight because they are afraid that if they examine it too carefully, it won't be there anymore. Well that's exactly why you should look at a new romance carefully in a lot of light in a lot of different settings and situations. You want to know that your feelings for this person can survive the *real* world.

## • Don't Have Sex Until the Relationship Has a Solid Base

My golden rule for good relationships is friendship first, lovers second, and honesty always. I think men and women should walk into sex slowly from a strong base of friendship. There are so many good reasons why I believe this. Here are some of them.

1. You want to know that you are operating in a "zone of personal safety." Personal safety is a large category. For example, you want to know *for sure* that this is not a potentially dangerous man in your bed. You want to know *for sure* that you are not placing yourself at risk for any sexually transmitted diseases or unplanned pregnancies. You want to know *for sure* that you're not foolishly risking your heart. To be *sure* of all these things takes time.

2. Men genuinely like a challenge. I have found in my experience that men have been conditioned to place more value on the sexual connection if they have to work to get it.

I've talked to many brothers who have complained about women trying to get them into bed. They say this kind of situation is too easy. One thing I've learned that men will never tell women: They are intrigued by a challenge. This is true no matter how much he may be telling you he must have you now. If he can't wait until the relationship develops, then he would have moved on anyhow. So once again, don't worry about losing your "last chance."

3. "When you're on your back, you lose your head." This is something my mama used to tell me when she was giving me reasons why women shouldn't rush into sex. What she was saying, and I think it's true, is that once a woman has made the sexual connection, she tends to feel bonded, she loses her focus of self-interest, and she can't think straight. These feelings interfere with good decision making. The rule is, make all your decisions about a man when you are still on your feet—and fully clothed.

## • Put Dating in Perspective

Such a big deal is made about a good date or a bad date. Dating, as it's currently practiced, is a concrete example of how Eurocentric values and thinking have confused our personal lives. Somehow Black men and women have come to believe that a good date is an expensive date. Thus, only men who have money or who are prepared to get into debt ask women out regularly. Consequently, sisters suffer from a lack of masculine attention. Forget about all the nonsense we see on television shows like *The Dating Game*. Encourage men to spend time with you in ways that don't cost money. Walk through the park or go to a Black art exhibit, street fairs, or free concerts in the park. Pack a picnic, visit friends or double-date with another couple, and arrange an inexpensive barbecue. Go for a hike in the woods or swimming at a public beach.

## • Get Rid of Financial Stereotypes About Who Pays

Don't be economically wrong-headed when it doesn't apply to your lifestyle. This issue of the man always being the one to cover the bill hasn't worked in the white community, so how can you use it as the measuring stick for a Black man who typically has even less money to spend on a date. Less money doesn't mean less man!

Don't be afraid to offer to split the cost of dinner or a date. Men appreciate it, and that way you can both pick a restaurant according to your budget. Working these kinds of financial details out during the early days of courtship is a good way to work out a relationship, and it will help eliminate the false embarrassment of talking about money.

## • Work at Making Male Friends

No, this is not a clever way to find romance. This is a sensible way to have a better life. Male friends are good for talking and socializing. If you have male friends, you will feel less lonely and less needy. Being with men who are "just friends" will increase your confidence and your sense of self-esteem. You will also gain more understanding of how men think and behave. Keep in mind that male attention need not be romantic to be fulfilling. Male friendship teaches us the value of intimacy without sex.

## • Use Your Own Judgment and Don't Be Embarrassed by What Your Friends or Family Say About the Men You Meet

"He dresses like a country boy." "He may talk sweet, but he'll break your heart for sure." "He's just looking for one thing." Many sisters are surrounded by people who always seem to have something negative to say about any man. If someone has some real information to share, obviously you should check out the facts. But if it's just idle judgments that are being passed, don't pay too much attention. Worrying about what others say or think about a man you could like isn't going to help you find the love you want. Take the time to draw your own conclusions about the men you meet and use those conclusions as your instruction. Experience is still your best teacher.

## • Change the Way You Rate Men When You Meet Them

First meetings lay the groundwork for everything that follows. Women typically notice good-looking men, men who wow them with a smooth line, and men who seem to have money or power. Here's a better way of rating brothers:

1. Notice how he thinks before you judge how he looks. We complain about men who chase after "obvious" women in tight clothes, yet we do exactly the same thing. We're programmed to notice the obviously good-looking men first. As part of your own romantic reeducation campaign, start paying more attention to what a man thinks about than how he looks. Before you focus on how sexy or handsome he is, find out what he thinks about life and love. Get his views on politics, religion, people, and the environment. Learn what he thinks about equality and sharing domestic responsibility.

Discover those areas in which you and he think alike. Find out where you have major differences of opinion. Too many women have married handsome men and learned the hard way. There's an old saying, "Pretty is as pretty does, and if pretty doesn't do right, pretty soon, pretty gets ugly."

2. Notice what he talks about before you pass judgment on what he wears. Trust me on this one. A few years into a relationship, when you and this brother are sitting around the table preparing to eat dinner and watch television, you're not going to care what he's wearing. What you're going to be

noticing is what he's talking about and whether or not he goes on and on about things that don't interest you.

Here are a few things to think about: Does he talk only about himself and his interests, or does he let you talk about your life? Does he seem interested in what you have to say? Does he contribute enthusiastically to a conversation? Is he fun? Does he have a sense of humor? Is he sensitive to issues that concern you? When you're thinking about a long-term relationship, these characteristics are more important than the label he's sporting on his new threads.

3. Notice the man, not what he's got in his hand. I don't mean to keep repeating this idea, but it's important. Pay more attention to a man's ability to love, commit, and share than you do to his car, his apartment, or his bank account.

# Avoiding Relationships That Hurt

"I feel like I've wasted the last fifteen years of my life in bad relationships."

—JALEELAH

At 40, Jaleelah doesn't want to spend any more time in destructive, dysfunctional relationships. Like many of you, she's tired of being in pain because of one man or the other. She's learned the hard way that bad relationships hurt, and she wants change.

I'm convinced that many sisters waste so much time focusing on difficult men that they never have the time or energy to find someone else. If you're always trying to work out a difficult relationship, you may be passing up a good one.

Always keep in mind: *The easiest way to bring about change in your romantic life is to avoid relationships that present compounded problems.* If you are already involved with one of these men, then you have to change your behavior with them—which is more difficult, but it can be done.

Here are some of the common behaviors that typically warn you that a relationship can cause you pain.

## Men Who Talk Holes in Your Clothes

"When I'm talking to a woman telling her what I'm going to be doing for her, I really mean it. It makes me feel good to talk right even when I know the minute I walk out that door, I'm not going to do right. But sure I believe that 'b.s.' in my heart while I'm saying it. That's why I can get the women I get."

—A 28-YEAR-OLD BROTHER

The world is full of men who will try to talk holes in your clothes. It's something males start preparing for in adolescence, when they first start applauding themselves and others on their ability to talk women into bed. It's a mistake to think that brothers like this are easy to spot because they are not. They don't necessarily sound arrogant or interested only in sex. In fact, many of these men are skillful at seduction because they have a practiced technique that solicits understanding and sympathy. They seem more sensitive than sexual.

A man like this may share his life story and ask a woman about her own life. He sounds sincere because for the moment he believes what he is saying. No matter how many women he has hurt, he thinks he has "feelings" for them. He may have feelings, but he doesn't have any follow-through. Men who talk holes in women's clothes have also been known to lie by saying "I love you" too soon in the relationship or by saying they have so much "control" that nobody needs to worry about birth control. The worst men in this category are probably those who assure women that they have a clean sexual bill of health when they do not.

I'm not saying that every man who is trying to talk you into bed is a no-good bum who is going to disappear the next day. All I'm saying is that you can't always separate the good from the bad by what men say. Your only protection is to let the relationship develop slowly and to find out as much as possible about the man over a period of time. Men who talk holes in your clothes are what I call "moment men." They are good only for the moment because the moment they see things are getting serious, they start backing off.

## Cultural Conflicts

Men and women meet, sparks fly, and reason goes out the window, at least temporarily. Then when the sparks cool down a bit, they look at each other and wonder: *How can I change this person so he or she will become more like me?* Some of the major disagreements in Black relationships seem to come from what can be termed cultural differences. Even if two people grew up in the same neighborhood, attended the same schools, and know the same people, they can have vastly different views on religion, politics, and ethnic values.

If you want to avoid relationships with conflicts in these areas, there are ways of determining whether a man may be locked into a point of view that will present serious cultural differences. Here are some clues:

1. Do you sense there are big differences in your attitudes and consequently find yourself avoiding conversations about potential topics of disagreement, such as religion or ethnicity?
2. Do you feel there is no room for you to have a different opinion than he does?
3. When you are talking, do all his beliefs and attitudes dominate the conversation?
4. Do you *value* different people and things? For example, does he think all your friends are "phonies"? Do you think all his friends are "lowlifes"? How strongly held are these values, and what do they reflect about each of you?
5. Do either of you have strong opinions about values that may seem superficial to others but are important to you? For example, do you have vehement and conflicting views about fashion, style, decorating, and where to live?

As you consider these issues, I think it's important to realize that no two people have the same views on everything and that compromise is always necessary. However, if you don't believe a willingness to compromise is in the cards, you need to think carefully before getting deeply involved. If you are already in a relationship and you want to try to work out your differences, you need to find new ways of talking to each other. Here are some examples:

To some women, Edward, a successful stockbroker, might appear to be a sister's dream walking. He owns a condo, he drives a BMW, and he skis in Aspen, but as far as Vanessa is concerned, he presents all kinds of problems. She calls him a Buppie and says that he may have African art on his walls, but his soul is stuck on Wall Street. She sees cultural differences as being the big problem in their relationship, and she worries that he will ultimately drop her for a woman who seems to be more of a trophy mate.

Marquita has a completely different kind of problem. Within the past few years, her fiancé has become a Muslim, which she feels is creating stress in their relationship. She doesn't want to go along with some of the practices and thinks his new emphasis on religion is too strict and time consuming. He has become so serious that she worries that he'll lose the flexibility and capacity to have fun.

Arnette's new boyfriend tells her that she is the first Black woman he has dated in a long time. He says he usually prefers white women because they are "less of a hassle." According to him, the white women he has known have been more "understanding." Although they have only been going out a short time, he has already informed Arnette that she is more "demanding" than most of the white women he has known.

All these couples have to learn to make joint decisions without calling in a United Nations negotiating team. Here are some suggestions to help them, and you, get started.

1. Realize that compromise requires two people.
2. Acknowledge that you can't change anyone's behavior but your own.
3. Write down the specific areas that you and your partner disagree on. Then make a sublist of the ways in which you still agree in those same areas. For example, if your disagreements revolve around child care, be specific about the ways in which you agree. Then work from these areas to try to find ways of compromising. Always start with the positive.
4. Don't make judgments or put your partner down for his views and values. We need to practice the tolerance we preach with one another.
5. Try to have calm discussions about your differences, not shouting matches, and make your partner aware of your willingness to reach a compromise.

Vanessa, for example, should discuss her need to maintain strong Afrocentric values in a nonjudgmental open-minded fashion. She needs to discover whether Edward is so self-promoted and self-involved that he can't appreciate any woman for who she is. Maybe after some conversation, she will learn that he is capable of relaxing and appreciating her point of view.

If Edward cares for Vanessa, respects her point of view, and isn't trying to change her, articulating her point of view might also make her feel more relaxed. She might even be able to make a difference in Edward's life by including him in activities to bring him more in touch with the values she wants to maintain. If he's not trying to restrict her or change what she believes, there is no reason why Vanessa and Edward can't share a life.

Vanessa also needs to think about some of the reasons why Edward may appear Eurocentric in his behavior. Only Edward knows the kind of tightrope he has to walk to further his career. As a Black man in a predominantly white field, Edward probably realizes the different levels of acceptance, fear, or prejudice that he may engender in his work environment. When Vanessa and Edward learn to speak honestly, they may both learn to change and grow together.

Marquita has to introduce the concept of the oneness of God into her discussions with her fiancé as a way of ending their fights about religion. If the relationship is to survive, they *both* have to learn to tolerate and accept each other's religious beliefs. It doesn't make sense to have long oppressive conversations about religion (or any other topic) if the conversations don't go anywhere. Both Vanessa and Edward have to respect each other's beliefs, as well as the rules and restrictions, dietary and otherwise, that go along with those beliefs. Practice saying: "I may not believe everything you believe, but I respect you as a person, and I respect your beliefs." Repeat this sentence to your partner and ask him to repeat it to you. Agreeing to disagree is a time-honored method of handling differences of opinion.

Arnette has to understand her situation. Any sister who finds herself caring about a man who talks about white women (or any other women) being "more" or "better" needs to be clear about what she's involved with. Men who talk this way are showing a disdain for *all* women. This kind of man is low-rating women and setting them up to compete against one another because such statements immediately put a woman on the defensive and feed his need to feel special.

Typically, this kind of man derives satisfaction from watching you try to prove yourself. The rule is, Don't compete and don't try to convince him of anything. Back off and don't defend all Black women because he's being hateful. It is possible that he is just going through a phase, but it's also possible that the phase of trying to get you to prove yourself can last a lifetime, and that's no way to live.

## *The Rolling Stone*

*Where have you gone*
*with your confident walk your*

*crooked smile the*
*rent money*
*in one pocket and*
*my heart*
*in another . . .*

—FROM THE POEM "WHERE HAVE YOU GONE" IN
*I AM A BLACK WOMAN* BY MARI EVANS

One minute you're with him, and you feel like the luckiest woman alive; the next minute he's walking out the door, leaving you with no sense that he will ever return. What can you do to protect yourself from this brother, and how can you make yourself feel better?

Rolling Stones may be charming, but they don't leave happy trails. It's up to you to find out more about his trail *before* you get involved with any man. How has he behaved with all the responsibilities in his life—women, children, work, friends. Yes, sometimes Rolling Stones grow older, sober up, discover religion, and change. But if he does, it's going to be because of something he wants, not something you want, so don't think you are going to be different and get special treatment. No woman gets involved with a Rolling Stone unless she thinks she's some kind of emotional mechanic who is able to repair his psyche. Don't make the mistake of thinking you are going to be able to do "repair work" on a Rolling Stone with any hope of success. Rolling Stones gather no moss or monitors.

If you are already involved with a Rolling Stone, I can't tell you to stop loving him, but I can tell you to start trying to separate emotionally a little at a time. He's not a reasonable person, so for your own good, you have to be doubly reasonable. If you insist on staying in the relationship, accept that you can't expect more from him than he is capable of giving. If you are going to have any peace in your life, you have to learn not to care when or if he shows up on your doorsill, and you have to learn to let him roll away whenever he so desires. I call this "the easy-come, easy-go flow."

Give this man passage; otherwise, he's going to flatten you every time he rolls on by. This isn't easy to do. That's why your best bet is to stay away from these men until they learn for themselves. The rule is this: A sister isn't going to instill terms of endearment in a Rolling Stone. The brother isn't stopping because he doesn't want to stop. The only thing that might make him change his mind is a woman who is moving so fast that he can't keep up with *her*. This is what is known as a woman who is setting her own pace.

## The Uncommitted Brother

Rolling Stones and uncommitted brothers have a lot in common. The main difference is that an uncommitted brother can sometimes appear to be more stable. Clarissa, a 27-year-old design trainee is a case in point. Throughout her relationship with Joe, a 29-year-old salesman, she has been paying too much attention to what he has been saying, and not enough to what he has been doing. Whenever he says anything positive about her or the relationship, she allows his words to build castles in her head. His words create the sound of music she wants to hear. She's so enraptured by what she expects will happen in the future that she is putting up with his day-to-day behavior. The lesson is this: When you're listening to the music, it's hard to watch the action. Music men drown out sincerity.

Clarissa and Joe met in a museum gift shop about a month before the Christmas and Kwanzaa holidays because Joe walked right up to her and asked her what he had to do to meet her. He seemed so sure of himself that Clarissa found it hard to believe that he wasn't already with a woman. However, she agreed to join him for some hot chocolate in the museum cafeteria.

There she discovered that he was feeling lonely and depressed over the holidays. He told Clarissa that he thought she was very beautiful and said he wanted her to meet his friends and his family. He told her that he hated to go to holiday parties alone and would feel so much better if someone like her was with him. Simply put, he made her feel as though she was the woman he had been looking for all his life.

That was a year and a half ago, and despite everything Joe said, he has made no attempt to share his life with Clarissa. In fact, although she hates to admit it, he sometimes makes her feel as though she is stashed away somewhere. What does he share with Clarissa when he's with her? Sex, intensity, feelings, and his secret inner life. He tells Clarissa what he feels and what he wants from life. He always talks about what's going to happen in the future. The problem is that the future never comes. Those castles in her head turned out to be castles in the sky.

In short, it is becoming apparent that Joe can't make a commitment. Clarissa is really torn. On the one hand, she believes that she and Joe were meant to be together. The attraction and the feelings are so strong she feels as though they are sharing a karmic destiny. On the other hand, she can't help but recognize that her relationship with Joe isn't moving forward.

Sometimes a sister believes that if she gets enough crumbs from a man, eventually she'll be able to build herself a whole cake. It doesn't work that way. Everywhere I go I hear stories about men who don't want to settle down and women who are accepting relationships that are making them insecure and anxious. Men with commitment problems and Rolling Stones both give women the sense that they could drift away from relationships without any warning, even when they seem to have deep feelings. In fact, such a man often leaves when he's feeling as much as he possibly can. The relationship has grown so close that he has run out of excuses and has no reason not to commit. But he associates love with a trap, so he walks away to put more space between himself and those feelings he can't control.

By definition, loving someone like this is going to trigger all your old separation anxieties. This sets up a vicious cycle. You respond to the fear of losing him by hanging on tighter. When you hang on tighter, he becomes even more nervous about commitment and moves further away, which makes you anxious, and so on. That's the pull-and-tug game he's playing.

Whenever you pay more attention to what a man is saying than to what he is doing, you run the risk of being set up for a major disappointment. A man can say many intoxicating things to convince you that the two of you have a deep connection. It's easy to trust that kind of talk. The problem is that even if you're not getting what you need from the relationship, you may be getting just enough so that you don't want to lose what you already have. Besides, you typically hope that if you stay with this man long enough, he will be able to fulfill all your dreams.

This is a good reason why you need to hold back emotionally at the beginning of a relationship until you are sure exactly what kind of man you are with. Meet his friends and find out how he has behaved with other women. If he's always going one step forward and two steps back, you'd better start walking backward yourself. Remember that words are easy and that you can't tell what a man is going to do until he's done it. You can be having the most intense, passionate relationship in the world, and a man like this can still want to get away. Some people call this behavior getting cold feet, but for brothers, I call it getting "winged feet" because when they feel this way, they want to "get in the wind."

What a sister like Clarissa needs to realize is that every time a man talks about something that doesn't happen or treats her as though she has no part in his public world, he is making a statement. If she goes along with it, the message she is giving him is that his behavior is OK. She is conveying to him that no matter how he treats her, she will always be there, waiting for him. This is an unhealthy interplay. My mama always said, "This kind of man will take the tail and hit the trail."

If you are in this kind of situation, what you need to do is to start building the kind of life you want for yourself without taking the man or his needs into account. You need to tell yourself that:

1. You deserve better.
2. You are not at fault; no matter how loving or patient

you are, he's not going to change and treat you the way you deserve.

3. You have to start acting as though you deserve better by treating yourself better.

Start separating emotionally and sexually from this man, in stages, if necessary. Find yourself a nonthreatening arena for growth, such a women's group. If you can't find one, start one of your own. Go to self-empowering lectures. Read books and listen to tapes that give you a point of view to help build self-esteem. Find some new friends. Force yourself to go to movies, plays, or concerts. Don't let yourself dream dreams about your future with this man. Be realistic and start trying to meet someone else. Don't issue ultimatums to this man until you no longer feel a need for the relationship. The truth is that these men often respond to ultimatums if they actually believe the relationship is threatened, but they can usually see through you. If you present such a man with an ultimatum that you don't follow through on even once, then he's going to treat it as a rehearsal, and he will be less frightened of the real thing.

## "Property Owners" and Control Freaks

"My wife doesn't do anything unless she checks it out with me."

—A CONTROLLING HUSBAND

The idea of woman as property didn't originate with Black people. It's universal. The really sad part is that women are almost as responsible as men for this situation because they often encourage this kind of thinking. When you're an adolescent and a boy acts like he has a say in what you do, it seems sweet, sexy, caring, and protective of you. It makes you think you've got a place in the world because you *belong* to somebody. Those adolescent boys see how girls respond, and they think, *Hey, kick it, this is the way to go.*

With some men, of course, this kind of thinking can

become extreme. A brother like this will act as though he is in charge of everything you do and everywhere you go—it's a real pain. He may want to check out what you wear and everybody you know; it seems as though he wants to crawl into your head and control your thoughts.

You can't always spot a control freak at the beginning of a relationship. He may sound like the most thoughtful man in the world until after the ceremony. That's one of the reasons why sisters need to take their time and get to know somebody really well. There are also different levels and kinds of control. All some men care about is controlling the thermostat and the bank account, whereas others are more concerned with their cars. It's when a man wants to control you—where you go and what you do—that you have a real problem.

Here are some ways to tell if a man is trying to control you:

- Does he try to sabotage your work because he doesn't want you involved in anything that doesn't concern him?
- Does he put you down, find fault with you, or make fun of what you do, so that he is the only person who can make you feel good or bad about yourself? (Experts tell us that criticism is the first wave of control.)
- Does he make so many demands on you that you have no time for anybody or anything but him?
- Does he threaten you with the possibility of his infidelity, so you are nervous all the time?
- Does he have so many moods that you are always on edge?
- Does he try to isolate you from your support systems—your family, work, and friends?
- Does he exhibit such extreme jealousy that you are afraid of every movement you make?
- Does he seem inappropriately involved with you to the point of obsession?

Controlling behavior is emotionally abusive. With some men, it goes over the line into physical abuse. These are what I call "the massa' men," slave-owner-mentality brothers who want to whip you into submission.

# The Abusive Relationship

Kit met her future husband, a handsome, well-educated brother who swept her off her feet, at her first job. About him, Kit says:

"I should have listened to my mother, who warned me up front. I knew he was moody, but I didn't know what that meant. Once we got married, he showed his real face. He turned into the bossiest man in Georgia. He never let up. He said I made him that way because of the way I was. He blamed me for everything that happened. He would leave me alone at parties, and if another man came up to talk to me, he would wait until we got home and then interrogate me about how I was 'planning to meet the man later.'

"He would tell me that I was a Black bitch and then would say that the whole world knows how American Black women try to push around their men. The first time he hit me, he had been drinking. Afterward he was all sorry and kept apologizing and trying to make it up to me, so I decided it was a onetime thing and didn't turn it into a federal case.

"I clearly remember the second time he hit me. We were packing up to go on vacation, and he hit me. I mean hard. He said it was because I wasn't listening when he was talking. I was watering the plants and he started saying something. I kept on doing what I was doing while he was talking. I mean, I can listen and water plants at the same time. But he didn't believe it. So wham!

"I had enough self-respect to know that there was no excuse for what he did, no matter what he said, but I wasn't strong enough to pack up and leave. My parents didn't raise me to take abuse, but I was too ashamed of what had happened to let them know. Also, as crazy as it may seem, I was afraid of losing him because I was afraid I would never find anyone else. So I kept brushing it aside and pretended, at least to the outside world, that it wasn't happening.

"My husband was smart enough not to want anyone to know either. He would punch me in the arm or shoulder, he would kick me down, and once he even broke my arm. But there was never a mark on my face for anyone to see. I tried everything. Sometimes I walked on eggshells to keep him from getting mad. Other times, I would confront him and create other intense situations. I must have packed up and threatened to leave at least a dozen times.

"Of course, it wasn't always that way. Sometimes months would go by with no problem. Then something would happen. If he had trouble at work, I would take the brunt of it. When I got pregnant, it was calm for a lot of the time. After the baby was born, it started up again, even worse, and that made it harder because I didn't want my baby to see Mommy and Daddy going at each other."

The need to keep up a pretense with everybody, including her child, put even more pressure on Kit. Finally, her job saved her because she knew that if she didn't do something, she wouldn't be able to continue working. So one day, with the help of a couple of friends, she packed a suitcase, picked up the baby and the cat, and hid out at a friend's house until she could get an apartment. It wasn't easy, and her husband tried to get her back, but she held firm.

Abuse happens to all kinds of women, in all income brackets. Neither shame nor economic dependence should keep you tied to an abusive man. Kit is fortunate because she had a good job and enough money to make it on her own. As we know, it's harder when you don't have enough money even to take a bus to a shelter.

Nonetheless, *no matter what your financial situation*, here's the rule: The first slap is a signal that you have real trouble. It's not a love tap. The first slap is a loud sound telling you that you both need to head for counseling. He needs to get with a group or a person who can help him handle and monitor his emotions. Every woman who has ever been hit will tell you that the man is always so sorry about the first time. But "sorry" typically doesn't stop the abusive behavior.

If the abuse in your relationship has already escalated, the first thing you should do is to remove your body from the situation. You cannot get back together until he is in counseling and learning better ways to problem solve. Much more attention is being paid to abuse in this country, and help can be obtained. For information about where to get help and find shelters, you can get in touch with the National Coalition Against Domestic Violence, P.O. Box 18749, Denver, Colorado 80218 (phone: 303-839-1852). In many areas, the phone number of a shelter is printed on the front of your telephone directory. If you can't find it, call the local police precinct for an emergency number for domestic violence. Obviously, if you need help right away, call 911, your local emergency number, or 0 for the operator.

An abusive man will try to lower your self-esteem to make you more dependent on him. He will also try to isolate you from your support system, so you will feel as though you have nowhere to turn. You do have someone to turn to, and that person is yourself. Get out and get help!

I want to issue another warning: Often abusive men are extremely jealous men who are always trying to get you to "confess" to some indiscretion, imagined or real. No man is equipped to handle information about another man. No matter how much such a man plagues you and promises that his behavior will change once he hears the "truth," *do not*, I repeat, *do not*, go along with his need for a confession. This is a man who is out of control, trying to get information (whether it's true or false) he won't be able to handle without beating you up or worse! And yes, the use of liquor and drugs is often connected with abusive behavior, but that's no excuse. A man for whom this is true needs to sober up as well as resolve his abusive tendencies. He will not be able to do one without doing the other.

# Looking at Who the Man Is— A Checklist for Evaluating the Men You Meet

"If I don't notice his bank account, his car, or his designer labels, what do I notice?"

—A SISTER WHO NEEDS A CHECKLIST

I believe sisters need to have a self-protective point of view about the men they choose to know. Sisters often ask me for specific ways of finding out more about a brother's character and his capacity to form a satisfying relationship. Here's a checklist of questions to ask about any man you meet:

## *Does He Treat His Mother with Respect?*

There's an old saying, "If he mistreats his mama, he'll stomp a mudhole in you." I believe there's a lot of truth to this statement. If you meet a man who's good to his mother (and also to his sisters), it means he know how to be good to women. Studies show, for example, that men who are raised in households with female siblings tend to be more sensitive to feminine issues.

I believe it is a big mistake to exhibit jealousy when a man is close to his mother. There is a difference between a man who is controlled by his mother and a man who respects his mother. The typical sister needs to get it clear in her head that a man's mother is not her rival. The fact is that you can't ever ask a man to treat his mother badly and expect that it won't come back to you.

## *Has He Respected Other Women in His Life?*

Men do change as they get older, and you don't want to hold a man's personal history totally against him. However, if you meet a man who has hurt other women, abandoned other women, or mistreated other women, there's a very good chance that he's not going to know how to treat you either. If at the beginning of a relationship with you, he treats you as though you are special or tells you that you are different, I wouldn't put too much weight on it. This is a sting operation that many men use to get women to do what they want. It's not real honey.

## *Does He Have a God-Consciousness?*

Does this brother recognize a higher authority that is motivating and affecting his life? If he doesn't, you need to worry about his moral and ethical underpinning. You don't want to spend your life with a man who has an "anything goes" attitude. Fairness, honesty, and integrity are necessary for a good relationship, so you definitely want to end up with somebody who has thought about the difference between right and wrong.

## *Does He Have a Work Ethic?*

A work ethic has nothing to do with being presently employed. It does have to do with wanting to work and demonstrating it with action, not just words. You want a man who is willing to pitch in to the best of his ability and to work as hard as he can to make life better for the family and the community. These are my cooperative labor laws.

## *Does He Have Strong Ties to His Family and His Community?*

When you first meet a man, he may seem to be a lone person without any attachments, but as you get to know him, you should be able to connect him to some family and community stability. You need to see a man in this environment to get a sense of how he is valued and how he values others. The

African saying is that "you can't separate a man from his village." If a man doesn't seem to have any real roots, it doesn't speak well for his ability to establish long-lasting, meaningful connections. It's also a possible warning sign for other more serious problems with his character. Con men and men who are on the run have typically alienated, with good reason, their family and friends.

## Is He Honest and Kind?

I'm not talking here about a "sweet-talk artist." What you want to know is that the brother has genuine feelings of empathy and caring for people, in general, as well as for you in particular. You want to spend your life with a man who has a positive view of humanity and shows it by being respectful and kind to the people he meets. You want a man who believes he should be truthful in his dealings with the world. It's a lot easier to live with a man who sees the world—including children, the elderly, and pets, as well as tradespeople and those who work in restaurants and stores—with a sensitive point of view.

## Does He Have Self-Respect and Good Manners?

Self-respect shows itself in the way a man treats himself. Among other things, this involves his health, his habits, and his hygiene. A man with genuine self-respect, for example, does not self-destructively abuse himself with alcohol or drugs. Manners also show that he respects himself, as well as others. Good manners are part of the African American tradition, based on African values. Many of us have lost too much of this heritage, and we've paid a price in our relationships. My mama always said, "Good manners will take you where money won't." We need to reconstruct these old reliable values to maintain a sense of ethnicity and core-culture pride.

## Does He Have High Ideals and Plans for the Future?

When you meet a man with ideas, ideals, and a desire to move forward in life and improve himself, it shows that there is more to him than meets the eye. A brother with the ability to project himself beyond his current condition and make plans for the future has the capacity for success. Also I believe that a man with plans is more fun and more interesting to be with. Please understand, however, that when I talk about somebody with plans, I don't want you to think I'm describing a big dreamer or a con man—because I'm not. Rather, I'm talking about a brother with concrete achievable goals, which is quite different from a con man whose goals are grandiose and unrealistic.

## Does He Understand the Importance of Communication?

Many good men have a hard time expressing their feelings, but you want a man who at least *understands* that communication is important and is willing to learn to talk about all kinds of things. After all, you want to spend your life with a man who can talk to you about the things that matter to each of you. You want him to encourage a verbal give-and-take in your relationship that is fair and reasonable. Delightful conversations set a romantic atmosphere that has nothing to do with sex. It can make you feel bonded and close. More men need to learn the loveliness of language.

You also want your partner to realize that verbal skills are essential in working out family problems, so you want him to be able to discuss matters that bother him calmly and not resort to temper tantrums or nonverbal communications, such as slamming doors, hurling objects, or shoving or pushing you.

## Is He in Good Health, and Is He Honest About His Health?

In today's world, health is a major issue. As we all know, there are a wide number of sexually transmitted diseases that, unlike HIV, are not life threatening, but are certainly chronic and physically debilitating. These diseases include herpes, genital warts, chlamydia, and strains of gonorrhea that don't readily respond to antibiotics. You want the man in your life to be honest and self-protective about his health, as well as protective about yours. You want him to see the importance of maintaining a healthy lifestyle.

Equally essential, of course, is mental health. You want to be sure that any potential partner has a stable personality and that he isn't given to untreated bouts of depression. You want to know that he isn't moody and that he doesn't have an uncontrollable temper. You want him to be able to discuss emotional health and well-being and recognize when professional help is necessary. My mental health rule is this: Strong Black men and women may need strong psychological counseling at some point. Needing such help does not make them weak, it makes them wise.

## Is He Able to Compromise?

Between two people, the spirit of compromise is what makes it possible to make good decisions about everything, from where you are going to live to which video you're going to rent on Saturday night. This may be the most important quality to look for in a mate because it tells you whether he is good-natured if everything isn't exactly the way he wants it. Explain to him that compromise is not giving in.

## Is He Supportive and Cooperative?

Does he want to help you achieve the goals you've set for yourself, and is he willing to back up his emotional support with a cooperative effort? For example, if you want to go to school, will he cheerfully pitch in with the children because he sees your relationship as a partnership? The opposite of supportive and cooperative is a man who is competitive and who views any of your successes as somehow taking away from him. This is a poor quality for a life partner.

## Does He Act Like You Are a Priority in His Life?

He may be the best man in the world, but if he's not serious about you, you're not going to end up where you want to be. With any relationship, here's an important question you have to ask: *Does he have good intentions toward you?*

This is an old-fashioned question, but it has meaning even today. When I say good intentions, I don't mean that the man has to be planning to propose marriage. Here's what I do mean.

- Does he treat you with respect, honesty, and dignity?
- Does he want what's best for you?
- Does he acknowledge the bond and connection between you every step of the way? (For example, when he's with you on a first date, does he give you the attention you deserve? If you're dating regularly, is he faithful and loving? When he talks about you to others, does he sound as though he cares?)
- Does he share his feelings about the relationship, and is he interested in building a strong equal partnership with you?
- Does he include you in his life and his plans in an appropriate fashion? If you've been seeing each other for six months, has he introduced you to his family and made you part of family and community gatherings?
- Is he well mannered and does he behave appropriately with your family and friends? Does he act as though he cares about them because he cares about you?
- And, most important, how is he with any children you may have? If a man can't get along with your kids, he's only going to make life hard for you. You've got to think

about his treatment of your children before you take the chance of having him cause chaos in your home.

## How Do the Cards Stack Up—an Exercise for Evaluating How a Man Makes You Feel

This little exercise can be used when you first meet and start going out with a man, or it can be employed in the middle of a relationship when you have some decision making to do. All you need to get started is a stack of lined 3 x 5 index cards, a pen for writing, and a commitment to personal honesty in evaluating yourself and your partner.

After each encounter, date, or phone call with this man, sit down and consider what took place. Think about how this interchange between the two of you made you feel. When it was over, did you feel that your partner gave something to you? Did you feel enriched, nurtured, cared for, entertained, amused? Did he cook for you, or plan something special for you? In other words, did he give something to you? If you feel he gave something, write *Giver* at the top of the card. Then write down what he gave. And on the other side of the card, write down how that made you feel.

Or did the opposite happen? Did you walk away from the experience feeling that you had done most of the giving? Think about everything you gave, and everything he took. Was he taking more than he was giving? Did he exhaust you emotionally or physically? Did you have to listen to him complain endlessly? Did you wait on him or work very hard to please him? In other words, how much did he take from you? If he took from you, write *Taker* at the top of the card and write down precisely what he took. On the other side of the card, write down how that made you feel.

Continue with this exercise for a specific period of time. Give it enough time (at least a month or more) so that you can get a real sense of what's happening in the relationship. At the end of the period, add up your cards. Don't share this exercise with him because he may think you are keeping score. That's not what this is about. This is about having a *written* record of your emotional state in the relationship. It's about being able to see for yourself clearly what's going on. You may add up your cards and realize that you're not giving enough. It could go either way. Or you could see that there is a good balance between the two of you. Obviously, if you have significantly more *Taker* cards than *Giver* cards, this needs some serious thinking.

# What About Prisoners?

Wanda, age 25, describes herself as the last person in the world to get involved with a prisoner, yet in many ways she is typical of the kind of woman who falls in love with a man who is doing time. Wanda, a psychology student, says:

"I still can't believe what happened. When I met Michael, it was my first time inside a prison, and I didn't know what to expect. I certainly didn't expect to fall in love. I went to the prison because my church group was visiting there each Friday night. We would be shown into this special room with about twenty or thirty men who would be waiting for us. Then we would have a little church service, and afterward our minister would ask the men if they had any special religious concerns or anything. Then we would have a discussion about the Bible and God and what the men were feeling. It was an amazing experience because so many of the men were so smart, so full of words and feelings. It was much more interesting than any other discussion like that I'd ever had.

"Michael attended even though he really doesn't consider himself a Christian; he leans more toward the Muslims. Basically, he considers himself a spiritual person and a thinking person. He says he tries to get permission to attend services with as many groups as possible.

"I fell in love with Michael before I knew why he was there. In prison nobody talks about what they're in for. It's not considered smart or something. It's going to be at least three more years before Michael can apply for parole. He thinks we should get married while he's still in prison, so we can get conjugal visits, but I'm questioning what I should be doing with this. This is a big jump for me, and I'm scared."

Wanda has every reason to feel nervous about starting a relationship with a man from whom she is separated by prison walls. All relationships are difficult, and the one she is considering has even more difficulties attached to it. However, many sisters have forged loving, loyal connections to prisoners, so I know that it can be done. Unfortunately, I also know that many others don't want to subject themselves to the special tests to which these relationships are subjected.

Brothers make up more than 47 percent of the population of state and federal prisons. This is a truly frightening fact, and it means that there are a large number of sisters who have loved or will love men who are behind bars. If you are one of these women, here are some things to consider:

• *How long will it be before he gets out?* You need to ask yourself if you can honestly withstand years without being with a man you love.

• *What was the nature of his crime?* I realize that prison manners dictate that men don't talk about the reasons why they are incarcerated. However, if you are going to get involved with a man who is in jail, I think it's important that you know why he's there. If, for example, his crime had anything to do with violence, in general, or women, in particular, I think you should think long and hard about the situation.

• *What will he be like when he gets out?* Has he prepared himself for life in the outside world? Does he have any skills to help him find work?

• *Is there a strong support system to help you both?* Has he maintained positive contacts with family members and friends who will help him lead a better life once he gets out of prison? Does he have ties to a religious group that will help him? Do you have a support network to help *you* make the necessary adjustments?

• *Does he have a true depth of commitment to his religious beliefs?* Many men in prison seek religion, and this is good, but it's difficult to evaluate what religion means to a man in prison. Is it something that he sees as a way of life, or is it simply part of a group involvement in prison and an outlet for interesting discussions? You want to be sure that he is able to act on his beliefs once he is out. You need to find ways to measure the level of his interest in maintaining a spiritual life.

• *Has he been willing to maintain his human responsibilities while in prison?* If he has children, has he written to them and tried to maintain contact? Has he maintained good contact with his mother or sisters or friends? Do they feel that he is a positive force in their lives?

• *Were drugs involved in his incarceration, and what does that mean?* Has he detoxed emotionally, as well as physically, or is he still drawn to that world?

Men in prison typically got there because they were living by their wits and not by the rules. Often an incarcerated brother will seem exceptionally smart and exceptionally appealing. What you need to think about is whether he has changed and is able to live by society's rules. To help you make a decision, see the resource list at the back of this book for the address of the NAACP Prison Program. This program, started by Leroy Mobley, should be able to give you more information and direct you to a local prison program.

# Finding Your Own Overlooked Brothers

The steady, reliable, hardworking but "all man" brother does exist, but you do need to expend some energy in order to find him. Here's a list of places to get you started. Remember, this man is not going to bowl you over with a good line. "Hello, my name is Theodore" may be all the come-on you'll get.

### SIXTY PLACES TO FIND OVERLOOKED BROTHERS

1. Church
2. Mosque
3. Conventions of fraternal organizations (Elks, Masons, Shriners)
4. Religious conventions
5. Gospel music festivals
6. Ethnic street fairs
7. Volunteer activities
8. African import stores
9. Caribbean, African, Hispanic, or Black restaurants
10. Parties
11. Parks and beaches
12. YMCAs
13. Supermarkets
14. Laundromats
15. Tennis clubs
16. Jogging trails
17. Roller rinks
18. Ski lodges
19. Black-owned resorts
20. Art galleries
21. Museums
22. Department stores or malls
23. Civil rights gatherings
24. Trains
25. Buses
26. Airline terminals
27. Health clubs/gyms
28. Travel tours
29. Theater group outings
30. Television talk-show audiences

31. Adult education for special interests (photography, sculpting, scuba diving, ceramics)
32. University extension classes
33. Doctors' waiting rooms
34. Hotels/motels/casinos
35. Work
36. Black expos
37. Family reunions
38. Libraries
39. Weddings
40. Bookstores in the section on African American studies or Black bookstores
41. Hobby groups
42. Sports events
43. Bowling alleys
44. Discos and public ballrooms
45. Sorority or Fraternity events (private gatherings or public dances)
46. An international house
47. United Nations, New York City
48. Black comedy clubs
49. Cookouts and picnics
50. Singles organizations like "Chocolate Singles"
51. Black award events
52. Concerts
53. Male fashion shows
54. College spring break activities and gatherings
55. College alumni events (even if you didn't attend that college)
56. PTA meetings
57. Through friends and family members
58. Military posts
59. Political campaigns
60. National Guard Armory events

# 9

# Men from Other Cultures

"Yes, I date white men. Not because I prefer them, . . . but right now it feels as though they are the only option available to me."

—BARBARA, 44

"Yes, my husband's Black, but he's from another country, and sometimes the differences between us are so great, it feels as though he's from another planet."

—LORETTA, 39

## Crossover Love

One Friday night, two girlfriends asked Carol if she wanted to go out with them and do the town. Carol, a single parent, can't afford to go out with friends often, so she had to think about it before she said yes. However, because she was about to celebrate her thirtieth birthday, she figured, why not? From her point of view, she deserved some fun. Besides she might even meet some men.

The plan was to go to a movie right after work and then head over to a restaurant-bar with a reputation as a Buppie hangout. The movie was hilarious, and by the time Carol and her friends reached the restaurant, they had been laughing so hard they were already relaxed. Carol had heard about this restaurant, but this was her first time there. Looking around, she noticed that the clientele was mostly well-dressed Black men and women in their late twenties to early forties. The others were equally well-dressed white men and women in the same age range. From the prices on the menu, it was apparent that this was not a fast-food crowd.

The three women decided to order drinks at the bar while they were waiting for their table. Gloria, one of Carol's friends, separated from them almost immediately. "I'm on a mission," she said. "I'm definitely going to see about getting into something," and she disappeared into the thick crowd hanging around the bar. Within minutes, Carol's other friend, Anne, ran into a man she had once dated. They started talking, and Carol was left standing there alone, holding a glass of chardonnay and looking at the crowd. It seemed like an interesting place, and there certainly were several men who looked attractive and appealing.

Carol was wondering how she could go about meeting one of them when suddenly a man was leaning down and talking to her. "You don't look like the kind of woman one normally meets at a singles bar," he said, "so I don't want to miss the chance to get to know you." His name was Pete, and Carol found out that he was a professional photographer with a job at an advertising agency. He was tall, he was good-looking, he was funny, and he was very attentive. The complicated part? He was white.

Fifteen minutes later, when the hostess came over to tell Carol that the table was ready, Carol expected Pete to leave, but he didn't. Instead he asked if he could buy her dinner. When she said she was with friends, he said he would buy them all dinner. And that's what he did.

Sitting with him at a table with Gloria and Anne, Carol didn't know what to think. On the one hand, he was a lot of fun, and she was having a good time. On the other hand, she had really wanted to meet some of those brothers standing at the bar. Just thinking that made her feel confused. After all, not only was Pete sitting there paying for dinner, he was acting like he couldn't take his eyes off her, even when she was chewing on a rib. When he excused himself to go to the men's room, Gloria said, "That man sure seems to like you."

After dinner, when they all returned to the bar, Gloria and Anne started talking with a group of men, leaving Carol alone with Pete, wondering what she was supposed to do or say. She barely knew him, and already she was confused about what was expected of her or what to expect from him. When they all finally left the restaurant, she worried that Pete was going to want her to continue on with him. At the very least, she expected him to try to kiss her, but he didn't. He just called a cab for everybody. When he said good night, all he asked for was Carol's phone number.

Since that night ten days ago, Pete hasn't stopped pursuing Carol. He calls every day, and she has already gone out with him a couple of times. If he had his way, they would have been together every night. When she is with him, he seems genuinely interested in her and her life. He even seems interested in hearing about her child.

Although he hasn't tried to get her into bed, the last time they were together, he started to get all heated up with kissing and hugging in the vestibule of her apartment house. Carol wasn't sure if she would enjoy kissing him, but she did. In fact, she became quite turned on.

It seems apparent that soon Pete is going to start pressuring for sex. Her friend Gloria has advised her to "just get into the wind" and see what happens, but Carol knows herself. Whenever she has sex with a man, she becomes more involved and more vulnerable. She doesn't know if she wants that to happen with Pete. In short, Carol isn't sure that she wants to be involved with a white man. How should Carol think out this dilemma? Is there truth to any of the stereotypes that she's heard? If she gets involved with Pete, will he be generous just because he's white? Will he take advantage of her just because she's black? What will his parents say? For that matter, how will her parents respond?

# Why Are So Many Sisters Dating White Men?

According to the U.S. Bureau of the Census, the number of marriages of Black women and white men has almost doubled in the past ten years. Are these interracial relationships going to work? The answer to this question, of course, is that some interracial relationships work and others don't.

My concerns about interracial relationships are not a result of racism, but are a product of my pride in the heritage of our people. I am truly proud of Black people and the Black culture, and I am always fearful that our connection to our past will be lost. That possibility saddens me deeply. Since I am writing for women here, I have to tell you that while it hurts me to see wonderful sisters complaining about lonely lives, it also saddens me to see decent, loving brothers who can't find partners. I feel strongly that in their quest for mates, sometimes sisters are overlooking some very fine Black men.

My other concern about interracial relationships arises from the fact that I have seen too many of them begin for all the wrong reasons and end painfully for the same reasons. No matter how much genuine love exists between the partners, you'd better believe that an interracial relationship is going to present some "special events." Too often, men and women become emotionally committed to each other with little or no understanding of the world they are entering. It goes without saying that a couple making this choice must be able to meet the challenges of two races, with their separate stereotypes, prejudices, and misunderstandings. It is one thing to take on such an endeavor with one's eyes open. It is another to pick an interracial partner just because he or she is "cute" or "available." This decision requires a lot of thought and careful consideration.

It certainly is not my intention to stop you or any sister from being with a white man. That is a choice only you can make. But if you do make such a choice, I urge you to do as much as possible to make sure that both you and your potential partner face up to the harsh realities you may confront in such a relationship. And I implore you to be honest with yourself and self-protective in your thinking.

# The First Question: How Well *Do* You Know Each Other?

The following are brief histories of the relationships of two couples who are planning to marry this year. Which sister has a greater chance of having her relationship stand the test of time?

*Couple One:* Bob and Tiffany met at work six years ago. They became friends almost immediately, but it took them another two years to become lovers. By the time they went to bed together, Bob and Tiffany knew they shared interests as well as friends. Bob says that he had no intention of falling in love with a Black woman, but he did, and he thinks it's great. His family loves Tiffany and thinks she is a terrific woman. Tiffany says that she had never considered marrying a white man, but this is the path her life has taken, and she is sure that she and Bob will be extremely happy. Although her family is less than thrilled with the relationship, they have told her that they will try to accept Bob into their hearts because he is her choice.

*Couple Two:* Ted picked Manitta up at a concert. He has always been attracted to Black women, and when he saw her, he was overcome by the attraction. Manitta wasn't as sure as Ted, but she felt as though many of her past relationships— all with Black men—were so toxic that she was willing to give Ted, a white man, a chance to prove himself. Without giving it much thought, she started a sexual relationship with him almost immediately. Things progressed so quickly that within two months, Ted moved into Manitta's apartment. However, Manitta still hasn't had the courage to tell her parents about Ted. When she told her brother, he became angry and accused her of just wanting a man, "any color, anyhow."

Manitta knows there are other places where Ted won't fit in. She, for example, is a strong churchgoer, and Ted has no interest in her religious convictions. As for Ted's world, he has told his parents about Manitta, but they haven't met her. His parents' hostility is so great that Ted wonders if Manitta and his parents will *ever* meet.

Tiffany and Bob, Manitta and Ted: Which couple do you think has the best chance for a lasting marriage? I'm sure you agree with me and would vote for Tiffany and Bob. Simply put, they know each other better and therefore have already been able to consider and confront some of the special issues they have to handle as an interracial couple.

Manitta and Ted, on the other hand, are avoiding the complicated stuff. If Manitta weren't so involved with the chemistry of the relationship, she would see for herself that there are major warning signs. But at this moment, Manitta is not thinking with both her feet on the ground.

At the beginning of a relationship, it's easy to sweep all the problems under the rug. "I'll deal with this tomorrow," you say to yourself. When you see potential disagreements, you look the other way and think, "Maybe this will change." Let me assure you, every time you don't deal with an issue honestly when it comes up, you create an environment for problems to grow and fester. This is true for all relationships, but it is even truer for interracial couples. Because all the normal male-female conflicts can't help but be compounded by the issues of race, you've got to be especially diligent about dealing with problems as they occur.

Knowing someone well means that you've had the chance to get past the chemistry; you've had the time to pick up that rug and dust around to see what the two of you could be hiding from each other. I firmly believe that sisters should be very sure before they start making major commitments to any man, no matter who he is. With interracial relationships, you have to take even more time to be certain that you're both thinking with your feet on the ground. In other words, you and your partner have definitely got more complicated stuff to figure out. Here are some questions to help you start doing just that.

## Do You View Dating White Men as Your Last Resort?

Frequently, a sister will say she's dating a white man because she doesn't believe she'll ever find a Black man to marry. She may see what she is doing as a big compromise. You'd better believe that no man wants to see himself as a compromise, so if you're indulging in what I call *last-resort thinking,* be warned that it's going to cause problems down the road.

Here's how last-resort thinking works. You meet a white man who says he thinks you're the best thing that's ever happened to him. You don't really know him all that well, but it feels good to have somebody give you so much attention. In fact, what you may like about him most is that he seems crazy about you. You think to yourself, "Why not make a commitment and give this a try? How bad can it be to be with a man who thinks I'm the best thing since Toyota, and he likes what I do for him?" You're so involved in what he seems to be thinking about you that you don't even notice what you think about him. You know only three things for sure: (1) he's white, (2) you're Black, and (3) you're prepared to make a compromise. This kind of thinking is not fair to him or to you.

If last-resort thinking has taken over, the white issue is so big in your head that you're not noticing anything else about him—*yet.* You're not noticing if he has a thousand little habits that will make you crazy; you're not noticing if he's a control freak or mean-spirited or just plain stupid. The fact is that you have become so caught up in your white-man compromise that you're not looking at anything else about him carefully. Of course, you could get lucky and wake up six months down the road and discover that you're with the best man on God's Earth, but you could also wake up six months down the road and say, "Who is this guy, and what was I thinking?"

## *Are* You *Harboring Any Stereotypes?*

In 1987 *Essence* published an article entitled "Guess Who's Coming to Dinner Now?" In it, the writer, Dorothy Tucker, said, "Many of us still have the mistaken impression that white men, generically speaking, have plenty of money, little penises and no rhythm. . . . These gross preconceptions are particularly interesting in light of the fact that if a white male states that *all* Black women were promiscuous, or on welfare, we'd slap him into next Tuesday."

Dorothy Tucker is right. We hate it when anyone stereotypes us. We know how ridiculous and stupid this kind of thinking is, yet most of us hold some stereotypes about white people. Before you get into a relationship with a white man, you need to take a hard look at any stereotypes, good and bad, that you may be harboring. Here are some questions to ask yourself:

• *Do you assume a man has money or more stability just because he's white?* If visions of financial security are among the hidden reasons you find a particular white man attractive, you have to ask yourself what it is you "see" behind the money. By that I mean, what fantasies are you conjuring up? Do you find him attractive because you *see* yourself in a big house in the suburbs with wall-to-wall carpeting, a Jaguar in the carport, and a live-in housekeeper woman swishing your undies in Woolite? In other words, are you indulging in soap-opera thinking and building fantasies around him that he will never be able to fulfill. Few people, white or otherwise, have the possessions or lifestyles you see on television. Just because he's white you can't automatically expect him to resolve all your financial insecurities.

• *Do you think white men treat women better?* Here's a fact: Some treat women better, some treat them the same, and some treat them worse. You can't make this kind of generalization about human nature. Expecting a white man always to treat a woman the way she wants to be treated is an invitation to disappointment.

• *Do you think because he's white he's going to make you feel more protected?* It's not fair to look at a man as though he's a security blanket, and it's not realistic. In truth, what you expect of him in this department may not correlate with his experience. For example, perhaps he comes from an environment in which he was encouraged to let women fend for themselves. He may even pride himself on what he regards as his nonsexist attitude toward women, whom he regards as equals who take care of themselves. Your expectations and his attitude may well collide.

• *Do you see him as a power symbol?* Coming out of the experience of growing up Black, it's easy to believe that white men are automatically more powerful in society. Dr. Nathan Hare contends that when a sister is attracted to a white man, her attraction frequently has more to do with his social potency than with his sexual potency. From the outside, it appears as though all white men have social mobility, status, and an obstacle-free chance at the employment market. There is an assumption that (a) he has power, (b) you will have power if you are with him, and (c) because of that your life will operate smoothly. This is the kind of stereotypical thinking that can provide real disappointments.

• *Do you believe the myth that white men "can't dance . . . can't make love"?* The stereotype is that white men aren't as good in bed, but they make up for it by being romantic or by being more sexually liberated and giving. I can assure you that sexual stereotypes are ridiculous and have no basis in fact. Everything depends on the individual man, but I can also tell you that if you make any man feel as though he is somehow failing you in bed, you're going to have trouble.

• *Do you believe that white men typically have stable lives and come from intact families?* Here again, the world does not resemble a television set. Divorce, alcoholism, addiction, financial chaos, poor parenting—all occur in white families, as well as in Black families. But you may not immediately recognize the dysfunctional elements because they reveal themselves in different styles of behavior.

• *Do you believe that white men won't present as much of a challenge?* The belief is that brothers are more competitive with women and resent sisters' goals and successes, whereas white men automatically cater to women and are supportive. The fact is that the kind of insecurity that makes a man jealous of a woman's success is color blind and can be found in all races.

## Are You Able to See This Man Realistically?

Generations of unequal footing can throw a sister off balance when she embarks on a relationship with a white man. By definition, this history of inequality creates confusion. You may, for example, have a tough time seeing him as a person with his own particular family background, education, experience, personality pluses, and personality flaws. Because his insecurities may show themselves in a style you don't recognize, his vulnerabilities may not be immediately apparent to you.

Sisters often tend to measure white men by impossible standards. They don't expect them to have problems, and they don't always identify with a white man's personal struggles or his pain. A white man's difficulties may not seem as real or important to you as they do to him. All of this can impact negatively on long-term intimacy. Understanding and empathy are necessary ingredients in any successful relationship, but it's not always an easy task to feel empathetic when you also feel the sense of historical imbalance.

## Do You Ever Feel Embarrassed Because You're with a White Man?

When the people around you are trying to shame you, it's tough not to feel downright apologetic about what you're doing. In our communities, hostility and resentment, particularly from men, may greet a sister who dates a white man. People may say unkind things, they may accuse her of suffering from "white boy fever," they may accuse her of trying to behave as though she is white, or they may make her feel as though she is somehow betraying her race.

There is a saying that comes out of the Black experience: "The only two people with real freedom are the White man and the Black woman." This fallacy creates a perception you're going to have to deal with in the community—that somehow because you're involved with a white man, you're sexually and emotionally freed up.

Often a sister responds to this backlash by trying to compartmentalize her relationship. For example, she may start making excuses for the relationship to her friends. Because she may be embarrassed to be seen with this man in all situations, she may exclude him from some events and gatherings. This behavior, of course, will be noticed by the man, who, in turn, may feel hurt and resentful. Ultimately, unless there is a lot of communication and understanding around these feelings, the relationship can't help but suffer. Some sisters, of course, go in the opposite direction and start avoiding their old friends as well as their families. I can guarantee that either of these extreme paths will create tension and stress.

The bottom line is this: A sister who is contemplating a long-term relationship with a white man has to be certain about what she feels and how she is handling those feelings. Most of us want to *share* our lives with the one we love. Don't shortchange yourself on that score.

## *Are You Trying to Make a Relationship, or Are You Trying to Make a Statement?*

A sister who is starting a relationship with a white man also has to be certain that she's not doing it primarily as an act of defiance. Sometimes a sister gets so discouraged and disgusted with the way things are that all she wants is to deal herself a different hand. Perhaps she's angry at a specific Black man who has hurt her, or perhaps for the moment she's feeling fed up with Black men in general. Perhaps she hasn't had a good relationship with the men in her family, particularly her father. Perhaps she doesn't want to repeat her mother's patterns. Whatever the reason, for the time being at least, she wants to sidestep tradition and distance herself from her family and her community. She believes that being with a white man will serve that purpose. And it will, temporarily.

If you're falling into this kind of thinking, the satisfaction of being different may not last. Once the shock value wears off, you may find yourself with a relationship that doesn't have any true staying power. So be sure that your love is as strong as the need to be defiant.

Also at this point I would like to remind sisters that your primal relationships with your parents lay the basis for all future relationships. If you have unresolved conflicts with your father, for example, it may well affect how you relate to all men. Old conflicts will not be resolved by avoiding Black men because they remind you of your father. Rather than avoiding Black men, I would suggest that you see a counselor and try to work out some of these unresolved issues.

## *Will Your Relationship Cause You to Put Too Much Distance Between Yourself and Your Community?*

"I live in a beautiful house in a wealthy community, but I'm so lonely I don't know what to do with myself. My husband works all the time, and there are only so many times you can rearrange your closets. My neighbors are polite, but nobody's inviting me over for coffee. Maybe that's just the way they are with everybody, but it doesn't matter because I still don't have anybody to talk to. My husband's friends are my husband's friends. It seems like all I have left are acquaintances."

—CONNIE, 48

Connie's complaints are not unusual. Black women who find themselves living in all-white areas, no matter how congenial, typically complain of a sense of alienation and discomfort. We all need our roots, so be certain that any relationship you enter gives you the freedom to stay connected to your family, your friends, and your community.

## Do You Have Color Issues That You're Not Examining?

We all know how loaded the issues of color are in our communities. Before you get seriously involved with a white man, ask yourself if you have been brainwashed into believing that lighter is better. Because you may not even be aware of these feelings on a conscious level, you have to think about the messages you received about skin color as a child to be sure you don't have your own hidden prejudices about what color means. In long-term relationships, everything tends to change once both partners get past what's on the surface and start dealing with each other's hearts and minds. So if you think he's an Adonis, and that's your primary attraction, you'd better get to know him well enough to make certain he doesn't have feet of clay.

## Do You Harbor Any Hidden Fears or Resentments That Can Erupt and Sabotage Your Relationship?

For our mothers and grandmothers, marrying a white man was an almost unheard-of option. In their experience, a white man's interest was almost exclusively sexual. Their memory banks were filled to the brim with horror stories of Black women who were raped by white men. On those rare occasions when there was mutual love, Black women knew that the love would be hidden and forbidden. These women carried with them a distrust and fear of white men that they couldn't shake, even if they wanted to. Of course, times have changed, but many sisters still carry a buried anger at the injustices heaped on Black people in a white society.

In a relationship with a white man, that anger sometimes spills out when one least expects it. I remember a friend discussing her marriage and saying, "I can't help it . . . We'll be arguing about some little thing, and all of a sudden I just get angry 'cause he's white and I'm Black and he's had it easier. I just switch on him and start railing about civil rights. When that happens, he doesn't understand what's made me so angry."

Given the nature of our society, it's almost impossible for a Black person not to feel some degree of anger and resentment. A sister who is considering a long-term relationship or marriage with a white man should be sure that she and her intended partner have discussed any hidden anger she brings to the relationship. Often premarital counseling is the best way to deal with this issue.

# What About Him?

You're not the only person in this relationship. Your partner may have his own hang-ups around the issue of race. Here are some questions to consider:

## Does He Love Black but Live White?

If he lives in an all-white world, he isn't going to be doing you any favors by making you live that way. The fact is that if a man isn't already living in an integrated world, he has no business being in an integrated relationship. Here are some questions to ask yourself: Are you the only Black person in his life? Does he have other Black friends and acquaintances, both men and women? How does he relate to them?

## Does He Compartmentalize Your Relationship?

It wasn't that long ago that white men who dated Black women kept their relationships hidden and separate. If a sister fell in love with a white man, she expected to be excluded from his world, no matter how hurtful that exclusion felt. But, once again, times have changed. If you're involved with a white man who doesn't want to bring you into his world and shows little interest in becoming part of yours, obviously this is a sure sign of trouble. However, the reasons for his attitude may be more complicated than they appear to be.

White women also complain about exclusionary behavior, and it really is a tried-and-true male technique for avoiding commitment. So if you are with a man who doesn't want to make you part of his whole life, whether this avoidance is because of his emotional problems with real intimacy or because of his racist problems is irrelevant. Any guy who doesn't want to share his *whole* world with you is trouble and should be ditched—fast. Here's something that sisters who want to protect themselves need to keep in mind: Men who have problems with commitment often become involved with women who they believe are inappropriate for a long-term commitment. If you go out with a white man who tries to compartmentalize the relationship, whatever the reason and no matter how close it may seem when you are together, you don't need him in your life.

## Is He Making a Relationship, or Is He Making a Statement?

There are many unconscious reasons why a white man might purposely choose a Black woman. Among them is a need to rebel against his family. If this is the case, and you are the woman, you will eventually discover that his need to hurt his family may be more important than his love for you. Here are some things to think about in this regard: How will your relationship affect his family, friends, ex-girlfriends, and others in his life? Will his mother tell him that it is "killing" her? Is he trying to get negative attention from his family?

There's another type of man you need to be aware of: this is the fellow who sees an involvement with a Black woman as a political statement. A sister on his arm is a kind of a trophy. Although he may not intend his actions to be hurtful, if you're the woman, you may eventually come to believe that you are not as important to him as a person as you are as a symbol. Feeling this way can't help but diminish you. Without your consent, you may even end up being a martyr to his generic-brand politics.

## What About His Family and Friends?

What are his family's views about Black women and Black people in general? If the views of his family and closest friends are not congruent with what his views seem to be, you may have a big problem on your hands. The color of your skin may turn out to be far more important to him than the color of your soul.

## What Do You Symbolize for Him?

Some white men say that they feel hypnotized by Black women. They say that the earthiness and power of Black women are overwhelmingly seductive. Now I know some earthy and powerful Black women, but I also know some earthy and powerful white women. Why are Black women so often cast in roles that are not of their own making? Here are some other questions to consider:

• *Does he see you primarily as a fellow "sufferer"?* Some white men who come from dysfunctional or troubled families say they prefer Black women because they believe sisters will be more understanding. Because these men feel as though they have been victimized, they believe that Black women, whom they perceive as downtrodden, will automatically be on the same "victim" wavelength. You may not want to be defined in this way.

• *Does he expect you to "mother" him?* Black women are often perceived as being more maternal and more nurturing. Psychologists know that many of the clues to our romantic attractions can be traced back to early childhood. We all know that many white men were cared for as babies by Black women. For these men, in many ways, their first loves—their first mothers—were actually two loves and two mothers—one white and one black. Twenty, forty, or sixty years later, the power of that love still holds. Is this a bad thing? Not necessarily. But if you don't want to play the mother role to a man, you'd better make sure that's not what he has in mind.

## Does He Have Sexual Stereotypes That Make a Real Relationship Impossible?

A Black woman is traditionally stereotyped as volcanic, eruptive, and erotic. The Earth is full of passion, and so is she, at least in the imagination of many men, both Black and white. Sometimes a man isn't even conscious of these feelings. Nonetheless, he may use the stereotypes as a form of aphrodisiac, and you may resent being expected to perform a sexual role. Ask yourself if he sees you as any of the following sexual stereotypes:

- A primitive woman, whose passion and sexuality are immediately on tap and on call whenever he feels the urge
- A nurturing "hot mama," who has been conditioned to cater to his every whim and need
- A promiscuous "Miss Loosey," for whom sex is the primary interest in life

If you're going to forge a successful relationship with a white man, you have to be comfortable with his view of you. You have to be certain that you don't symbolize a sexual role that you may not want to live up to. No sister can become a fully functioning human being while trying to fulfill these unreal roles. You want to be with a man who sees you as a whole, complete woman with many dimensions, not just as a cardboard stereotype that fits his sexual agenda.

## Is He Trying to Fulfill Some Sexual Rite of Passage by Being Involved with a Black Woman?

Some men believe they are entitled to one woman from every possible type—a blonde, a redhead, and so on—before they settle down. This is even truer when it comes to some men's attitudes toward Black women. For example, historically, in the South, sex with an African American woman was considered an almost necessary rite of passage for young southern males.

In his book *Sex and Racism in America,* Calvin C. Hernton refers to the complicated and confused feelings of southern men toward Black women:

> In every southern white man, whether a racist or not, there is, just below the level of awareness, the twilight urge to make love to a Black woman, to sleep with the alter mother, to consume her via the act of intercourse, thereby affirming his childhood affinity for Black flesh and repudiating the interracial conflict of his masculinity. Because of Jim Crow and racism, whatever genuine sexual desires the southerner might have toward Black women are twisted and distorted.

Obviously not *all* white men, southern or otherwise, are harboring at-least-one-time sexual urges toward Black women. However, it would be foolish to discount the importance of sexual feelings in determining action. To protect yourself, before you get in over your head, make certain that this man is as interested in the relationship as he is in the sex.

# Time Is on Your Side, So Take It

If you're about to embark on a relationship with someone you don't know well, you will serve yourself and your interests best by taking a lot of time. I once talked to a sister who said she didn't see what the big deal was about falling in love with a white man. "After all," she said, "when your eyes are closed, a kiss feels like a kiss, and a hug feels like a hug."

My reaction to that remark is to remind you that what you want to do is fall in love with your eyes open, no matter what color the man is. Sure it may be hot, hot, hot when the lights go out, but you need to make sure your worlds intersect in the bright light of day. You need to know that there are other things besides the "wild thing" holding you together. That takes time.

# The Same, but Different

Recently I was reading a book called *Crossings: A White Man's Journey into Black America* by Walt Harrington, who I met when we were both guests on *Geraldo*. Harrington, who is married to a Black woman, writes about traveling through Black communities all over the country, trying to understand the African American experience through a white man's eyes. Near the end of the book, he writes, "I know now that Black people are like me and unlike me at the same time."

I think this statement is an important one to keep in mind if you're falling in love with a white man. Yes, human nature is human nature, and we all feel love, pain, and jealousy. However, we are also different. To have an honest, solid relationship with a white man, you have to know the ways in which Black people and white people are different as well as the ways we are the same.

When you're going out with someone from another culture, you need to see everything about him. It's not enough to meet his family; you have to *know* his family. It's not enough to plan where you would live if you were together; you need to visit that place and try it on for size. You have to know that because your experiences have been so different, you and he will sometimes use the same words, but not mean the same thing. It's not enough for you to want to make this relationship work, you need concrete proof that he's prepared to invest his time and his good intentions in making a relationship work with you. And, once again, you need to make sure you're seeing each other as complicated individuals, not as stereotypes.

# He's Black, but He's Not American

"I met my husband at college, and in that atmosphere, he was just another student, who acted like all the other students. I knew him for a while before we started going out, but I didn't examine his views or anything. It was a rapid courtship, and when we decided to get married right after graduation, my parents were worried, but they didn't try to stop me. His father lives here, but his mother stays in their country. So there were very few of his relatives at the wedding, and I didn't get to talk to them.

"After marriage, he started changing almost immediately. He started accusing me of embarrassing him, and he started to monitor everything I did. I would say it was jealousy, but it was more pervasive than that; it was just controlling and strange. As I began to meet more of his friends and their wives, I noticed that most of those women were very obedient to their husbands. I got the feeling that some of them were abused and that everybody thought it was OK. It's not like anybody came out and said, 'We condone ass-whipping around here,' but you definitely got a picture. I get the feeling with some of his friends that they all want well-educated wives who are willing to act like doormats.

"I'm not happy with him, and the cultural thing is definitely the reason. He knows how I feel, and I can see that he's trying to loosen up, but it's hard for him, too. I think I jumped into this too quickly. I still love him, but this is more work than I ever imagined."

—TALISHA, 29

If you're about to get involved with a Black man from another country, you may discover, as Talisha did, that a cross-cultural relationship can present both shocks and challenges. You need to be self-protective in these relationships. Otherwise one day you could be an all-African American woman hip-hopping along happy as could be listening to Whitney Houston singing "I Want to Run to You," and the next day you could be standing there crying, not knowing *where* to run or what to do.

## When It Comes to Relationships, Culture Overrides Color

It's easy to assume that just because the man is Black, you and he are on the same track. But it's simply not true. Men from African cultures, for example, bring with them a continuity of culture that we have no experience with. Their cultures have given these men a series of traditions that mold their behavior and weigh heavily on their choices. How a man treats you as a woman, as a mother, as a lover, and as a family member are all shaped by his culture.

In America, we tend to be guided by the rights of the individual. A man from Africa is accustomed to thinking in terms of family, and the family that takes priority is his own birth family. Therefore, as his wife, you will be expected to give his family a level of attention and respect that may seem strange for someone from this country. Family needs may override your personal desires. A book you may find interesting on this subject is Marita Golden's *Migrations of the Heart*.

## A Different View of Women

Men from some African nations may have attitudes toward women that seem archaic at best. Furthermore, sometimes these attitudes don't reveal themselves until after the wedding. Africans are typically raised to think of men as the authority figures. Thus, as his wife, he may expect you to behave like the proverbial obedient child who is seen but not heard. He may firmly believe that all child care, housework, and cooking are done only by women. You should also bear in mind that many African societies are patriarchal. This means that in their view children belong to the father. This is an issue that will have real meaning if you and your African husband divorce. Even if you are living in this country, there is always a possibility that your husband may try to remove the children and take them back to his native land, where he may be protected. This can also be true of men from Arabic nations.

## Which Home Is Home?

Many men from other countries, whether the countries be in faroff Africa or the Caribbean, find it difficult to adjust to life in the United States on a permanent basis and ultimately convince their American wives to return with them to their homelands. Then it is up to the wives to adjust, and it's not always easy. The social mores are different, the language is different, the lifestyle is different, and the plumbing may be *very* different. In Africa, an American woman may be considered more of a social liability than an asset, and she may find it painfully lonely and isolated.

If you continue to live in this country, on the other hand, you may discover that your foreign-born husband is perceived as receiving an unfair advantage. Many African Americans are extremely resentful of foreign-born Blacks who find adequate employment, for example. This may be an issue that you will have to deal with with your friends and your community. Looking at it from his point of view as a foreign-born Black, your husband might incorrectly believe that American Blacks lack a strong work ethic. He may find it hard to understand your struggles, and you may find it impossible to comprehend his attitude.

## If You Feel You Are Madly in Love

I certainly don't want to talk any woman into forgoing what she believes is her chance at true happiness. However, before you enter a permanent relationship with someone from another country, I would like to urge you to do a great deal of research about what your life with this man would be like. Here are some things to consider:

• *Where would you live?* Take the time before you are married to visit his country and see what it's like. Stay there long enough so that you have a real sense of what the amenities are and how well you cope with them. Even if this man says he wants to stay in the United States, recognize that his attitude may change, and you should be prepared.

• *How would his family treat you?* It's not enough simply to meet his family. You must spend enough time with them to see for yourself how women are treated in general, how daughters-in-law are treated, and how you would be treated as a foreigner.

• *Can you adapt to the food and the lifestyle?* Some of this may seem irrelevant, but so many African American women have mentioned the strain of trying to become accustomed to a completely different kind of diet, that I think it's worth mentioning. There are other things you need to think about. The lack of air-conditioning, electricity, television viewing, and other sources of entertainment will all impact on your life. Will you be able to live this life long-term?

• *Can you fulfill this man's expectations of how a wife should behave?* You need to see how men and women relate to each other in his country. What would your responsibilities be? No matter where you end up living, would he expect you to wait on him hand and foot? Would he expect to control your behavior? Would he expect you to behave as though his word was law?

• *What about the children you may have?* I can't urge you enough not to rush into motherhood. Before you have children, you need to be certain that your marriage is stable and that your husband's attitude toward you is loving and supportive.

• *Does he have a tendency to regard women as property?* This kind of thinking may make you feel protected and pampered at the beginning of a relationship. It may seem masculine and charming. Later, when you realize that it affects everything in a relationship, from the way he views sex to the way he views the family finances, it may make you very unhappy.

## Green-Card Love

Obviously, not every immigrant who proposes to an American women does so in order to gain a green card. However, every now and then, I run into a sister who has told me that she was lied to by a man who married her only so he could get permanent residence.

Typically, such a man will move quickly to convince the woman that they should get married. Usually, he is not shy about expressing his "love" and commitment. However, once his residency status is secured, he changes. When a sister is exploited this way, she can't help but feel hurt and enraged.

Once again, your best protection is time and a great deal of information about the man. Whenever a man sweeps you off your feet, you've got to be careful that he's not trying to steal your shoes. This is one of those instances in which an ounce of prevention is worth a pound of cure.

# Now for the Positives

After saying all this, I want to tell you very emphatically that I've seen many happy, fulfilled marriages between African American women and men from other cultures. In fact, some of the best marriages I know are between people from the United States and people from the West Indies. I've also known some fabulous relationships between Africans and Americans. So I want to assure you that these relationships can thrive and flourish despite the cultural differences. Every sister who decides to enter one of these relationships will discover that it's an individual journey with its own special rewards and obstacles. If you decide this is a journey you want to make, let me wish you *Na nek sa weurseuk*, which means "good luck" in Wolof, the Senegalese national language.

# 10

# Sing Your Own Song

I truly believe each of us has her own song to sing and a life to glorify through that song. When our African ancestors first arrived in the Americas, whether they landed in North America or were dropped off in South America or the Caribbean, they were amassed together with no thought of tribal cohesion. Consequently, they could no longer communicate with one another. As a people, our different languages were taken away, but remaining in our ancestors' consciousness were their songs and drumbeats. They learned to communicate with one another with little thought of tribal differences, and music played an essential role. The ancestral sound of music has stayed with us, individually and as a group. No matter how musically talented or tone deaf you may be, there is music in the rhythm of your internal life, and no one can take that away from you.

Music carries an expression of the continuity of living. It brings joy and exaltation and celebrates the sound of personal and group freedom. I am convinced that each sister has a sacred inner song emanating from her soul. This music provides a divine African link to the land and traditions of our ancestors.

In Africa, the sound of music was used to celebrate life, death, the land, and the people, as well as the individual experience. Since *we are all different and special*, each sister has to find her own unique voice and the song she was meant to sing. The song you specifically were meant to sing proclaims who you are, where you came from, tells you what you're about, and shows where you are going.

As you go through life, you need to gather *your* own lyrics, make *your* own arrangements, and write *your* own scores. Here are some beats to follow to help you make sure your song is as clear and beautiful as it was meant to be.

# Listen to the Strength of Your Inner Power

"I feel as though every man I've ever been with is deficient in the knowing-how-to-be-a-man department. None of them has treated me right, and no matter what I do, I'm always getting stomped on in some way."

—KEYNETTA, 30

My mother and father came from a town called Woodstock in Bibb County, Alabama. Growing up, I spent a lot of time there visiting family, including my great-aunts, the Woodstock Women of Alabama, as I called them. When the Woodstock women heard another sister complaining about her life, as Keynetta is doing, they would say, "You know why she always looks so pitiful and mistreated? That's 'cause she hasn't come to herself yet." I remember them telling me that nothing in your life would ever go right until you "come to yourself." This is the best kind of village-chorus correction.

If your life is in disarray and you always have a feeling of being at your wit's end with men, relationships, and personal confusion, this is a high indicator that, as my great-aunts would say, you may not have come to yourself yet. The Woodstock women didn't know contemporary terms like *empowerment* and *self-esteem*, but that's what they were talking about. They saw that if a sister couldn't seem to nail things down in her life and was frequently unhappy, confused, and disappointed, the first thing she needed to do was to *stop operating on someone else's principles* and come back to herself, so she would be in touch with her own inner sense of power.

In *Tapping the Power Within: A Path to Self-Empowerment for Black Women*, Iyanla Vanzant describes yellow as the color of the mind, intellect, optimism, forgiveness, and vision. Women with low self-esteem should concentrate on the color yellow and then seek all the colors of the universe. Use yellow to remind you of the strength of your inner values and your inner power. Tie a yellow ribbon on one of your doorknobs and use it to remind you to keep coming back to yourself, so you can find the song you were meant to sing.

# Start on an Inner Journey of Your Very Own

When a sister finally "comes to herself," she realizes that the knowledge and direction she is looking for is inside her and has been there all along. To find some *real* answers, all she has to do is take an inner journey and trust what she finds. Women typically have serious problems with inner journeys. They understand outer journeys; they understand the journey from the cradle to the grave; they understand having babies and doing for others; and, most of all, they understand reacting and responding to what's going on around them. But when it comes to setting her own pace, her own time, her own direction, and her own schedule, the average woman is still insufficiently skilled.

A sister needs to get in touch with her inner compass so she won't lose her way. To help you make an inner journey, start by setting aside thirty minutes of "thinking" time each day. You can do this while you're doing other things—washing dishes, setting out your clothes, or taking a shower, for instance. But devote your inner thoughts to your inner value and loving and claiming your inner self.

Remember that love is what you carry inside like a sentinel standing guard over your life. It is your inner love affair that never ends. Bad relationships tend to make you think that love has failed you. Not so. Love never fails; people do. Love is a spiritual quality, not the primary possession of one person. If you keep finding yourself attached to the wrong man, keep telling yourself the following: I WAS A PERSON BEFORE HE CAME INTO MY LIFE; I AM A PERSON WHILE I AM WITH HIM; I WILL BE A PERSON IF HE DEPARTS. Remind yourself of all the ways in which you are a special person with a unique song.

# Change from a "Reactor" to a "Contributor"

"This summer was really whacked, and I didn't get to do much. First I thought my boyfriend, Andre, was carrying on with my best friend, but it turns out they really are just friends. Then he had this test he had to take, so we spent weeks studying. Finally, the last few days, he had some time so we got to go to the beach."

—TENESHA, 21

Listen to the way Tenesha describes her life. It's all about someone else! Tenesha has been socialized to be a *reactor* and a *responder*. A man wants to go to the beach, she goes along; a man has to study, she helps him; a man gets sexy, she responds.

The capacity to respond and react to people and the world is a wonderful trait, but many sisters go too far: They forget how to initiate for themselves and all their fine energy becomes focused on others.

In fact, some sisters, if they're not running around doing for others, don't know what to do with themselves. This is true even of high-powered career women; the only difference with these women is that instead of some man telling them what to do, they're listening to an employer or a corporation. A woman like this is allowing someone else to take over her inner world and fill her with someone else's words, thoughts, and directions.

If this is what you have a tendency to do, it means you've turned over ownership of your life to someone else. If there is nobody around who you think owns you, you feel like a piece of lost property sitting on a shelf waiting to be claimed, existing but not really living. Waiting for the highest bidder is an example of the auction-block mentality.

To change these feelings, *practice divinely ordered thinking.* To be divinely ordered is to be psychologically, emotionally, and spiritually assembled around your own best interests. I call this attitude the "assembly of the sensible self" because the sensible self always follows the first law of nature, which is self-preservation. Everyone knows that sometimes relationships can be unreliable. That's why it's important to have your own core life in order with or without a man. If you are practicing divinely ordered thinking, you will love yourself, empower yourself, and correct yourself.

# Make the Song You Sing One You Want to Hear

What kind of song are you singing right now? Are you singing a song of woe-is-me? Are you singing a song of joy? Are you singing a song of defeat and doom and gloom? Are you singing a self-destructive song? Are you singing a calming, soothing song? Are you singing a bottomless song that says there is nothing in this world for me? Are you singing songs of hope for the future? Are you singing a loving song? Are you singing baby songs that say, "Somebody please come take care of me—sooooon"? Are you singing a song that says, "I'm so strong, I don't need anybody"?

As we walk through this world, by the way we walk, talk, and move, we leave an impression of who we are and where we are going. This is the song people hear emanating from us. Watch yourself and listen to yourself. Decide what qualities you possess that should receive the most attention. Put these qualities in your words and your life, and they will become part of your permanent song. Maintain your own copyrights; don't be a copycat.

# "Love the Ground You Walk On"

By now, anyone reading this book has figured out that I put a lot of stock in the advice my mother gave me. As I said before, my mama was a very smart woman, and much of what she said is worth repeating. When she told me that a sister has to love the ground she walks on, she wasn't advocating a selfish or self-centered lifestyle. What she was saying is that as a Black woman, if you're going to hang on to your center and well-being, you've got to have respect for your value in the world. When you value yourself, you'll be valued by the people around you. When you value yourself, you'll see the importance of your role and your place in the world. When you value yourself, you'll see the importance of maintaining a continuity of good values in your life, in your home, and in your community.

Loving the ground you walk on is about keeping your essential inner core, so you'll always know what's important. Any sister who wants to have a satisfying life has to pay a great deal of attention to the value that begins in her own center. Loving the ground you walk on means:

- You are sure of who you are
- You are sure of what you deserve
- You trust your own decisions
- You know how much of value you bring to relationships
- You know how much you contribute to the world
- You know what you are willing to accept from others

- You know what kind of behavior is unacceptable
- You know you deserve the best kind of loving

Unless you have this kind of rock-solid love for the ground you walk on, you run the risk of always being vulnerable to people and situations that come and go in everyone's life. If you have a strong center and a strong sense of your value, you'll always be able to operate from your own place of internal power. That way even if relationships come and go, you won't be losing yourself in the search for love.

# Find Your Own Safe-Place Feeling

"The only time I feel really happy and comfortable is when my boyfriend and I are sitting together on the couch watching TV. It makes me feel safe and peaceful. When he gets up to leave, I feel really terrible."

—TONI, 34

Most sisters can identify with Toni's feelings. Women are socialized to believe that they need to be with a man to feel comfortable and at peace with the world. They believe that the only time they can feel safe is when they are in a man's arms or at his side, secure in the "female" role. Without steady infusions of this safe-place feeling, they feel separated from themselves, as well as from others.

I believe that every sister can find these feelings of peace and security by creating her own safe place in her own head, where it can't be removed by someone getting up and leaving. For me, the safe-place feeling began in my childhood, where the safest place I knew was back in Woodstock, Alabama, in my Great-Grandmother Vinnie Caffee's old country homestead. Great-Grandmother Vinnie was one of the pillars of Woodstock womanhood, and each summer we would go visit her. Because I was the smallest child, I would get to sleep with her in her big featherbed. I remember snuggling up next to her, surrounded by the smell of biscuit dough in her white bleached-out flour-sack nightgown. I felt completely enfolded and protected. Any time I need to, I can call back that feeling. It's my permanent safe place, and I carry it with me, no matter where I go.

Safe-place thinking is one way to counteract the all-by-myself, no-one-loves-me feeling that sisters get from time to time. When you get that feeling, remember that love isn't just about romance and reflect on your own safe place. Find a nonromantic place in your head, where you felt loved, protected, and cared for. Perhaps you were fortunate enough to get it as a child, or perhaps you have been fortunate to find it as an adult through friendships or work. Perhaps you have been fortunate enough to find it through your spiritual beliefs and know that the God you love loves and cares for you as well.

When you find your own safe place, build on it by adding other memories of times when you've felt love and warmth. You can add memories of times when you've felt pride in your own accomplishments or times when you've been particularly happy. Once you've located your own personal safe place, remember how you got there, so you can call it back whenever you need to have a place where you belong, with or without a man.

# Forgive Yourself

Each of us has made more mistakes than we want to remember. Each of us has done things that make us cringe and wince and weep. And each of us carries too much guilt, too many regrets, and way too many "I'm sorry"s. The only thing that's really important about our regrets is that we are honest with ourselves about our shortcomings and we try to learn our lessons and move on. A mistake doesn't represent the whole person. A mistake is nothing but a small adjunct and shouldn't be confused with the essential self.

I'm convinced that women need a ceremony of self-forgiveness to help them move forward toward the best kind of loving. If you are like most sisters, you are probably so accustomed to feeling responsible and guilty that you don't know how to give yourself a break. It's time to start changing all that: If life dealt you a hand and you played the wrong cards, forgive yourself. If one of your children is in trouble even if you did everything you could to raise him or her right, forgive yourself. If a relationship ended and you have that old I-did-something-wrong feeling again, forgive yourself. There's an added plus to forgiving yourself: It helps you achieve the power to forgive others. A few years back when I read Tina Turner's book, *I, Tina*, I couldn't help but be impressed by the way she broke the chains of a destructive life and started her recovery through chanting and Buddhist ceremonies. I have always believed that ceremonies should be an essential part of the life of any person of African descent because they are part of the African tradition.

No sister should be dragging her chains of guilt with her all her life. Try this simple water ceremony as a way of erasing your regrets. Because water cleanses and heals, let water be the symbol of your ceremony for personal healing: Dip your index finger into a glass of water; place the water on your forehead; and say, "I forgive myself right here and now. I release myself from chains of guilt and fault-finding. I set myself free in mind, body, and spirit. Hallelujah!" This water ceremony reminds sisters that as far as their guilt is concerned, they should dip it, skip it, and drop it.

# Don't Use Up Your Life Wailing Over Some Man

When a sister is singing a bad, boring, redundant, not to mention sad, song, more often than not she's singing it about some man who has treated her badly. This is the only life you've got. Each of us spends only a short time on this planet; it's up to you to make your own life sweet. Here are suggestions to help you avoid Johnny-one-note songs about men who do women wrong.

## • Don't Be So Quick to Believe in That Old Black Magic

*It was Magic*
*The way your love captured my heart*
*Snatched me up into a whimsical trance*
*Didn't realize that this*
*Was only an act*
*In one of your short stories.*

—FROM THE POEM "IT WAS MAGIC"
BY DAPHNE HAYGOOD-BENYARD

Daphne Haygood-Benyard, a promising sister poet, describes a man whose magic act caused more pain than pleasure. I learned to take men and the magic spell they produce with a large grain of salt from my cousin Buddy. Buddy was a good-looking, sweet-talking navy veteran who lived with us when I was a teenager.

I loved Buddy because he treated me as though he was my protective older brother, and he was always eager to give me a play-by-play account of his romantic conquests along with line-by-line warnings of how I shouldn't be so foolish as to believe everything a man told me. He used himself as a good example of a brother who had such a practiced act and line with women that he couldn't even stop himself. One of Buddy's stories made an indelible impression on me, and I hope it will on you, too. Buddy prefaced this story by telling me that he didn't want me to be so stupid that I didn't understand the sweet-talk game and the man-woman interplay.

Here's Buddy's story: It seems he had gone out with a couple of friends, and they were on their way to a big party they were looking forward to, but because they had an hour to kill, they stopped off at a sister's house to pass some time. They played some music, had some conversation, and started to dance. Buddy began to talk trash to the woman he was dancing with. Then he said he would really like to go upstairs with her. To his shock, she said yes. Later, he told me, "I didn't expect her to say yes so fast. Damn, I was just asking."

He said this sister was just a big dummy who didn't

understand the sweet-talk game. The answer he expected to his question about going upstairs was neither yes nor no. He expected her to know how to play the sweet-talk game for the sake of heightened erotic and verbal foreplay—a literal dance of intimacy. He didn't want to go "upstairs"; he was on his way to a party, and he wanted to get there. What he wanted was to spend more time dancing with words—to enthrall, that's all.

## • Learn the Difference Between "No" and "No-for-Now"

I think this last story provides a very good lesson for women. It shows that you don't have to say yes and that "no-for-now" isn't about rejection. When you first discover you're attracted to a man, you can engage in verbal foreplay until both you and he know what you want to do with this relationship. Sisters worry that if they say no once, a man will never ask again. That's not so. Besides, if he doesn't come back, he would have gone his way anyway. It's better to have it happen before you get overinvolved. Practice saying "no-for-now" and learn to say it so what the man hears is a promise for the future, rather than a turndown in the present.

Obviously "no-for-now" applies only when you want the relationship to continue. There are plenty of times when you want to say *No!* and mean it. It's not unusual for a man to have the perception that inside every woman's no is a yes waiting for him if he is persistent enough. Recognize sexual harassment when it's happening and don't believe that just because a man is persistent, you owe him something. Also don't believe that just because a man is persistent, he's serious about something other than sex.

Many women who have had sexual relationships in the past need permission to say no. They've internalized a misbelief about women as "used goods." They assume because they said yes to one man, they can never say no again. Once their virginity is gone, they think that their "excuse" is also gone. Your body can't be stripped down like a used car. Let me tell you that you don't need an excuse to say no. A woman says no because she has a strong sense of self, and she doesn't want to rush into a sexual relationship until she has more information about the man and the way he behaves in the world and toward her.

## • Stop Going for the Okeydoke

Okeydoke is an expression that never seems to go out of style, and it always seems to mean the same thing: Some man is running a mind game on some woman for his own advantage. When a sister tells me this has happened to her, almost invariably she also says that all along she sensed what was happening. However, she didn't want to lose him, and she wanted to believe something good was happening. That's why she went along with his game against her better judgment.

There are still a lot of manipulative men trying to make sure that women continue to believe what they say even when they are only playing games. They are attractive, otherwise they wouldn't be able to get away with so much; they place a high premium on themselves because they know they are in demand. Manipulative men train themselves so they can play women like pieces on a chessboard, and they are often moving several women around at the same time. This is not a movement of the heart; it's a movement of the hand. A man like this plays sleight-of-hand games with feelings, providing sisters with a new definition of being manhandled. That way, your hope chest becomes his chessboard.

Don't let yourself become one of these high-profile brothers' chess pieces being moved around on a board. The only reason a man can practice this kind of manipulation is because you have handed over ownership of yourself to someone else. The minute you claim *you* for *you*, no man will ever again have this kind of power over you. State your own claim on love and happiness.

*Don't believe any song lyrics that tell you that you're not going to be able to live without "him."* All kinds of songs have been written saying that you're not going to "breathe again," "live again," "smile again," or "love again" unless the one you currently love is in your life. Don't believe it, and don't go along with it. No man can walk away with little parts of you! This is happening in your head, and you have the power to change it. Once again, you're the owner. Claim your territorial rights.

# Don't Disrupt Your Precious Life with Heavy Mouth-Battling

It's difficult to sing a sweet song if you and the man in your life are always arguing. Yes, I know men and women sometimes don't seem to know how to talk to each other without getting into shouting matches. However, if you want a life filled with the best kind of loving, it's imperative that you rethink and relearn the way you problem solve in relationships.

Here are some guidelines for resolving relationship conflicts:

• *Don't interrupt.* I've listened to a lot of brothers say things like "She's always jumping in and cutting me off." So let him finish what he's saying before you speak.

• *Try to repeat his ideas.* When the brother is finished speaking, ask, "Did I hear you correctly? and then try to repeat what he said. Do so without adding "attitude" or sarcastic inflection, no matter how little you think of his point of view. You want to make sure that there are no misunderstandings and that you are hearing each other correctly.

• *Ask him to repeat what you said.* You also want to make certain that he understands what you are saying. Try to stay calm when you are doing this because there is a good chance that he's not hearing you correctly either.

• *Stop trying to get the upper hand in your arguments.* If you're always trying to be right, you're not trying to communicate. Sometimes men and women argue with each other as though some unseen judge is going to come down and claim one of them the winner. This isn't about right and wrong; it's about resolving problems.

• *Don't ever, ever get physical.* Hitting, kicking, punching, slapping, spitting, and hair pulling are not ever part of a good relationship.

• *Don't make any generalizations about him.* When you start generalizing and saying things, such as "All men" or "All Black men," you're not talking to your partner, you're talking about past history. So don't put labels on him because it's not fair and it's counterproductive!

• *Don't make indictments.* If you indict a man, he's going to respond with a strong, often angry, defense. Don't treat him as though he's guilty. Instead, act as though you are both innocent parties trying to resolve a *common* problem.

• *Don't turn off when he says something you don't want to hear.* It's normal to want to avoid hearing something unpleasant, but it's necessary if you're going to move to a better place in your relationship. So when your partner criticizes you or tells you things that are upsetting, stay with it and hear him out. If you're always lowering your antenna, you can't pick up on anything.

• *Don't say hurtful things because they're never really forgotten.* When you lash out and say things that are designed to wound, that is exactly what they do. The problem is that those wounds leave scars that don't ever go away. So watch your words and remember that you get more bees with honey. The rules are these: No name-calling! No put-downs!

• *Treat him like he's the man you want him to be.* I once saw a sister greeting her partner with the following sentence: "Hi, honey, every time I see you coming, I know something good is going to happen." When I asked her about it, she said: "I know where it is I want to go—someplace good. I don't know where the hell he wants to go, but I hope if I reinforce the positive, it'll keep turning out right."

Learn from this wise sister, and reinforce the positive. Try saying things like "I would love to be with you on the beach (choose your own, anything from Coney Island or Venice Beach in California to Kingston, Jamaica). I can see you now, your brown body on the white sand with the blue water and me." Learn how to build positive mental images in his mind without challenging him. Keep reinforcing the positive. The glass is always half full, not half empty.

• *Don't always fight his plans.* A few weeks ago, I walked by a quarreling couple, and the sister was saying in a loud voice, "What do you mean we're going to see the movie you want? You know that's not what I want to see." The brother she was with was looking uncomfortable and unhappy. Don't have this kind of dialogue.

Try this wording instead: "Hey, now I know why you like karate films. It was interesting. Thank you for sharing it with me. Maybe next week we can see that new romantic suspense film. I'd love to get your masculine reactions to something different." This kind of conversation sets the ground for cooperation in making plans, and that's what you want—isn't it?

Understand that when a man seems contrary, it's probably nothing personal. Many men have a knee-jerk reaction that makes them oppose female guidance, direction, or suggestion—no matter who the female is. This reaction may have started with his mother, his sisters, or his past relationships. It doesn't matter. All that matters is that this is the way he behaves, and it makes your conversational exchanges more complicated. So try not to jump in with your own defensive reactions.

• *Try to keep your voice pleasant.* I know this is difficult, but try anyway. All men hate hearing harsh female voices, but brothers seem particularly sensitive to them because angry outbursts make them feel even more under attack. Besides, men tend to stop paying attention to women who are yelling at them. Remember, suggestion, not direction, is the way to go.

• *Don't turn off when he's saying something you don't want to hear.* Listen to his complaints about what makes him unhappy, and don't act like he doesn't know what he's talking about. His complaints are important to him, so they should be important to you even if what he is complaining about is something about you or the way you've become.

• *Finally, one last time, don't let money drive you apart.* For Black people, money has always been elusive, no matter how hard they've worked or how much they've contributed. Therefore, money has more emotional and psychic value than it deserves. Getting it, having it, and spending it all provide heightened major arenas for conflicts. We can't allow things over which we sometimes have so little control to have control over us. Fighting about money complicates relationships in ways that defeat you.

• *Get rid of what I call "victim-speak."* When we compete and argue with each other about our failure or success in our careers, we are focusing attention on each other, rather than on the system that oppresses Black people. We have to stop victimizing one another and join forces for mutual support and progress.

• *Get counseling if your arguments are becoming more intense or more frequent.* Don't be afraid to get some guidance as a couple to resolve your conflicts. Counseling is available from several sources, including religious groups and community mental health centers. Even if your partner doesn't want to join you, get counseling for yourself because it will help you make better decisions about dealing with the situation. Counseling may improve your coping skills.

# Celebrate Your Sexuality and Give Up on Dot Sex

Sometimes when I do seminars, I take a big piece of paper and make a black dot on it. Then I hold it up and ask people what they see. Just about everybody tells me that they see the dot. Then we talk some about why people see the dot. Here are some typical answers: "The dot is more prominent." "The dot sticks out." "The dot is black, so it's easier to see against the white paper." Then I ask, "What about the piece of paper?" People say things like "Yeah, we see the paper, but our eyes were drawn to the dot." This dot-on-paper exercise is similar to the way people think about sex. There's a whole body, yet we tend to focus only on the genitals. Your first dot-sex experience probably happened when you were very young, and your parents saw you with your hands on your dot and told you not to play with yourself. That incident immediately placed great emphasis on your dot. After all, you could touch the rest of your body, why couldn't you touch your dot?

It's essential that we do away with this "dot" mentality and stop focusing only on our genitals for sexual pleasure. Your entire being is sexual; if you love another person, all of that person is sexual. Your gender identity may be located in your dot, but your sexuality is located in the total you—mind, body, heart, and spirit. This point is important because so many men think they are men because they have erections. An erection doesn't make a man—even babies have erections.

When relating to men, we women sometimes have to learn how to help them lift their minds out of their genitals.

Too many brothers think manhood and identity are packaged in their penises. One sister put it this way, "Brother get your mind up out of your behind; talk to me, not my titty." Not that long ago I read a piece in *Essence* called "Looking for a Man" by Black writer Kevin Powell. In it, he talked about the hand-on-penis displays of many brothers today, describing this behavior as part of the sex and manhood thing that is also attached to baby making as a rite of passage. I call this physical behavior "sexual hand signals," similar to the hand signals of those who direct traffic. The message the brother is sending is that he wants to be your handyman and "Sex You Up," as the lyrics of a familiar song describe.

Sometimes it's up to us as women to make it clear that we want more from our relationships than just sex. It's up to us to communicate that we value a man's ability to express himself and that we're willing to listen when he does. How about you? Are you singing the wrong kind of sex songs and getting little out of relationships except a bootie bounce without any real intimacy. If so, change your lyrics and bring your mind and body up to the high notes, so you won't attract or be attracted to the wrong kind of hand signals—or the wrong kind of music. Try being your own symphonic life conductor.

# Celebrate Your African Heritage

On my office wall are these Latin words, *Vita Celebratio Est:* "Life is a celebration." Sisters need to restore African-based celebrations of life and love. Our tradition is one of celebrations: of life, nature, the harvest, rites of passage, our ancestors, and the healing arts. We magnified all of these celebrations by including music, the drumbeat, and dance.

Ceremonies and celebrations are part of African life and tradition. Without ceremonies and celebrations, each of us is nothing more than a creature of routine and habit. Celebrations affirm your tie to the sacred and the existence of the unseen spiritual world.

When I visited West Africa a few years ago, I found that the celebration of life continues in Africa today. Life itself is a celebration as the people work, build, and keep the village spirit alive. During my stay in West Africa, I was a part of the African majority for the first time in my life. It was a strengthening experience for me because the Black collective experience is an empowering one. By keeping our relationships together, we celebrate the African collective, which was our strength in ages past and will be our hope in years to come. Separated from our village, we're individuals; coming together makes us whole again.

# Celebrate the Gifts of Your African American Ancestors

When I was returning from West Africa, I remember walking through the airport pulling a big rice bag full of African art to bring back to the United States, when I passed under a sign that said, in effect, this way for people with American passports, another way for everyone else. There were four white men going through the gate and they thought they were going through alone, except that they must have heard me clanking and banging as I dragged this big bag. When they looked at me in surprise, I realized what my African American ancestors had given me: The right to walk through the gate marked American Passports Only.

I'm intensely proud of everything my ancestors gave me. But like most people, I have to remind myself to feel pride in everything Black people gave this country. The American economy was built by free slave labor. For three hundred years, the energy and exertion of our ancestors provided the underpinning on which an economy was based. No other group can claim this contribution. No other group contributed as much with as little reward.

Stay proud and conscious of the gifts of our African

American ancestors. Slavery was an evil, peculiar institution of oppression and repression. Nonetheless, it proved the great spirit of Black people. We managed not only to stay alive, but we also managed to keep some sense of sanity, order, dignity, and community. As far as I'm concerned, this is a great lesson in the power to overcome adversity, not just for us, but for all ethnic groups, as well as anyone who claims to have an interest in the strength of the human spirit.

# Celebrate the Future Through Your Children

Children are our only projection into the future. They are the hope and the promise, and you want them to be confident and secure in themselves. If you're a parent, your children are in your care for a short time, but this time prepares them for everything else that will happen in their lives. It's important that all of us educate ourselves about child psychology and rear our children so they will be ready for the best kind of loving. Here are some simple guidelines to remember:

• *Give your children empowering messages.* Praise all their accomplishments, no matter how small. Notice the good and sweet things they do or say. Give them support and encouragement in school and in their projects. Reinforce their good behavior and let them know that you feel proud and happy to have them as your children. My alphabet formula is give more A's than C's—more acceptance than criticism.

• *Don't frame your children's destiny in a destructive manner.* Don't think criticism is the way to build character or make a child "shape up." It's not. Reinforcing what they do right is the way to go. Don't always be telling them what they do wrong. Don't punish them with unnecessarily harsh words or actions.

• *Don't ever call your children names.* Telling your daughter that she is a bitch or a tramp is leaving her vulnerable for abuse as an adult. Telling your son that he is "no good" or "just like his daddy" is setting the stage for him to become the wrong kind of man. Don't ever lay self-fulfilling-prophecy statements on your children. There is a correlation between what we expect from others and what we get.

• *Separate the child from the behavior.* No matter what your children do, let them know that you love them. Affirm the child even while you are correcting his or her behavior. Say, for example, "I love you dearly, but what you did is unacceptable, and I expect better from you because I know you know better."

• *Try to remember what you felt as a child.* Let your children know that no one is perfect and that you made mistakes as a child. Emphasize that learning one's lessons is a mark of courage and character. Remember the things that gave you pleasure as a child and try to share them with your child.

• *Find activities that you and your child can do together.* There are so many ways to spend time with your children. You can read together, for example. A friend told me that one of her most cherished memories is going to the library once a week with her mother, each of them picking out a book to read during the week, and then going out for ice cream. Get your children to help you cook. Find movies you'll all enjoy. Make one night a week family night. Share sports. Watch the same television programs and *talk* about them. There is an added plus to this because it allows you to monitor what they watch. There are hundreds of activities. All that counts is that you are spending time together and talking.

• *Keep your children connected to their African American heritage.* Incorporating children into the African American community is essential in building character and values. Teach your children that solid values and respect for others, as well as themselves, is part of our heritage. Teach them to be proud of our history and our major contributions to this country. To stimulate that kind of racial pride, every African American child, for example, should know that a Black man named Garrett A. Morgan invented the gas mask as well as the American traffic signal that each year saves thousands of lives.

• *Teach your children the importance of love and respect for others.* This is particularly important in our communities because the African perception should be that family is community and community is family. This kind of thinking will eliminate the family-feuding mentality that creates Black-on-Black crime, as well as situations that exist in places like Rwanda. There is a legend that the Ashanti empire was created because of the love between a young man and woman from different tribes who were at war. This love transformed the destiny of a people. Black men and women need to use all their fine energy to get ahead, not to war with anyone, particularly each other. This legend was told to me by a poet and playwright from Ghana, Kabu Okai-Davies.

I agree with Dr. Martin Luther King, Jr., who, in an address to the Episcopal Society for Cultural and Racial Unity in St. Louis, Missouri, on October 12, 1964, said: "All I am saying is simply this, that all life is inter-related and, somehow, we are all caught in an inescapable network of mutuality, tied in a single garment of destiny; and whatever affects one, directly affects all indirectly."

• *Teach your children to show extra respect for their elders.* Show your children that you value and respect all older Black Americans for their life experience and their contributions to the community, no matter how small. There was a time, not that long ago, when the African American community was regularly applauded for the degree of respect that we showed toward older men and women. It's essential that we all try our best to return this value to our community. The importance of this became particularly clear when Rosa Parks, who is considered the mother of the Civil Rights Movement, was assaulted in her own home by a young man from the community. Mrs. Parks was then in her eighties. This kind of behavior is shameful, and we need to make sure our children know it.

• *Teach your children to be joyful as well as responsible about their sexual identities.* If you have daughters or granddaughters, you can help them love and accept their womanly bodies by showing them that the menarche or onset of menstruation needs to be celebrated in a tangible way. Young Black women need a landmark event for womanhood in the African tradition. My mother gave me a family feast and celebration for my menses and I passed on the gift to my daughters. I recommend a family dinner or gathering to celebrate what it means to be a woman. This can help shape a womanhood responsibility that has nothing to do with teenage pregnancy.

Young African American males also need African rituals to help them deal with manhood in an appropriate way. We need to give young males guidance concerning the responsibilities associated with masculine sexuality. Sharing manhood and womanhood events with young people invites them to be responsible members of the village community. Young Black males need to know that man making comes before baby making.

• *Help your children form realistic, attainable goals.* Tell your children about the importance of education and good planning for the future. Show them that there are many ways to achieve success. Even if they are gifted athletically or musically, encourage them to build math, science, and other skills as well, so they will always have options if their hopes don't work out.

• *Let your children know how beautiful you think they are.* Give your children full-length mirrors for their rooms, so they can watch themselves grow and appreciate their looks. Giving children mirrors tells them that you love their reflections. Love of self is a defense against immoral and violent behavior toward others.

A friend of mine once asked her mother, "Mama, when I'm leaving the house, why do you always stand at the door and watch me until I disappear?" Her mother replied, "I love looking at you, and I want to see you as long as I can." It's wonderful to feel that kind of parental love and acceptance, and that's what you need to give your children. The thing to remember is that nobody ever died from too much love, but children have been known to perish from too much neglect.

# Celebrate Your Connections to Other Women

During and after slavery, it was the communal sister support spirit that brought Black women out of a wide variety of depressing and degrading circumstances. I believe we need to reconstruct those strong relationships among Black women. Sisters gave each other emotional support and encouragement as well as genuine physical support with child rearing and household chores. Even if a sister wasn't getting the help she needed from a man, she knew she could count on other Black women. In fact, men would often resent this support and refer to "the hen's club—cluck, cluck, cluck." Right now, African American women need each other as much if not more than ever. Here are some ideas about how to keep your ties to your sisters strong for what I call the "Second Reconstruction."

*Don't think a no-man plan means there's no plan.* Women are sometimes afraid to make commitments to other women because they worry they won't be available if a man suddenly appears and wants to do something. Yet, the truth is that many of us can make our lives considerably more pleasurable and easier if we bond together to make plans on all levels. In truth, our female friendships often outlast our relationships with men. So treat them with the respect they deserve, and if you make a plan, no matter how small, to go to the movies or shopping, treat it as though it has value, because it does.

*Don't condemn another sister's life journey.* Slavery tried to make us believe that the only way one sister could get ahead was to climb over another. Don't buy into this myth. Don't put down other Black women; don't compete for the same men; don't target another sister's husband; don't assume you are better or more deserving; don't measure each other by beauty standards set down by Eurocentric thinking; don't buy into the kind of sexist games that blame the woman for the man's manipulations.

*Consider the ways that sharing a life with another single woman might make yours easier or more satisfying.* Growing up, most sisters expected they would end up with men and families. As life is turning out, it isn't always happening that way. Sisters are discovering that they can go for long periods without permanent male companions, in residence or otherwise. This fact opens up a great many options for living that sisters need to consider. Some are short range, but others involve long-term planning.

For example, if your immediate family is small or doesn't live nearby, you might want to consider joining with one or more women and forming your own extended family for holiday celebrations. If you have children, you and some other sisters might form baby-sitting clubs for taking care of each other's kids for a night or even a weekend. With or without children, think about planning joint vacations, renting summer houses, or buying time-shares with other single women. Some sisters have already discovered the benefits of renting, or even buying, large houses or apartments together and sharing expenses, chores, and child care. And there are many sisters who have formed successful businesses with one another. Futurists predict that eventually many people will be living communally to combat rising costs, as well as for companionship. Communal living is just a way of creating stability and reducing overhead.

*Seek the advice of a nonbiological village mother and mentor nonbiological female children.* Every sister needs a village mother. It is part of our African heritage to seek the counsel of our elders. Maintain this tradition in your own life. Oprah Winfrey, for example, on television, described poet Maya Angelou as her mother-adviser.

# The Most Essential Celebration: Celebrate Who You Are

Here's a statement to write down and put on your wall. "You are an African Queen, not a Greek tragedy! You've got to adore and celebrate yourself, not weep and wail and moan." Wrap yourself in the royal robes of self-pride.

Love should never ask you to relinquish your own spirit. Love should help you gain a more positive identity and self-esteem. When your love is balanced, you are protecting your own inner song, as well as the other person's. *Kuumba*, which refers to creativity, is another of the Seven Principles of Blackness. It suggests that we use our creative talents to leave our world better than we found it. We can do this by defining ourselves, speaking for ourselves, and making our own decisions.

Sisters need to give up all forms of sorry self-denial, as in "I'm sorry I'm not what you want me to be." "I'm sorry for not having thoughts that are in agreement with yours." "I'm sorry I don't measure up to your standards." "I'm sorry I'm not as pretty as your first (or last) girlfriend (or ex-wife)." Loving someone doesn't ever mean losing your identify or apologizing for being the person you are.

Celebrating who you are is speaking up for yourself in symbolic ways. It's defining yourself, approving of yourself, and giving yourself permission to be the best person you possibly can be.

Here are some ways to start your celebration of the person who matters most in your life—*YOU:*

## • Give Yourself the Credit You're Due

I remember once standing outside church next to a very attractive sister and complementing her on her beautiful dress. "Oh, sugar," she said, "I need to lose some weight." I find this tendency to be self-deprecating is common among Black women, and it's something you need to work against. Black women as a group have contributed a great deal to this country, and I'm sure you individually contribute to your world.

So always stop and give yourself credit for your good decision making, your common sense, the lessons you've learned, the work you're prepared to do, the better person you've become, and the beauty you carry with you. Give credit where credit is due—to YOU!

## • Celebrate the Way You Look

The fact is that there is no ideal body, and the beauty messages we've all been fed are destructive and don't even apply to the people who create these erroneous images. Women come in different sizes, different shapes, and different shades. We are tall, short, and medium. Unfortunately, racism, sexism, and ageism have convinced sisters that there are only a few desirable physical shapes, sizes, and shades. This kind of thinking is an assault on all of us, so don't go along with it.

The fact is that thinking you're unattractive is *very* unattractive, and any woman who walks and talks and moves as though she thinks she's beautiful is beautiful. During my visit to West Africa, I couldn't help but notice the way the women moved. These African sisters haven't been force-fed a lot of nonsense about good body type and bad body type. They walk as though they know their bodies represent a celebration of life, and they look gorgeous because of this inner knowledge. The following poem appeared in *Essence.* I think it's wonderful and hope you do, too.

### IN CELEBRATION OF MY ASS

*I'm here tonight to celebrate my ass*
*Yes, my ass*
*This nice round intrusion strapped to my lower back*
*You see this ass and I have been*
*enemies for years*
*For three decades I have attempted*
*to remove this little intruder*
*from my life*
*For years I did those*
*masochistic exercises in hope*
*of reducing my full set of*
*round hips, my derriere*

*I was attempting and it was*
*a pathetic attempt to create*
*the European flat ass*
*Now even though I've always been*
*baffled by the phenomenon of*
*how one keeps from slipping*
*off the chair with everything*
*being so flat*
*Yet I was attempting to duplicate a European structure*
*on this Afrikan body*

*Mind you this Frankenstein attempt*
*to replace my natural hip line*
*would never work*
*I have legs so long and a waist so short*
*can you imagine being flat too?*
*So in my attempt to clone*
*my Afrikan gluteus maximus into*
*the European butt*

*I discovered*
*I became*
*I grew to like adore*
*my Afrikan ass*

*So you see I stand*
*here not to criticize*
*my ass but to celebrate it*
*To rejoice at my round hips*
*which have held life*
*To praise my ass*
*which has allowed me to wear*
*those skirts which make Afrikan*
*men drop to their knees with desire*
*To thank my behind for providing me with support*
*and not allowing me to fall*
*off my chair*
*I'm here to praise*
*I'm here to honor*
*I'm here to celebrate*

*My Afrikan heirloom ASS*

—Shquestra

Shquestra is a poet, but even if you have never tried writing anything down, why don't you use her poem as an example, and write down some of your thoughts in celebration of your body. Choose characteristics and body parts that may have bothered you in the past and give them the praise and celebration they deserve. West African women drape scarves around their breasts, buttocks, and waists to draw attention to their bodies, whether they are tall, short, small, or large. You might want to try dressing so that you accentuate those body parts that you're accustomed to trying to hide. You may discover that these parts of you are desirable, adorable, and appealing.

Take the same approach toward your skin shade and your hair type. Make the most of whatever God gave you and treat it with respect and love, like you want to be treated by others. Your body is your temple. Don't act like it's condemned housing.

### • Celebrate Your Physical and Mental Well-Being

Every sister needs to take care of herself. Taking care of yourself means learning about nutrition and vitamins and eating accordingly. It means finding a way to get regular checkups for general health, as well as gynecological health. It means breast examinations and mammograms when your doctor advises. It means checking for blood pressure and diabetes. It means finding a way to get counseling for your mental health when your problems become unduly stressful or feel overwhelming. And it means attending to your spiritual health through prayer, meditation, and/or ecclesiastical consultation.

### • Celebrate Your Strength

As a Black woman, your strength is your beauty mark. It is like a tribal mark, etched not on your face, but on your soul. So don't let anybody tell you that you're not feminine enough. Yes, starting with picking cotton in the field, Black women proved they are able to handle cross-gender roles. Someone once said that Black women are like tea bags: You don't know how strong they are until you put them in hot water. Yes, sisters proved they can manage food-stamp families or large departments in Fortune 500 companies. But we've also proved time and time again that we can put on our Flori Roberts makeup, show off our great design sense or our fabulous African hairstyles, and walk through the world looking drop-dead gorgeous and completely feminine. It's what I call androgyny and mahogany in perfect harmony.

### • Celebrate Your Age

Racism, sexism, ageism. It seems there is no end to the way Black women can feel discriminated against. However, the truth is there are enormous benefits to becoming more mature. It's great being a woman of childbearing age, but it's also great when you finally can stop planning your life around your menstrual period. It's great feeling the rush of young hormones, but it's also liberating when you don't have to fight those same hormones to make good decisions about men.

Many women have discovered that menopause makes them clearheaded—not less sexual, but more sure. Older women learn to make decisions on the basis of what they have learned, which gives them more control. In the African village, the older women were always cherished for their wisdom and their capacity to help younger sisters make decisions. African tradition teaches us that everybody has a journey, and all that matters at the moment is where you are in your journey. There's a saying about getting older: "Age is mind over matter, and if you don't mind, it doesn't matter."

## • Celebrate Your Sense of Humor

Laughter always creates a lovely song, and it's a great part of our African American heritage. Humor was a coping mechanism our ancestors used. Our ancestors laughed so they wouldn't cry. This ability to find the irony and the humor in situations that are sometimes far from funny is a great heritage, and as everyone in America knows, it has produced some amazingly funny comic artists, male and female.

Humor is a terrific asset in a relationship because it diffuses anger and helps put situations in perspective. Humor gives your body a chance to destress itself, and it teaches each of us not to take oneself too seriously. Humor is a wonderful antidote for disappointment, and, most important, it is an empowering tool because it can help release us from the moment-to-moment strain of life's burdens.

## • Celebrate Your Commitment to Yourself

Not that long ago, I read about a single sister who decided to show her love for herself by "marrying" herself. She had a ceremony, she wore a beautiful gown, she had a wedding cake, and she invited all her friends. She even bought herself a ring. It was a fine party to celebrate her ongoing relationship with herself. I was so impressed by this celebration! Every woman can learn from how this sister treated herself. So don't be afraid to shower yourself with good things and prove that you take your relationship with yourself seriously. Having a ceremony to celebrate yourself is not about a rejection of men—it's about an acceptance of self.

# It's Not Just You and Me, Babe

When Black people talk about relationships, it's not just about you and me, babe. It's the whole nine yards of African kinte cloth—you, me, and the family tree, with its roots in the motherland. Coming together as a couple is just one small step in the monumental task of maintaining the strength of the extended family in the midst of alien values.

Our ancestors journeyed here not by choice. Right now, we, as their children, are standing on our North American frontier surrounded by values and attitudes that are eroding our strengths. There is a Wild West Show taking place in our cities and neighborhoods, and some of the bandits are living right next door. The terrifying situation of Black-on-Black crime is in direct opposition to our history of extended families. What the killing cotton fields of slavery could not do, we are doing to each other.

Our male-female relationships represent the foundation of better living in our communities. Our focus has to be on strengthening our family and cultural values. Here are some suggestions for keeping Afrocentric values in our lives:

## • Understand Black Wealth

For African Americans, Black wealth is more than just cash flow. After slavery, we were each supposed to receive forty acres and a mule as payment for those long, hard years of servitude. That's why Spike Lee named his production company Forty Acres and a Mule. Lee understands the concept of Black wealth, and he built an empire on it. If our ancestors had received this payment, we would be standing on real, not just estimated, wealth.

My advice is to maintain a wealthy attitude in the midst of economic inequity. We serve a God of riches, we have a rich heritage, and we are rich in wages and tax benefits that we have never received. I call this state of being "rich poverty," and you are a rich person no matter what your cash flow. A Black man or woman with a wealthy outlook can overcome the poverty of spirit that is at the core of most failures. I believe the failure to understand the degree to which your ancestors had and earned great wealth leaves you with a vastly underrated view of your own wealth and your own worth. This view creates an emotional poverty, which doesn't jibe with the facts. Whether you know it or not, you are a rich person. Many rich people never carry cash, but they are wealthy just the same. Black people have what I call cultural cash assets.

## • Maintain Your Cultural Attachments

Every experience you have in this culture chips away at the underpinnings of your cultural attachments. It doesn't matter whether that experience is waiting in line for a welfare payment or waiting at the bank to cash a five-figure corporate paycheck. If you don't maintain your ties to your community and your culture, when a crisis hits your life, you run the risk of bottoming out.

This point is vital for all of us, but it's especially important for the many young Black men and women who are on predominantly white campuses or working in white environments where they may feel isolated. I always remember a letter I received at *Essence* from a woman who described her workplace by saying she felt like she was in an "ocean of white foam."

The fact is that it is easy at first not to notice the sense of isolation and separation that can exist when you lose your ties to your community and your culture. At first, one doesn't even necessarily miss the sense of Black community. In fact, it may feel like a relief. Then time passes, and all the situations in which you may find yourself being treated not as a person, but as a representative of your race, combine with always having to live up to other's imagined standards, and the whole thing becomes overwhelming. You start to miss the people, the warmth, the humor and the sense of belonging. It's important for you to stay connected to your culture, and it's important for your culture. Culture carved out a place for you in a strange land, so you could sing your song.

Don't just pay lip service to your cultural values. Try always to make sure that your cultural values and your cultural attachments are in sync with one another. Try to give back to your communities. Remember that ethnocentrism is a normal condition. In fact, it's abnormal not to be ethnocentric. Cultural attachments make you self-affirming. When people call you a minority and you're living in Los Angeles, you think that's all there is. But when you see your Afrocentric connections from a larger view, you know that you are not a minority in the world. A strong cultural attachment will protect you from other people's definition of who you are. Wade Nobles, Ph.D., national president of the Association of Black Psychologists, believes we can rightfully be referred to as the BUSA tribe or BUSA people (Blacks in the United States of America) to help maintain our Afrocentricity.

If you are away from your own community or in a strange city or town, locate the nearest Black church or religious group. This group will give you physical evidence that you are not alone. The church or mosque or temple will model for you again the sense of family, community, and the village.

### • Form Your Own Kupenda Group

This is Dr. Nathan Hare's suggestion, and I think it's a wonderful one. *Kupenda* is the Swahili word for love. What Dr. Hare suggests is forming nonsexual, nonrelationship-related groups for men and women to support each other's lives and nourish each other's spirits and cultural connections. A

Kupenda group ideally would mirror the African village in giving us an extended human system on which to depend. You can form these groups in the workplace, on campuses, or in your communities.

### • Free Up Your Value Logjam

Make sure that your values mirror an Afrocentric point of view. Remember what's important. Stop judging people materialistically. Stop leading your life so that it's materially driven, and start focusing on your beautiful African spirit and values.

# Find the New Sister Inside

Through each phase of our lives and relationships, if we want to feel healed, we must always remember to talk about what we have learned and how we can move forward to the next phase. I firmly believe that women tend to evolve in phases. At regular intervals, each of us has a new woman inside who is ready to emerge with new ideas, new priorities, new goals and objectives, new outlooks, and new ways of thinking.

We have to remember that for each of us, faith is the glue that holds our lives together. With a man, or without a man, faith is what empowers a sister. When a sister has faith, she has love. With faith, she knows that love doesn't leave, even if Jim, Jason, or Jamal walk out the door. The Swahili word for faith is *Imani*.

# Keep Striving for the Best Kind of Loving

Always wanting the very best has been part of the cultural fabric (or kinte cloth) of the African American experience. Historically, brothers and sisters were always told they had to be twice as good and work twice as hard to achieve their goals. Brothers and sisters were taught that if they were going to get anywhere, they had to be the best there was. Being the best could make one's life go beyond all the predictions of failure assigned to Black people. I was always told to take the obvious and do the opposite. When someone predicts your failure, become even more determined to prove that prediction wrong.

Now brothers and sisters must decide not to settle for anything less than the BEST in their personal lives. This kind of thinking will keep us collectively in a like-minded direction and give us purpose, or *NIA*, which is one of the seven principles of Blackness. There are positive indicators that we have started the process of healing ourselves and our relationships.

So the next time someone asks you what you want from life, tell them, "the Best." Even if you are not at the top right now, that doesn't mean you want less than the best for your future. You may not be in charge of your circumstances all the time, but you are in charge of your thinking and goal setting. Think BEST, talk BEST, aim for the BEST, expect the BEST, and never settle for anything less. You deserve it.

# Resource List

The following organizations are available to assist sisters and brothers in locating professional counseling, culturally attached therapeutic support, prison programs for inmates and their families, legal defense, Black historical information, welfare rights, political empowerment, women's support groups, education, housing and employment opportunities and advancement of the cause of Black women's health. Contact any of these groups for help and referral:

Association for the Study of Afro-American Life and History
1407 14th Street, N.W.
Washington, DC 20005-3704
(202) 667-2822

Association of Black Psychologists
P.O. Box 55999
Washington, DC 20040-5999
(202) 722-0808

Black Psychiatrists of America
2730 Adeline Street
Oakland, CA 94607
(415) 465-1800

National Association for the Advancement of Colored People
Director
The Prison Program
4805 Mt. Hope Drive
Baltimore, MD 21215
(410) 358-8900

National Association of Black Social Workers
15231 West McNichols Avenue
Detroit, MI 48235
(313) 836-0210

National Association of Black Women Attorneys, Inc.
3711 Macomb Street, N.W., 2nd Fl.
Washington, DC 20016
(202) 966-9691

National Council of Negro Women, Inc.
1001 G Street, N.W.
Suite 800
Washington, DC 20036
(202) 628-0015

National Medical Association
1012 10th Street, N.W.
Washington, DC 20001
(202) 347-1895

National Political Congress of Black Women, Inc.
600 New Hampshire Avenue
Suite 1125
Washington, DC 20037
(202) 338-0800

National Urban League, Inc.
500 East 62nd Street
New York, NY 10021
(212) 310-9000

Schomburg Center for Research in Black Culture
515 Malcolm X Boulevard
New York, NY 10037-1801
(212) 491-2200

National Black Women's Health Project
1237 Ralph David Abernathy Boulevard, S.W.
Atlanta, GA 30310
(404) 758-9590

# Reading List

Akbar, Na'im. *Chains and Images of Psychological Slavery.* Jersey City, N.J.: New Mind Productions, 1984.

Cobbs, Price M., and William H. Grier. *Black Rage.* New York: N.Y. Basic Books, 1968.

Davis, Larry E. *Black and Single: Meeting and Choosing a Partner Who's Right for You.* Chicago: The Noble Press, Inc. 1993.

Delaney, Sarah and Elizabeth, with Amy Hill Hearth. *Having Our Say: The Delaney Sisters' First 100 Years.* New York: Kodansha International, 1993.

Golden, Marita. *Migrations of the Heart.* New York: Ballantine Books, 1987.

———. *Wild Women Don't Wear No Blues: Black Women Writers on Love, Men and Sex.* New York: Doubleday, 1993.

Hare, Nathan and Julia. *Crisis in Black Sexual Politics.* San Francisco: Black Think Tank, 1989.

Harrington, Walt. *Crossings: A White Man's Journey into Black America.* New York: HarperCollins, 1992.

Hernton, Calvin C. *Sex and Racism in America.* New York: Doubleday, 1992,

Hopson, Derek and Darlene. *Friends, Lovers, and Soul Mates: A Guide to Better Relationships Between Black Men and Women.* New York: Simon & Schuster, 1994.

Khanga, Yelena, with Susan Jacoby. *Soul to Soul: The Story of a Black Russian American Family 1865–1992*. New York: W. W. Norton & Co., 1992.

Kunjufu, Jawanza. *The Power, Passion and Pain of Black Love*. Chicago: African American Images, 1993.

Loewenberg, Bert James, and Ruth Bogin (eds). *Black Women in the Nineteenth Century American Life: Their Words, Their Thoughts, Their Feelings*. University Park: University of Pennsylvania Press, 1976.

Madhubuti, Haki. *Black Men: Obsolete, Single, Dangerous? One African American Family in Transition, Essays in Discovery, Solution and Hope*. Chicago: Third Word Press, 1990.

McMillan, Terry. *Waiting to Exhale*. New York: Viking, 1992.

Morrison, Toni, *Jazz*. New York: A Plume Book, 1992.

Wade, Brenda, and Brenda Lane Richardson. *Love Lessons: A Guide to Transforming Relationships*. New York: Amistad Press, Inc., 1993.

Welsing, Frances Cress. *The Isis Papers: The Keys to the Colors*. Chicago: Third World Press, 1991.

Vanzant, Iyanla. *Tapping the Power Within: A Path to Self-Empowerment for Black Women*. New York: Harlem River Press, 1992.

# Index